"Alex Guarnaschelli is one
firsthand. Alex has the bes
words come to life in her b
on my kitchen shelf at hor
Cooker Brownies alone . .
kitchen, including mine."

—**BOBBY FLAY,** CHEF

"I trust Alex with my taste buds. In *Cook with Me,* every dish has an aha moment of unexpected flavor and texture. What's not to love? The recipes are comforting—and daughter-approved!"

—**CARLA HALL,** CELEBRITY CHEF AND AUTHOR

"There has never been a time when Alex Guarnaschelli has invited me to her home for dinner that I didn't jump on the opportunity. Her meals are as special as her friendship, and now with this cookbook I don't have to wait to be on the East coast to enjoy her delicious and inspired dishes."

—**GIADA DE LAURENTIIS**

"What I love about Alex is not just her amazing knowledge as a chef and her passion for food, but she's also the greatest combination of storyteller and teacher. With this book, you'll learn something new on every page while also feeling like you're cooking alongside a close friend."

—**MOLLY YEH,** BLOGGER AND FOOD NETWORK HOST

"*Cook with Me* is 100% Alex — whip-smart, honest, unfussy, and exactly how I want to cook (and live!). Each recipe overflows with love and purpose, technique and soul, and, most of all, genuine joy for nourishing the people in your life who matter most. This book is a must for every kitchen!"

—**GAIL SIMMONS,** FOOD EXPERT, TV HOST, AND AUTHOR OF *BRINGING IT HOME: FAVORITE RECIPES FROM A LIFE OF ADVENTUROUS EATING*

"Every once in a while, I read a cookbook that makes me want to drop what I'm doing and rush into the kitchen. Alex Guarnaschelli's *Cook with Me* is one such cookbook. It's filled with love, family stories, and sophisticated yet extremely doable recipes for home cooks."

—**JENNIFER SEGAL,** AUTHOR OF *ONCE UPON A CHEF*

Cook with Me

Clarkson Potter/Publishers
New York

COOK *with* ME

150 RECIPES FOR THE HOME COOK

Alex Guarnaschelli

PHOTOGRAPHS BY JOHNNY MILLER

Published in the United States by Clarkson Potter/
Publishers, an imprint of Random House, a division of
Penguin Random House LLC, New York.
clarksonpotter.com

CLARKSON POTTER is a trademark and POTTER with
colophon is a registered trademark of Penguin Random
House LLC.

Library of Congress Cataloging-in-Publication Data
is available upon request.

ISBN 978-0-593-13508-2
Ebook ISBN 978-0-593-13509-9

Printed in China

Book and cover design by Ian Dingman
Cover and interior photography by Johnny Miller

10 9 8 7 6 5 4 3 2 1

First Edition

THE ONLY PLACE SUCCESS COMES
BEFORE WORK IS IN THE DICTIONARY.

—STUBBY CURRENCE

This book is dedicated to my dad, may he rest in peace (with two huge slices of lemon meringue pie); my mom, who is the most brilliant person I will ever know; my daughter, Ava, who makes my life worth it; and my boyfriend, Michael, who makes me laugh.

Contents

INTRODUCTION

My father was a man who, above all things, loved the Fourth of July. Fireworks are illegal in New York, so we would drive out to Mom and Dad's modest country house in Milford, Pennsylvania, and, on the way, stop at the local fireworks warehouse for "supplies." I think he actually chose to buy a house in that spot because fireworks were legal there. He'd load the car with small, low-key fireworks, drive them home, and set them off on the front lawn, lighting each one and stepping back in sprightly, boyish wonder as it shot up with bursts of light. He literally looked like a little kid. I realized right then and there that we never know our parents as children. Instead, they are the custodians of our childhood and as such always seem larger than life as we grow up. Parents can do anything, fight anyone, buy anything, and, in my case, cook absolutely anything. That "cook anything" part became pretty significant to me as time went on.

Everyone seems to have grandmothers or a mother who cooks and passes down recipes (or maybe, more infamously, doesn't pass down recipes). I have received so many letters from people who wish they had gotten their grandmother's secret trick to great coleslaw or had asked their mom what that missing ingredient was in her legendary cinnamon buns. I always think there is no secret or missing ingredient to these hand-me-down recipes, only the absence of the person and the comfort you felt as they cooked them. In my case, I only wish my father would come back and be alive and cook for me. Eat with me. I can't accept that he won't. That's not a very "tidy" feeling. It leaves too many loose ends and questions and wishes, so this book is for him.

I know a cookbook isn't necessarily the place for tragedy. It's just that, for me, the parent and the food are inextricably connected. In my family, food marks the spot; we use food for all occasions and all states of mind. My father had a sort of oddball role in the kitchen of my childhood. He did the less glamorous cooking: the weeknight dinners of Risotto with Tomatoes and Parmesan Cheese (page 153) and Whole Roasted Fish (page 218), the "on the fly" cupboard dinners like a Whole Roasted Chicken (page 76), and the penny-pinching meals we needed, too. My dad would have cooked the whole chapter of One & Done dinners (pages 60–73), while my mom would likely be stuck somewhere in the middle of the Baking for Breakfast (pages 235–46) or Cookies & Such (pages 265–87).

My dad also taught me that you have to do what you love for a living and that, ideally, your professions, passions, likes, dislikes, and hobbies, should be rolled into one. That was his idea of a free life lived on one's own terms. To my dad, freedom meant never sitting at a desk, never donning a suit or a uniform, and always waking up with a desire—even if you are exhausted or have a cold—to go and do the day's work. "Do what you love," he said, "because you're going to be doing it a lot and for a long time." He was right about that. I dove headfirst into a career in cooking and never looked back. But I didn't grow up wanting to become a chef. I didn't have a closet full of aprons and chef jackets. I didn't handwrite recipes with crayons as a kid. I didn't win any local hot dog cook-offs in fourth grade. I started out after college.

I began with a "basic skills" class at the now-closed Peter Kump's New York Cooking School and then took a once-a-week cooking class for five weeks. We did communal cooking and then ate the food we made and discussed it. My teacher? Peter Kump himself. He was wonderful. The most important thing happened on the day of my enrollment: I went to the school store and bought my first knife. A huge Wüsthof-brand chef's knife. I tore open the box and examined my purchase. There must've been twelve inches of blade. Too much for a hotshot like me. I stowed the knife carefully in my bag and brought it home to my mom and dad to show them what I intended to do. "Look, Ma," I said, digging around in my bag to show her. I found the knife and pulled it out from under a mess of papers. The blade cut through the skin of the three middle fingers on my right hand, and I watched in shock as blood seeped from my fingers and soaked my bag. Was this the first lesson? I think so.

We chefs have such hang-ups about arrogance and vanity. There's something we find commendable about being pale, hungry, somewhat malnourished (ironic for chefs, right?) or hungover (probably both), and definitely sleep deprived. This is a good "look" and symptomatic of the job. The chefs that roll up in ski parkas with their knives wrapped in elegantly woven wool pouches, sporting suntan marks that can only have come from ski goggles? Well, you do the math on that—how much time have they spent in their kitchens? I guess that first encounter with a knife awoke something deep inside me: the awareness that I was leaving childhood and school behind and trading it in for a savage profession, one that would demand all my attention. The price if I took my hands off the wheel? After my first knife misstep, I did everything I could to avoid the answer to that question.

I cooked so much for the next sixteen or so years that I rarely ever made anything to eat for myself—I cooked as if there were repercussions for not cooking. One night, I wanted some tea and had to boil the water in a stainless-steel measuring cup because I didn't own a pot. The instruction sheet for how to use my oven was still inside it the day I moved out of my West Village studio in 2006. Some chefs don't cook for joy or to feed themselves. They cook for sport. They cook for everyone who comes to the restaurant. They report to work for the camaraderie and to forget whatever they really need to get done in their larger life picture. Peeling 200 pounds of beets and cutting them into a 1⁄16-inch dice can be easier than facing a sick parent or an angry spouse. Work is a place to go to stay off the streets, a place to find community and stay out of trouble. It can be a rewarding refuge from one's own life.

Do I sound grumpy? I don't mean to. I'm trying to describe my personal pursuit of passion and expertise. I wanted to become an expert at something, to master a craft. I wanted to wake up with desire and passion and to push through any conflict that impeded my path. I have come to accept that it may be the constant seeking of knowledge and striving for satisfaction with my work that drive me toward success. Becoming an expert is lonely and, in many cases, so can be the life of a chef. But our strange reality is something we must embrace—we have to in order to survive and thrive. This isn't always a convenient philosophy for significant others, husbands or wives, and friends who don't work in the industry and therefore have a hard time understanding its peculiarities. But it is a point of view that can change. In fact, all of that changed for me when I gave birth to my daughter, Ava.

Did having a child change my cooking? My knee-jerk response is no. But I think I'm wrong. I think that's when I realized that even if you are a chef who basically lives at the restaurant and not at home, having a child changes the meaning of home. I can't go to my apartment, eat frozen yogurt on my bed, and doze off to an episode of *Chopped* with my coat still on. Now when I get home, there's a little human looking up at me. It took a while for this reality to pervade my cooking, but that's definitely when the idea of myself as a home cook came to life.

My first book on this topic, aptly titled *The Home Cook*, explored home recipes that I imbued with a chef's sensibility and techniques. *Cook with Me* embraces the food and experiences I had with my mother and father when I was growing up, and blends the dishes we ate together with dishes I never ate with them but that I now want to explore with my daughter. It's sort of a crossroads between Mom's Quiche Lorraine and Lobster Newburg, Dad's Stuffed Shells and Risotto with Tomatoes and Parmesan Cheese, and my own Fried Green Tomatoes with Marmalade and Lentil Cookies (probably recipes that neither of my parents would care to make or eat—and that's okay). This book is who I am now as a home cook—the dishes are a road map to who I am today as a cook, parent, and daughter. These recipes are the evolution of me.

I see clearly where my mother and father have influenced my cooking: the French dishes from Julia Child and Mom, the Italian dishes from my dad's Neapolitan roots. I also see how years of my own cooking in France shaped the types of sauces and vinaigrettes I turn to time and time again. Here's what I am only starting to learn: the influences of my daughter, Ava! She comes home asking for foods she ate at school; she watches a PBS show about Chinese food and wants to learn all about it. As I evolve as a cook, I am also making new discoveries about myself, like my newfound hobby: baking. It took me a long time to realize that making some good powdered sugar doughnuts or a cake with goopy frosting would be so therapeutic for me after cooking so many bass fillets and chicken breasts.

Truth is, no matter what I'm making, all I really care about is flavor and getting the most of it from whatever I cook. In this book, I teach you how to bring that approach into your home kitchen. You'll find lots of "chef" tricks, like dehydrating Parmesan cheese to make parm dust for popcorn. I'm taking years of cooking experience and personal history and distilling the best of it into a collection of 150 recipes for you to enjoy, conquer, and play with. So, let's cook.

PS: Cooking is tough. Sometimes it means doing a whole lot and sometimes it means taking a step back and letting the ingredients get to their destination. I still burn stuff and cut myself. I have great, tasty successes and some epic failures, too. Don't fear the stove or the kitchen. You're the boss.

I find inspiration everywhere—the amazing cooks and staff at Butter, my parents, and other chefs who I get to cook and create with—but no one inspires me more on a daily basis than Mike and Ava.

THE ZEROLL CO
TOLEDO, OHIO
PERONI
ITALIA

COOKING TOOLS AND EQUIPMENT

Here are the tools and equipment you will need to make the majority of the recipes in this book. The same tools appear time and time again. Most of them are simple; a few can seem daunting, but don't let that deter you. Remember—you're the boss in your kitchen and tools are here to help you, not to get in your way.

KNIVES: I generally shy away from boxed knife sets because they always include knives that I'll never touch. For me, all I need in my kitchen are a good paring knife, a serrated bread knife, a boning/meat knife, and a chef's knife. These blades will get you through all jobs. If you have a knife you bought at a discount store ten years ago and the handle is slightly cracked but you love it, cook with that! Cut food with knives that give you confidence and make you happy rather than with knives that you think you should use or that someone else tells you to use. Go to the store. Hold the knife in your hand; ask for a cutting board to practice how it feels when you go through the motions of chopping and dicing. Knife-shopping is like test-driving a car. Comfort and handling are everything.

"JAPANESE" (GREEN OR BEIGE) PLASTIC MANDOLINE: There's a reason why these slicers come with a guard to protect your fingers, but while you should be cautious when using one, you don't need to be afraid of it. The mandoline slicer can do many things, from shaving radishes paper-thin to cutting apple and potato matchsticks. You will get thinner and more even results than you could ever get from a knife, and even cuts mean evenly cooked food.

MICROPLANE GRATER: There are a few different styles on the market. Some produce a fine and fluffy, powdery grate; some grate thin, fine strips. These graters are all worth having in your toolbox. I use them most often for grating (and essentially liquefying) garlic so it cooks faster and more evenly. The same goes for removing fibers from fresh ginger. I grate hard cheeses for pasta dishes. I even grate vegetables like radishes and turnips and mix them into sauces to give thickness and mustardy zing from a plant-based source.

A BOX GRATER: This is a clunky, old-school piece of equipment that I find myself using more and more. From grating potatoes for potato cakes on the "large hole" side to finely grating aged pecorino cheese on the "small hole" side, this piece of equipment is a great multitasker that you can buy for a few dollars.

SPIDERS, SLOTTED SPOONS, AND A COLANDER: Using a spider or slotted spoon to fish vegetables from boiling water or doughnuts from hot fryer oil makes these tools invaluable. I like to place a colander in an ice bath for quickly chilling blanched vegetables—all you need to do is lift the colander out of the bowl instead of rooting through tons of ice cubes for those last green beans. These items will make you more efficient.

HEATPROOF SILICONE SPATULAS: Better to buy one or two pricey spatulas than a bunch of cheap ones. They enable you to complete more delicate tasks at the stove, like scrambling eggs, without scratching the surface of your nonstick skillet.

FOOD PROCESSOR: A standard 6-cup food processor can do a lot of heavy lifting. I love it less for chopping and more for making doughs.

BLENDER: My unsponsored love of the Vitamix blender is pure. I adore this machine—you can puree and aerate literally anything with it.

KITCHEN TOWELS AND PAPER TOWELS: I like to use a few kitchen towels to drain and dry ingredients. Sometimes I call for paper towels when the draining will likely make the cloth towel a single-use towel.

HALF SHEET PANS (A.K.A. MEDIUM SHEET PANS): I use these 18 by 13-inch rimmed multipurpose pans as baking sheets, aka sheets for cookies, as well as for cooking savory dishes like a roast chicken (shallow pans mean lots of browned, crispy chicken skin). You'll see them in all of the recipes in the sheet pan chapter on pages 63–73. I recommend buying a couple—they're inexpensive.

MY ALL-THE-TIME INGREDIENTS

Just as you have kitchen tools and gadgets that help you simplify or elevate the techniques in your cooking, you will also need some basic ingredients to build and layer flavors. Sometimes a dash of salt or a splash of vinegar in the right place can change a whole dish.

ACID: I love sharp, pungent, acidic liquids in all forms, and I call for a few different ones in this book. In general, I live in a world bathed in vinegar made from red wine, white wine, and apple cider, as well as your basic distilled white and balsamic vinegars. I generally stick to the cheap stuff with red wine vinegar because I want it to offer blunt-force acidity. The "finer" red wine vinegars sometimes add too strong or too distinctive a flavor, and the acid becomes overbearing. For balsamic, it's good to buy authentic from Modena, Italy; stick with the simple stuff. Aside from vinegar, I also love lemons, limes, and citrus in general.

SALT: I mostly use two types of salt when cooking: Diamond Crystal kosher salt and flaky Maldon sea salt. The kosher "forgives," so you can use a lot and rarely overseason. (You can play a more nuanced game with salt by seasoning as you go, layering ingredients and flavors as you add salt.)The Maldon salt has a great flavor and the large flakes crackle in your teeth as you chew a rib-eye or cauliflower steak. It's a finishing salt that gives great texture and a final burst of seasoning when you're ready to serve a dish.

GARLIC AND ONIONS: I use a lot of garlic and onions. I don't have a standard way that I cut these ingredients. I correlate the cuts—be they minced, grated, sliced, or chopped—to the other ingredients I'm adding them to, so the dish makes sense and comes together cohesively.

SOUR CREAM: I like full-fat sour cream, which has only 20% fat. It offers great tang and richness. Use a brand without additives.

CRÈME FRAÎCHE: This is a richer (30% fat) and less tangy cousin of sour cream.

SHIRO MISO (WHITE MISO PASTE): This is a light, mellow fermented soybean paste. It adds salt and caramel notes without sweetness. You can also use darker miso, but that's intense stuff. Start light and work your way up!

HOT SAUCES: I have a place in my heart for every hot sauce. The two I tend to add most frequently are Tabasco (because it's American to the core and provides a tingle of heat as well as acid and pungency in so many unexpected places, like in scrambled eggs) and *sambal oelek*, an Indonesian chile paste (because it packs serious heat but also lifts up the other flavors it mixes with).

WORCESTERSHIRE AND LOW-SODIUM SOY SAUCE: My dad cooked with the darkest soy sauces when I was growing up. I love their intense flavors, but they are often tough to cook with because they raise the salt level of a dish very quickly; they must be used judiciously. A splash of low-sodium soy or Worcestershire can make food taste like it has been cooking on the stove for hours instead of minutes. I prefer classic Worcestershire with anchovy in the base, but there is also a good vegetarian version. These two sauces are saviors, especially when you taste a dish just before serving only to realize it is underseasoned or a little "thin" in flavor. Try it . . .

THE MOST IMPORTANT INGREDIENT OF ALL IS CONFIDENCE: Confidence in the kitchen is demonstrated when you can touch something and tell if it feels done. Like when you press the center of a seared steak and instinctively know what temperature it is, or lightly press the center of a cake to know when the spring-back is just right. Use your sense of smell, too. You can smell when tomato or barbecue sauce hasn't cooked enough; those canned-tomato and undercooked-vinegar aromas hang heavy in the air of your kitchen. Be on the lookout for them. Confidence in the kitchen is also knowing not to take the food (or yourself) too seriously. It robs the kitchen of the joy of experimentation and learning. A mistake can be delicious, too.

I love to see what's actually growing and blooming nearby. It often inspires what gets put on the dinner table.

SNACKS & DIPS

These are the kinds of small plates that a chef like me collects over the years—they are great connectors between the start of a meal and the main course. I most often find myself putting a few of these plates out on the counter while I cook so my guests can graze at their leisure, and then I serve a main course and sides family-style afterward. I think it's a reaction to growing up in a house where appetizers for dinner parties were often plated, usually in a frenzy, in a too-small kitchen, and for too many guests! When I started working in restaurant kitchens, it felt the same, only instead of a couple of appetizers, we were plating a hundred. My way of serving small plates seems way more casual and friendly to me. Try these recipes out as snacks, as openers to a meal, or just for fun.

Flaming Broiled Provolone

WITH GARLIC-PARSLEY TOASTS

Broiling provolone cheese until it's molten and browned, then dousing and flambéing it with gin is pure drama, which is why this dish is so fun. The tang of the cheese and the lingering herbaceous note that the gin leaves behind make the duo work so nicely together. I like to start with a loaf of sourdough bread that weighs at least a pound. You can arrange the parsley-sprinkled garlic toasts on the table and just broil the cheese when you're ready to serve. I love how communal this dish is. The flame element makes me feel like I'm on vacation at a restaurant overlooking the ocean, and I'm a firm believer that food always tastes better by the ocean.

SERVES 4 TO 6

- ¼ cup extra-virgin olive oil
- 2 large garlic cloves, minced
- Kosher salt
- 5 or 6 (1-inch-thick) slices sourdough bread, halved lengthwise
- 8 sprigs fresh flat-leaf parsley, finely chopped (stems and all)
- 2 pounds provolone cheese, cut into 1-inch cubes
- 2 ounces gin (such as Bombay Sapphire)

Preheat the oven to 350°F.

MAKE THE TOASTS: In a medium bowl, whisk together the olive oil and garlic with a pinch of salt. Brush the garlic mixture over one side of the bread slices and arrange, oil-side up, in a single layer on a sheet pan. Place the pan on the middle rack in the oven and bake until the bread is browned, 8 to 10 minutes. Remove the pan from the oven, arrange the toasts on a platter, and sprinkle with the parsley; keep the oven on.

BROIL AND SERVE: Arrange the cheese in a single layer in a 9-inch broiler-safe baking dish, place in the oven, and bake until melted, 18 to 22 minutes. Set the broiler to high and broil the cheese until it's browned, about 2 minutes. Watch so it doesn't burn. Remove the baking dish from the broiler, sprinkle the cheese with salt, and place the dish on a trivet next to the toasts. Standing back, carefully pour the gin over the cheese and light it until it flames. Let the flame burn until it dies out, then dig in with the toasts.

Beef and Roasted Poblano Empanadas

This is one of the first recipes I ever devised at Butter, my restaurant in New York City. I imagined that the meaty taste of the beef would come through more powerfully if boosted by tart cream cheese and the heat from roasted poblano chiles. I even dreamt about it, and I was right: the subtle addition of these two ingredients takes the filling to the next level. I often make the dough and fill and shape the empanadas the day before baking and serving them so the flavors get a chance to meld together. Take care when cleaning poblanos—they are deceptively spicy, so wear gloves (or small plastic bags over your hands) when removing the ribs and seeds.

MAKES 24 TO 26 TWO-BITE EMPANADAS

DOUGH

6 cups all-purpose flour

5 tablespoons unsalted butter, at room temperature

1 tablespoon kosher salt

1⅓ cups room-temperature water

EMPANADAS

1 tablespoon canola oil, plus 1 quart (4 cups) for frying

1¼ pounds ground beef (80% lean)

Kosher salt

1 tablespoon unsalted butter

2 medium red onions, diced small

3 large garlic cloves, minced

3 medium poblano chiles

4 ounces cream cheese, at room temperature

½ teaspoon ground cumin

½ teaspoon cayenne pepper

All-purpose flour, for dusting

2 cups tomato salsa, for serving

MAKE THE DOUGH: In the bowl of a stand mixer fitted with the dough hook, combine the flour, butter, and salt and mix on medium speed until the ingredients are fully blended. Slowly add the water, continuing to knead on medium speed until the dough is soft and pliable, 3 to 5 minutes. Transfer the dough to a sheet of plastic wrap, flatten it into a 6-inch round, wrap it tightly, and refrigerate it for at least 30 minutes or up to 4 hours.

MAKE THE FILLING: In a large skillet set over medium heat, heat the 1 tablespoon oil until it smokes lightly, 2 to 3 minutes. Remove the pan from the heat and add the ground beef in a single layer. Season it with a few pinches of salt. Return the pan to the heat and cook, stirring occasionally, until the meat is cooked through, 5 to 8 minutes. Turn off the heat, use a spatula to push the meat to one side of the pan, and pour off any pooled fat. Add the browned meat to a medium bowl.

In the same skillet, melt the butter over medium heat. Add the onions and garlic, season with salt, and cook until they are soft and translucent, 8 to 10 minutes. Add the onions and garlic to the cooked beef, cover the bowl with plastic wrap, and refrigerate.

ROAST THE POBLANOS: Meanwhile, over an open flame or on a grill, roast the poblanos on all sides until charred, 3 to 5 minutes per side. Cool just enough to handle. Wearing gloves (or small plastic bags), slice the peppers open from top to bottom and remove the seeds and ribs. Lay the poblanos on a flat surface, charred-side up. Use a kitchen towel to wipe off the charred skin, then cut the chiles into thin strips. Set aside.

recipe continues

ASSEMBLE THE EMPANADAS: Remove the beef-onion mixture from the refrigerator and stir in the cream cheese, cumin, and cayenne; set aside. Lightly dust your work surface with flour and roll the dough into a ⅛-inch-thick sheet, flouring the surface beneath the dough as needed to prevent sticking (make sure you flour only one side of the dough; if you flour both sides, the dough won't stick together when you're crimping the empanadas). Let the dough rest for 10 minutes. Use a 3-inch round cookie or biscuit cutter to stamp out rounds as closely together as possible. Place a strip of poblano down the center of each round and top it with 1 tablespoon of the beef mixture. Fold the dough in half to make a half-moon and crimp the edges together by gently pressing them with the tines of a fork to seal. Take the cookie cutter and place it over the empanadas to trim the excess dough. Place the empanadas on a half sheet pan lined with parchment and refrigerate for at least 1 hour or up to 4 hours. (Note: The empanadas can be wrapped and frozen at this point; once frozen, transfer them to a gallon-size resealable bag and freeze for up to 2 weeks. Defrost them in the refrigerator for a few hours, or until somewhat soft, before frying.)

Preheat the oven to 250°F.

COOK AND SERVE: In a heavy-bottomed medium pot, heat the 1 quart canola oil over medium heat until it reaches 350°F on an instant-read thermometer. Drop a few empanadas into the hot oil (don't crowd the pot) and fry until they are golden brown on both sides, 3 to 5 minutes total. (A note about frying: Use a slotted spoon to move the empanadas around in the oil so all sides fry evenly.) Use a slotted spoon to transfer the empanadas to a wire rack set over a sheet pan (to allow any excess oil to drain off). Sprinkle with salt. Repeat with the remaining empanadas and arrange them all in a single layer on the rack. Place the sheet pan in the center of the oven and heat for 5 to 8 minutes to ensure the centers of the empanadas are warm. Serve with tomato salsa on the side.

Grilled Clams

WITH BACON AND SHAVED FENNEL

When I visited Charleston, South Carolina, a few years ago, I watched (I will admit, in horror) as a chef arranged some whole oysters on a piping-hot grill. As a native of New York City, home to so many great oyster bars, I always thought oysters should be served raw to preserve their briny freshness. This chef pulled one off the grill and handed it to me along with a small tangle of fennel tossed with lemon. Wow. That oyster was deeply delicious, taking on a smoky complexity that a fresh oyster can't offer. This dish is inspired by that single oyster. Who would ever think to put clams on the grill? There is, to me, nothing better for pure flavor than cooking seafood in its own shell. I use my mandoline on a "thin" setting to slice the fennel so it's tender when I take a bite of the bacon and clams. Be patient with the clams—sometimes they can take a few minutes to open on the grill. Whenever I give up and turn my back, that's when they open!

SERVES 4 TO 6

- 6 thin bacon strips, cut into 1-inch-wide pieces
- 36 littleneck clams (5 to 6 pounds), thoroughly washed and scrubbed
- ¾ cup panko bread crumbs, plus more if needed
- 6 tablespoons (¾ stick) unsalted butter, at room temperature
- 4 scallions (green and white parts), thinly sliced
- 2 large garlic cloves, minced
- Kosher salt
- 1 lemon: zest grated and lemon cut into quarters
- 12 sprigs fresh flat-leaf parsley, finely chopped (stems and all)
- 1 small fennel bulb, tough outer layers removed and discarded, cored, and sliced as thinly as possible (preferably using a mandoline)

Preheat a grill to medium-high. Preheat the oven to 350°F. Position a rack in the center of the oven.

COOK THE BACON: Place the bacon strips in a single layer in a large skillet and cook over medium heat until crispy, 8 to 10 minutes. Drain the bacon on a plate lined with a paper towel, reserving the fat in the pan.

COOK THE CLAMS: Have a pair of tongs and a large platter ready. Scatter the clams on the grill in a single layer. As they open (anywhere from 5 to 8 minutes), use the tongs to transfer them to a sheet pan, taking care to lift them by the top half-shell so you don't lose any of the precious clam juice pooling in the bottom shell. Discard any clams that don't open. Let the clams cool for a few minutes and then twist off the top shell from each one. This leaves the clam "meat" in its bottom shell. Slide a small knife under the clam meat to loosen it, but leave it in the original spot in its shell. (That way, when they are eaten, the clams will come off the shell easily.) Cover the sheet pan with plastic wrap and refrigerate the clams while you make the bread-crumb topping.

TOAST AND SEASON THE BREAD CRUMBS: Spread the bread crumbs in a single layer on a sheet pan and place in the oven on the center rack. Toast the bread crumbs until they are golden brown, 5 to 8 minutes.

Meanwhile, place the butter in a medium bowl and combine it with the scallions, garlic, a pinch of salt, the lemon zest, juice from 2 lemon quarters, and the parsley. Stir in a tablespoon or two of the reserved bacon fat, and then stir the toasted bread crumbs into the mixture.

recipe continues

SABATIER

THE TASTE TEST: Place a little of the bread-crumb mixture on a sheet pan and bake it until it is golden brown and bubbling, 3 to 5 minutes. Taste and adjust the seasoning if needed. Too greasy? Add more bread crumbs. Too dry? Add more bacon grease.

HEAT AND SERVE: Remove the clams from the refrigerator and discard the plastic wrap. Add a spoonful of the bread-crumb mixture on top of each clam in its shell, loosely molding it into a somewhat compressed mound. Bake the clams until they are hot to the touch and smell of garlic and toasted bread, 8 to 10 minutes. Remove the clams from the oven and arrange them on a serving platter. Squirt the juice from the remaining lemon wedges over the clams and top with the bacon and the fennel. Serve immediately.

Chicken Skewers

WITH SPICY PEANUT SAUCE

I love how the richness of the peanut butter absorbs the heat from the spice and the freshness of the lime that is added last minute. It's one of the first dishes I ate when I found out I was pregnant with my daughter, Ava. The doctor told me to stay away from spicy, rich sauces, so naturally I ran straight toward them. *Sambal oelek* is a chile sauce that comes in a small jar; professional chefs keep lots of it all around the kitchen to dollop over steamed rice or grilled beef. I like to stir it into other sauces, like tartar sauce or chicken-wing glaze to add a little (or a lot of!) heat. Want this sauce to be extra spicy? Top it with thin slices of fresh jalapeño. You can use metal or wooden skewers for the chicken—just make sure they will fit flat in your pan before threading the chicken onto them.

SERVES 2 TO 4
(14 TO 16 SKEWERS)

- 1 pound chicken tenders (about 8 pieces)
- Kosher salt
- ½ cup unsweetened coconut milk
- ¾ cup smooth peanut butter
- ⅓ cup low-sodium soy sauce
- ¼ cup apple cider vinegar
- 2 tablespoons toasted sesame oil
- 1 tablespoon sambal oelek chile sauce
- 1 tablespoon honey
- 1 large garlic clove, grated on a Microplane
- 2 tablespoons canola oil
- 1 tablespoon unsalted butter
- 2 tablespoons sesame seeds
- 1 large lime, cut into wedges

Preheat the oven to 350°F.

PREPARE THE CHICKEN: Season the chicken tenders with salt and cut them crosswise into 1½- to 2-inch pieces. Thread the chicken pieces onto skewers, fitting 2 or 3 pieces on each skewer.

MAKE THE SAUCE: In a large bowl, whisk the coconut milk with the peanut butter, soy sauce, vinegar, sesame oil, sambal oelek, honey, and garlic. Taste for seasoning, and if the sauce is thick like peanut butter, add a splash of water to loosen it. You should be able to spoon the sauce over and coat the chicken pieces. Set aside.

COOK THE CHICKEN: Heat the oil in a large skillet over high heat until it begins to smoke lightly, then reduce the heat to medium. Remove the pan from the heat so the meat doesn't flame up as it hits the hot oil, and add the skewers in a single layer. Return the pan to the heat and cook the chicken on one side until golden brown, 3 to 5 minutes. Then turn the skewers over and cook on the second side until golden brown, 5 to 6 minutes. Transfer the skewers to a rimmed sheet pan, place in the center of the oven, and bake for 5 to 8 minutes to finish cooking.

TOAST THE SESAME SEEDS: Meanwhile, in a small sauté pan, melt the butter over medium heat. Add the sesame seeds and toast them, stirring, for 1 minute, until the seeds are light brown. Drain the seeds, reserving the butter. Transfer the sesame seeds to a paper towel and season with salt.

SERVE: Remove the skewers from the oven, squeeze the lime wedges over the chicken, then drizzle with the reserved butter and slather with the peanut butter sauce. Sprinkle the sesame seeds over the chicken and transfer the skewers to a serving platter.

Spicy Crab Dip

Some chefs choose their profession because they grew up in a house steeped in good food and cooking. Other chefs cook in reaction to bad cooking or limited variety. I would say I am a mix of both types. There were a number of things my mom didn't cook when I was growing up. Basically, if my dad didn't like it, we didn't eat it! I never had fresh chiles until my late teens. Green bean casserole at Thanksgiving? Never heard of it. Guacamole was something I had eaten only a handful of times (and never at home). In fact, my mom, who famously made all kinds of delicious dishes from the cookbooks she was editing, never made dips, either. It probably explains my midlife obsession with them. I also really like to maximize an expensive ingredient like crab, and dip is one smart (and tasty) way to go about it. Buy the best crabmeat you have access to; it's front and center in this dish, and spending the extra money is worth it. I love jumbo lump crabmeat when I can get it. This dip is spicy, but you can tone that down if you want: just omit the cayenne, Tabasco, and jalapeño. You will need a 1-quart baking dish (any shape) for this.

SERVES 4 TO 6

1 tablespoon unsalted butter

4 scallions (green and white parts), thinly sliced

2 large garlic cloves, minced

Kosher salt

8 ounces cream cheese, at room temperature

½ cup mayonnaise

1 tablespoon Worcestershire sauce

2 teaspoons Tabasco

½ teaspoon cayenne pepper

10 ounces cooked fresh crabmeat, picked free of any shells

1 large lemon, cut into wedges

1 sleeve butter crackers (35 to 40 crackers)

Preheat the oven to 350°F.

COOK THE SHALLOTS AND GARLIC: In a small sauté pan set over medium heat, melt the butter and then add the scallions and garlic along with a pinch of salt. Add a splash of water and cook, stirring occasionally, until the scallions and garlic become tender without becoming overly brown, 3 to 5 minutes. When the water is cooked out and the scallions are translucent, remove the pan from the heat and set it aside to cool.

MAKE THE DIP: In a large bowl, whisk together the cream cheese, mayonnaise, Worcestershire, Tabasco, cayenne, and a pinch of salt until smooth. Put the crabmeat in a medium bowl and season it with a pinch of salt and a little lemon juice; then gently stir the crabmeat into the dip. Spoon the dip into a 1-quart (4-cup) baking dish.

COOK: Place the baking dish in the oven and bake until the dip is warmed through, 20 to 25 minutes. Squeeze the remaining lemon wedges over the top and serve warm, with the crackers alongside.

I grew up with an exceptional cookbook editor for a mother. Our bathroom reading was unproofed galleys of cookbooks or manuscripts that consisted of hundreds of pages of recipes. My mother's process for editing was to cook her way from one end to the other of every manuscript. Talk about thorough editing! I think that watching Julia Child cook and replicating her recipes or cooking from old-school cookbooks was actually my mother's recreational form of cooking—her "off-duty" work when she wasn't working on a book. Cooking was a great hobby of hers, but also an obsession. She could only understand an author if she cooked the recipes and tasted the results. The standard she set? Nothing short of kitchen greats like Julia Child, Edna Lewis, Bruce Cost, Craig Claiborne, and Marcella Hazan.

Herbed Pigs in a Blanket

WITH MUSTARD SAUCE

This recipe is just enough cooking for those times when you feel like doing a project but you don't want to spend all day at it. Grab some buttery puff pastry sheets in the freezer section of your supermarket. Pick up those mini hot dogs (you know the ones). You will see such a difference in flavor when you roll and bake these yourself rather than buying them pre-made (it's a lot cheaper, too). The real sleeper is the sauce—the pop of the mustard seeds mixed with the hot sauce, vinegar, and sweet honey is so good. Everyone loves these. So will you! Stop lying to yourself and dig in.

MAKES ABOUT 4 DOZEN AND ½ CUP OF SAUCE

- 2 (12-ounce) packages mini hot dogs (48 pieces)
- 2 large egg yolks
- All-purpose flour, for rolling the pastry
- 1 (1-pound) box frozen puff pastry, thawed
- 8 sprigs fresh flat-leaf parsley, finely chopped (stems and all)
- ¼ cup grainy Dijon mustard
- 2 tablespoons honey
- 1 tablespoon Tabasco
- 2 teaspoons red wine vinegar

PREPARE THE HOT DOGS: Use a paring knife to make a few small cuts into the casing of each hot dog. (This will prevent the hot dogs from bursting when you bake them.) In a small bowl, whisk the egg yolks with a splash of cold water. Line two sheet pans with parchment paper.

MAKE THE BLANKETS AND ROLL THEM: Sprinkle some flour on a work surface. Place one of the puff pastry sheets on the floured surface and flatten the seams with a rolling pin. The goal is to thin out the pastry a little and smooth the edges. Cut the pastry into strips about 1¼ inches wide and 2¼ inches long (about 24 strips per puff pastry sheet, so you have 48 total). Place the cut strips on one of the lined sheet pans and refrigerate them while you cut the other sheet of pastry into strips.

Sprinkle some parsley down the center of each strip. Set a hot dog crosswise on the short end of a pastry strip, making sure it is centered on the pastry. Dab some of the egg wash on the other end of the pastry strip, roll the hot dog up in its dough "blanket," and press the free edge onto the blanket to seal it closed. The dough should overlap slightly on itself. If need be, pinch the two edges to firmly close them. Place the pigs in blankets, seam-side down, on one of the prepared sheet pans, leaving some distance between them for browning. Leaving them on their seams will help keep the dough from unfolding. Repeat with the remaining strips, setting them on the lined pan once rolled. Refrigerate the pigs in blankets for at least 30 minutes or up to 4 hours.

MAKE THE DIP: In a medium bowl, whisk the mustard, honey, Tabasco, and vinegar with a splash of warm water. Taste for seasoning and adjust as you like. Set aside.

Preheat the oven to 375°F. Arrange oven racks in the lower-middle and upper-middle positions.

BAKE: Place the sheet pans in the oven and bake until the pastry is golden brown, 25 to 30 minutes. Serve the pigs in blankets with the dip on the side.

Steamed Pork and Rice Pearl Balls

The first time my dad lifted the cover of the steamer to reveal these pork and rice gems, I marveled at them—they really did look like large glistening pearls. "The rice is pressed onto a little pork meatball made with water chestnuts, ginger, and scallions," he explained, gently lifting one out for me to taste. The almost crunchy layer of rice on the outside gave way to the meaty, flavorful filling. An important detail is the cut of the meat: buy pork shoulder and ask your butcher to grind it.

To cook these, I like to place about 15 dumplings in each layer of the steamer (you can use the one that came with your pasta pot or a bamboo one); the timing varies if both steamer trays are full. You can also cook one layer and serve those while the next batch is steaming. Note that the rice needs to soak for at least 1 hour before making the dumplings.

MAKES 30 DUMPLINGS AND ⅔ CUP OF DIPPING SAUCE

DUMPLINGS

1 cup sticky rice or sweet short-grain glutinous rice

4 large dried Chinese black mushrooms (about 1 ounce)

12 ounces ground pork shoulder

2 scallions (green and white parts), minced

Generous ½ cup canned water chestnuts, rinsed and diced

1 large egg, lightly beaten

2 tablespoons low-sodium soy sauce

1 tablespoon grated fresh ginger

2 teaspoons kosher salt

SOY AND GARLIC DIPPING SAUCE

¼ cup low-sodium soy sauce

2 tablespoons distilled white vinegar

1 teaspoon honey

1 large garlic clove, minced

1 teaspoon toasted sesame oil

SOAK THE RICE AND MUSHROOMS: Soak the rice in 4 cups of cold water for at least 1 hour and up to 4 hours. Drain the rice in a colander and rinse it under cold running water to remove all of the excess starch.

Meanwhile, soak the mushrooms in hot water for at least 20 minutes to hydrate and plump them. Drain the mushrooms, remove the stems, and chop the caps into small pieces; place them in a large bowl.

MAKE THE DUMPLINGS: To the mushrooms, add the pork, scallions, water chestnuts, egg, soy sauce, ginger, and salt. Stir gently to combine (overmixing will make the meat tough). Line two sheet pans with parchment paper. Spread the drained soaked rice out on one of the sheet pans. Use a teaspoon to scoop about 2 teaspoons of the pork mixture from the bowl and roll the meat into a ball (it should be about the size of a mini meatball). Gently roll the ball in the rice to coat the outside. Do not press the meat into the rice and don't get multiple layers of rice on the ball. You don't want to end up with several layers of rice that potentially aren't cooked. Repeat with the remaining pork mixture, placing the rice-coated balls on the other parchment-lined sheet pan.

STEAM THE DUMPLINGS: Fill a large pot with about 2 inches of water. Add a steamer basket to the pot and arrange the dumplings in a single layer in the basket. If you want, add a second steamer basket on top and fill it with more dumplings. Cover the pot and bring the water to a simmer over medium heat. Steam the dumplings over low heat for 1 hour, replenishing the water if it gets low. The goal is to cook the rice completely without overcooking the meat in the center.

MAKE THE SAUCE AND SERVE: While the dumplings steam, in a medium bowl, whisk together the soy sauce, vinegar, honey, garlic, and sesame oil. Taste for seasoning and adjust as needed. When the dumplings are done, drizzle some of the sauce over each dumpling and serve them directly from the steamer basket, with extra sauce on the side.

Corn Fritters

I love biting into a fresh ear of corn slathered in butter, salt, and sugar—those first few bites are so luscious and sweet. I make these fritters to taste like individual bites of corn right off the cob. The secret to a tasty fritter is seasoning the corn before it's battered and fried. I use fresh corn when I can find it. I also use frozen by simply defrosting the corn and draining the water from it before cooking. The two spark plugs in this recipe? The brown sugar, which gives the corn a caramel-y flavor, and the cayenne pepper in the batter, which lends a burst of heat.

MAKES 15 TO 20 FRITTERS

1 tablespoon unsalted butter

4 cups fresh or frozen corn kernels, thawed if frozen

4 tablespoons dark brown sugar

Kosher salt

2 tablespoons granulated sugar

1½ teaspoons baking powder

2 large eggs, lightly beaten

½ cup whole milk

½ teaspoon cayenne pepper

¾ cup all-purpose flour

1 quart (4 cups) canola oil

1 large lime, cut into 8 wedges

SEASON THE CORN: If you are using fresh corn, melt the butter in a medium sauté pan set over medium heat, add the corn, and season it with 2 tablespoons of the brown sugar and about 2 teaspoons salt. Cook, stirring occasionally, until the flavors meld together and the corn gives off steam and shrinks slightly, 2 to 3 minutes. Drain the corn in a colander or sieve and set it aside to cool.

If you are using frozen corn, toss it with the melted butter, brown sugar, and salt and skip to the next step.

MAKE THE BATTER: In a large bowl, whisk together the granulated sugar, baking powder, eggs, milk, 2 teaspoons salt, and the cayenne. Gently stir in the flour and then add the seasoned corn. Set the batter aside to rest at room temperature for 15 to 20 minutes before frying.

FRY AND SERVE: Pour the oil into a large, deep, heavy-bottomed pot and heat it over medium heat until the oil reaches 360°F on an instant-read thermometer. (Or test the oil by dropping in one dollop of batter. Once the batter hits the oil, it should rise to the surface fairly quickly, and begin to bubble and fry. If it doesn't, wait for the oil to heat more before frying.) Line a sheet pan with a paper towel. Use a tablespoon or a small ice cream scoop to drop the batter, one scoop at a time, into the hot oil. Don't crowd the pot—for most pots, frying about 6 scoops at a time is enough. Use a slotted spoon to gently swirl the oil as the fritters fry. (Swirling allows the fritters to move around a lot, ensuring that they fry more evenly on all sides.) Once the fritters are light to medium brown, after 3 to 5 minutes, use the slotted spoon to transfer them to the paper towel to drain. Sprinkle the fritters immediately with salt and more brown sugar, and serve them with the lime wedges while they are still warm. Bring the oil back up to temperature before frying more fritters.

Crunchy Tomato, Pepper, and Anchovy Toasts

There are so many anchovies to choose from at the supermarket. I always aim for the ones in a glass jar or in any packaging where I can actually see the fillets. I look for pristine, firm fillets, with their silvery skin or without, that look like an invitation to eat! For this recipe, I like the pure taste of fish simply packed in a neutral oil or olive oil and without excessive herbs or spices.

Piquillo means "little beak" in Spanish. Named for their shape, these peppers are sweet and come fire-roasted and peeled. The result? A luscious ready-to-eat red pepper with great texture.

I like to put the cold, straight-from-the-fridge anchovies on the warm toast for a temperature contrast.

SERVES 4
(MAKES 12 TOASTS)

- 3 tablespoons extra-virgin olive oil
- 2 tablespoons red wine vinegar
- 12 sprigs fresh flat-leaf parsley, coarsely chopped (stems and all)
- 3 medium garlic cloves, minced
- 20 to 24 cold anchovy fillets (about 5 ounces), plus their oil
- ¼ teaspoon dried red pepper flakes
- 1 (12-inch) baguette, cut on a diagonal into 1-inch-thick slices
- 4 tablespoons (½ stick) unsalted butter, at room temperature
- ½ cup drained piquillo peppers, thinly sliced crosswise into rings
- 1 medium-size ripe beefsteak tomato, cored and finely chopped
- Maldon salt

PREPARE THE VINAIGRETTE AND ANCHOVIES: In a medium bowl, whisk together the olive oil, vinegar, parsley, garlic, and 1 tablespoon of the oil from the jar of anchovies. Remove the anchovies from the jar and drain them on a paper towel. Place them in the vinaigrette, add the red pepper flakes, and marinate for at least 20 minutes or up to 4 hours (refrigerated).

Preheat the oven to 350°F.

PREPARE THE TOASTS: Arrange the baguette slices in a single layer on a sheet pan and toast them in the oven until golden brown, 5 to 8 minutes. Turn the slices over and toast for an additional 3 to 5 minutes, until they are dry and crunchy.

SERVE: Spread the butter on the toasts, top each toast with some piquillo peppers, and then spoon on some tomatoes and vinaigrette. Add 2 anchovy fillets on top, and drizzle with more vinaigrette. Season with Maldon salt. Serve immediately.

Spicy Browned Butter and Sambal Potato Skins

The skin has always been my favorite part of a baked potato, so why not devote an entire recipe to potato skins tossed with butter and then roasted until crisp like chips? When I was a kid, I would wait for my mother to eat the last bits of the inside of an Idaho baker or a sweet potato, and then I'd scavenge the precious skins from her plate. I always felt like the skins deserved their own moment to shine. So tasty. Earthy. I love butter with potatoes, and it makes perfect sense to use butter for crisping the skins. It's critical to cook these at the last minute, just before serving, to allow people to devour them hot! I usually make a quickie potato salad or even a small batch of mashed potatoes with the insides of the cooked potatoes. I have also made mashed potatoes from the insides and then topped them with the crispy fried potato skins. Note: If you try this with sweet potatoes, leave a little more of the flesh on the inside of the skins for sweetness.

SERVES 4 TO 6

6 medium Idaho baking potatoes or sweet potatoes

3 tablespoons unsalted butter

Maldon salt

1 to 2 tablespoons sambal oelek chile paste

Preheat the oven to 450°F.

COOK THE POTATOES: Place the potatoes on a sheet pan. Place the pan in the oven and bake until the potatoes are tender when pierced with the tip of a knife, at least 1 hour. Cool but do not refrigerate.

CUT THE POTATOES: Place the cooled potatoes on a flat surface and cut each one lengthwise into 6 wedges. Gently scrape the flesh from the inside of each wedge, leaving a very thin layer of flesh inside the skin for some texture. Set the flesh aside for another use.

CRISP AND SERVE: In a large heavy-bottomed roasting pan, melt the butter over medium-high heat. Add the potato skins in a single layer, skin-side down, leaving some space between them. Place the pan in the oven and roast until the skins start to firm up, 10 to 12 minutes. Remove the pan from the oven and turn the potato skins over. Return the pan to the oven and roast until the skins are crisp to the touch, 10 to 15 minutes more.

Remove the pan from the oven and transfer the potato skins to paper towels to drain. Sprinkle with salt. Add the sambal oelek to the remaining (now browned) butter in the pan and give it a good stir. Drizzle the sauce over the potato skins and serve hot.

My Favorite Salami and Cheese Platter

I love French food. It's really what I cook. But I am also an Italian American who grew up with a mother who would hand me bowls of fresh ricotta sprinkled with sugar as a snack. Sometimes she would just hand me some thin slices of soppressata or a slab of fresh mozzarella. When I get in the mood for a platter, I go to Di Palo's on Grand Street in Manhattan's Little Italy and treat myself to an amazing assortment of cheeses and cured meats that takes me straight to those Italian childhood moments. I've been going to Di Palo's since the counter loomed large above me at the age of seven. Decades later, I lean on the counter and nibble on the different "seasons" of Parmesan cheese (spring milkings yield flowery notes; fall milkings taste of fallen leaves) and newspaper-thin slices of peppery salami while talking shop with Lou and telling jokes with Sal Di Palo. Give them a call. Tell them I sent you.

To make a platter that is abundant and inviting, serving 4 to 6 people, plan on about 1 pound of thinly sliced cured meat total (I keep it easy and buy about ¼ pound of each variety) and a ¼- to ½-pound wedge of each cheese. I usually serve four types of cheese. I like a mix: one creamy cow's milk, one goat cheese, at least one firm, aged cheese, and a tangy blue. Serve them with olives, mixed marinated peppers, cherry tomatoes, giardiniera, cured anchovies, crackers, and, of course, the best, freshest bread you can find.

continues

I also love a crudités or fruit platter with these meats and cheeses, depending on the overall meal.

MEATS

SPICY SOPPRESSATA

Soppressata is a cured pork sausage that's made in many regions of southern Italy. I like the ones made in the traditional style, with coarsely ground pork belly so there are big pieces of fat and meat that give the final product a lush, rustic texture. Most soppressata has a slightly aged flavor, unlike most regular salami. Sliced super thin, it's addictive.

PROSCIUTTO DI PARMA

Imported Prosciutto di Parma, which is a giant cured and aged pork leg, is my favorite cured meat. It's rich and nutty but also salty. I like the heat of the soppressata followed by the salty and slightly gamy taste of prosciutto.

SALAME ABRUZZESE

This pork sausage is made with black pepper and cured in the Abruzzese style. It's air-dried and salty in the best way. It melds really well with spicy soppressata because of its mellow flavor. I love the pop of the occasional black peppercorn, too.

SALAME CALABRESE

Cured in the style of Calabria, where my mom's family is from, these salami are typically packed with some heat—one famous variety is our American pizza favorite, pepperoni. This sausage combines the heat of spicy peperoncino chiles with ground pork and is air-dried, giving it a deeper flavor.

CHEESES

BLACK PEPPER PECORINO

This sharp and crumbly pecorino is made from sheep's milk and matured for about 40 days before being covered with a thick crust of ground black pepper gives it a tingling heat and brings out the salty notes of the cheese. Whatever I have left over from the platter usually gets grated over pasta dishes or tossed in a salad. The pleasantly sharp taste of the cheese is especially good with prosciutto.

GORGONZOLA DOLCE (SWEET GORGONZOLA)

Dolce means "sweet" in Italian, and Gorgonzola Dolce is a soft, rich blue cheese made from raw cow's milk. The cheese took its name from a small town near Milan, where it is said it was first made in the twelfth century. The cheese is buttery like Brie but has a little tangy blue-cheese note as well. It carries the DOP (Denominazione di Origine Protetta) certification, which means that the cheese was locally made and packaged by artisans using traditional methods.

LA TUR

A creamy blend of goat, sheep, and cow milks, this cheese has the most sublime texture. La Tur is made in the Alta Langhe region of Piemonte, near the border with Liguria. The rind is edible and gives a pleasantly bitter note to this luscious cheese.

FRESH RICOTTA

Ricotta is a fresh Italian cheese made from the whey left over after pressing cheese curds into a mold. The whey can come from sheep, cow, goat, or buffalo milk. Since the casein (milk protein) is filtered out of the whey, ricotta ends up being mild and creamy. It's also surprisingly low in fat and high in protein and tastes smooth and mildly sweet.

BURRATA

Burrata is made from fresh cow's milk (occasionally buffalo milk) and cream. The outer shell is firm like mozzarella, while the inside is rich, creamy, and loose in texture thanks to the cream. This cheese is served fresh and is best at room temperature.

Cheesy Truffled Popcorn

Sometimes it's the smallest nuance or change to something you have done for years that can make even the simplest recipe more inspiring. This recipe came to be when I grated some Parmesan for a salad and forgot about it. Later, upon absentmindedly nibbling on it, I discovered that the cheese had dried and become just slightly crunchy, like a flavorful salted cousin of panko bread crumbs. I immediately imagined this atop hot popcorn. While you may love butter on your popcorn, I suggest trying popcorn dry and liberally seasoned with this cheese. The only rule? Serve the popcorn immediately after popping so it's still warm.

I suggest buying black truffle oil, which I generally find more flavorful than white; but white truffle oil will do just fine if you don't have the option. I like the flavor of Urbani truffle oil. You can find it at urbani.com if your market doesn't carry it. If you want to go lighter and cheese-less, try sprinkling the hot popcorn with a few teaspoons of apple cider vinegar instead—acidity is surprisingly delicious on top.

SERVES 4 TO 6

1 (3-ounce) wedge Parmesan cheese

2 tablespoons extra-virgin olive oil

½ cup popcorn kernels

Kosher salt

2 to 3 teaspoons black (or white) truffle oil

"DRY" THE PARMESAN: Using a fine Microplane grater, grate the Parmesan over two sheet pans, forming a thin layer of cheese on each one. Leave the pans out on the counter at room temperature for at least 30 minutes or up to 4 hours to let the cheese dry and become almost slightly crispy.

POP THE POPCORN: In a medium heavy-bottomed pot with a tight-fitting lid, heat the oil over medium heat. Add the popcorn kernels to the hot oil and place the lid on the pot. Cook, shaking the pot slightly from time to time, until the popcorn begins to pop, 2 to 3 minutes. Once the popping is steady, remove the pot from the heat to allow the popcorn to finish popping without scorching and burning.

FINISH AND SERVE: Gradually transfer the popcorn to a large bowl, salting it and drizzling it with the truffle oil as you pour it into the bowl. Use a large serving spoon to toss the popcorn while seasoning it with the cheese. Serve immediately.

Charred Eggplant Dip

Eggplant dip, also called baba ghanoush, is everywhere these days—and I love it. What I have discovered through my experience in charring peppers and tomatoes on the stove is how much I love a vegetable that is super juicy on the inside and yet charred and bitter on the outside. That goes for eggplant, too. Mix the smoky scooped-out eggplant flesh with some vinegar and tahini and you are literally cooking with gas. You can also cook the eggplant on the grill, with the lid closed, until it is almost falling apart. The most important part of this recipe is fully cooking your eggplant and salting it. Don't rush it. Buy eggplants that are firm and medium-size—the larger ones have more seeds, which contribute more bitterness to the dip. For this recipe, I like either a meaty graffiti eggplant or a classic globe eggplant because both have thin skin and flesh that is surprisingly sweet and relatively low in seeds. Note that we salt many times in this recipe because eggplant can be bland. Salt will bring it to life. Taste for seasoning as you make this dish.

SERVES 4 TO 6

4 medium eggplants (preferably Italian or small globe eggplants; 3½ to 4 pounds)

3 tablespoons mayonnaise

3 large garlic cloves, minced

Grated zest and juice of 1 large lemon

3 tablespoons tahini paste

2 tablespoons apple cider vinegar

½ teaspoon hot paprika

Maldon salt

4 large pita breads, cut into 8 triangles each, toasted

Preheat the oven to 350°F.

COOK THE EGGPLANT: If you have gas burners, turn them to medium heat and place the eggplants directly on the burners. Using tongs, turn them often until they are charred on all sides, 10 to 15 minutes. Transfer the eggplants to a sheet pan lined with foil, place it in the oven, and roast until they are completely tender when pierced with the tip of a knife, 30 to 40 minutes. If you don't have a gas burner, char and cook the eggplants on a closed grill or simply roast them in the oven until tender. Set aside to cool completely.

MAKE THE DIP AND SERVE: In a large bowl, whisk together the mayonnaise, garlic, lemon zest and juice, tahini, vinegar, paprika, and a pinch of salt. On a cutting board, split the eggplants lengthwise and scoop out the flesh. Coarsely chop the eggplant flesh, mixing in a little of the charred skin. Drizzle it with all of the tahini mixture and a generous sprinkle of salt, mixing to combine. Taste for seasoning, adding more salt if needed. Transfer the baba ghanoush to a serving bowl. Serve the dip sprinkled with salt and with the toasted pita on the side.

Fried Green Tomatoes

WITH MARMALADE

There used to be a wonderful no-frills restaurant in Charleston, South Carolina, called Hominy Grill. It was there that I experienced a few Southern dishes for the first time—like shrimp and grits, hoppin' John, and fried green tomatoes. The tomatoes were coated in layers of cornmeal and fried until that cornmeal hugged those tomato slices like a skintight pair of jeans. I loved the gritty texture of the cornmeal as I chewed and found the tender tomato inside. As I ate, I longed for something tangy to brighten up the flavors but just couldn't figure out exactly what. One morning, a few months later, I was at home scraping a knifeful of butter over my toast, and the texture reminded me of the cornmeal coating on the fried tomato. I scooped some marmalade onto the bread and chewed, imagining it was a fried tomato slice, and that is how this dish was born. You will want to cook these close to when you serve them. They don't hang around very well once they are crisped up and sauced.

SERVES 4 TO 6

- 6 medium green tomatoes, cored and sliced into ½-inch-thick rounds
- 2 tablespoons sugar
- Kosher salt
- 2 cups old-fashioned finely ground cornmeal
- ½ cup all-purpose flour
- 1 teaspoon Hungarian paprika
- 1 cup whole milk
- 1 to 1½ cups canola oil
- Coarsely ground black pepper
- 3 tablespoons orange marmalade
- 2 teaspoons Tabasco
- 1 large lemon, cut into wedges

Preheat the oven to 325°F.

PREPARE THE TOMATOES: Arrange the tomatoes in a single layer on a sheet pan lined with parchment paper and sprinkle both sides with the sugar and a little salt. In a medium bowl, combine the cornmeal, flour, and paprika. Pour the milk into another bowl. Submerge a tomato slice in the milk and then dredge it through the cornmeal mixture, making sure it is evenly breaded on both sides. Arrange it on the sheet pan. Repeat with the remaining tomato slices, keeping them in a single layer on the sheet pan.

COOK THE TOMATOES: Set a large skillet over high heat and add about ½ inch of the oil. When the oil begins to smoke lightly, after 2 to 3 minutes, turn off the heat (this ensures that the oil won't get too hot or burn; burnt oil doesn't taste good) and add a single layer of tomatoes (you'll have to fry them in batches). Do not crowd the pan or the tomatoes will steam instead of crisp. Turn the heat back on to medium and cook the tomatoes on one side until they get lightly browned and crispy, 2 to 3 minutes. Using a slotted spatula, turn them over and cook until browned and crispy on the other side, 2 to 3 minutes more. Remove them from the skillet and drain them on a paper-towel-lined sheet pan. If your pan is low on oil, wipe out any bits of browned cornmeal left behind, then add 2 tablespoons more oil and heat over medium until it smokes lightly. Repeat the same cooking process with the remaining breaded tomatoes. While the next batch fries, keep the fried tomatoes warm on a sheet pan in the oven—leave the door ajar so they don't get soggy or overcooked.

SERVE: Season the tomatoes with salt and black pepper to taste. Warm the marmalade in a small saucepan over medium heat until its texture loosens, 1 to 2 minutes. Stir in the Tabasco and drizzle the sauce over the tomatoes. Serve with the lemon wedges.

THE NEW MEATS: CAULIFLOWER, SQUASH, BROCCOLI & CABBAGE

I love a slab of steak or a juicy chicken breast as much as the next person, but I also love how meaty vegetables can be. A cauliflower steak has almost become a cliché for a reason: it's fantastic. When cooked right and seasoned right, it is really tasty and satisfying. You can also take some of these heartier vegetable entrées and serve them alongside grilled fish or roasted chicken. I honestly never once had a vegetarian main course growing up. The most vegetarian dinner we ate was an omelet when the fridge was low on supplies. Ava takes well to these types of dinners, but not all the time. She is twelve and loves steak, burgers, and chicken. It can be challenging to introduce something like a whole cauliflower as dinner. That's why it has to be extra delicious.

Eggplant Steaks

WITH TAHINI AND BASIL

Eggplant wants to be meat when it grows up. I just know it! This dish is all about highlighting the earthy, sweet flavor of the eggplant, using the creamy, nutty tahini and zingy red wine vinegar as bookends. I serve this luscious dish as a main course with wedges of crusty bread, and pass out serrated knives for cutting, as if it were a rib-eye steak (the shape of the uncooked eggplant steak really reminds me of this cut). The tahini does wonders to add the creamy component we crave here, while the sunflower seeds and basil add sweetness and crunch. Don't buy eggplants that are soft or too large. Large eggplants are often cottony and loaded with bitter seeds. I love graffiti eggplants or the medium-size classic globe type.

SERVES 3

½ cup shelled sunflower seeds

4 large eggplants (about 1 pound each)

8 tablespoons extra-virgin olive oil

Kosher salt

¼ cup tahini paste

1 tablespoon plus 1 teaspoon red wine vinegar

Juice of 2 large lemons

⅔ cup fresh basil leaves

Preheat the oven to 400°F.

Scatter the sunflower seeds in a quarter sheet pan and toast them in the oven until they are fragrant and lightly golden, 5 to 6 minutes. Remove from the oven and set aside; keep the oven on.

PREPARE THE EGGPLANT: Place an eggplant on its side on a flat surface. Using a large knife and picturing that you are creating a large "steak," trim a little lengthwise slice off each rounded side so the eggplant sits flat on its side and measures 1½ to 2 inches thick. Repeat with the other eggplants.

SEAR THE EGGPLANT: Heat 2 tablespoons of the olive oil in a large skillet over high heat. Once the oil begins to smoke lightly, add the first eggplant steak. Sear until it browns on the bottom, 3 to 4 minutes. Transfer, browned-side up, to a sheet pan lined with parchment and season it generously with salt. Repeat with the other eggplants, adding 2 more tablespoons olive oil to the pan before searing each and transferring them to the sheet pan as they are done.

COOK THE EGGPLANT: Place the sheet pan in the oven and roast until the eggplant steaks are completely tender when pierced in the center with the tip of a knife, 25 to 30 minutes. Remove from the oven.

MAKE THE DRESSING: In a medium bowl, whisk together the tahini, vinegar, and lemon juice. The dressing should be thick enough to coat the eggplant but thin enough to spread over the eggplant as you spoon it on. If it is thicker than that, thin it with a splash of cool water. Taste for seasoning.

SERVE: Arrange the eggplant, browned-side up, on a serving platter and sprinkle with salt. Spoon the tahini dressing directly over the steaks and top with the basil leaves and toasted sunflower seeds.

Spiced Ruby Red Cabbage Steaks

WITH WHITE WINE AND GRAPES

I love red cabbage so much because it takes on flavor so well. The cabbage just drinks up the apple juice and white wine here and leaves you with no crunchy part left—just wilted tenderness. Cutting into this cabbage steak and taking that first bite offers a burst of brightness from the green grapes and wine, but it is also meaty and satisfying. The toasted walnuts bring a welcome contrast to the cabbage's silkiness.

SERVES 2

- ¼ cup walnut pieces
- 1 large head red cabbage (about 2 pounds)
- 4 tablespoons (½ stick) unsalted butter
- 2 teaspoons cumin seeds
- 2 teaspoons caraway seeds
- Kosher salt
- 3 medium shallots, halved and thinly sliced
- 1 cup dry white wine
- 1 cup unsweetened apple juice
- ¼ cup golden raisins, chopped
- 1 cup medium-size seedless green grapes, halved

Preheat the oven to 375°F.

Scatter the walnuts on a quarter sheet pan and toast them in the oven until they are fragrant and lightly browned, about 8 minutes. Remove from the oven and set aside; keep the oven on.

PREPARE THE CABBAGE: Place the cabbage upright (stem-side down) on a flat surface. Using a large knife, slice off the rounded part from two opposite sides so that, after slicing, each half will lie flat. Cut the cabbage in half.

BROWN THE CABBAGE: Melt 2 tablespoons of the butter in a large skillet over medium heat. Add the cumin and caraway seeds and toast them lightly for about 30 seconds. Do not let them brown. Immediately add the cabbage steaks. Swirl them in the butter and spices, and season with salt. Cook until they brown lightly on the first side, 5 to 8 minutes. Use a spatula or tongs to turn the cabbage steaks over and cook until they brown lightly on the second side, about 5 minutes. Transfer the cabbage to a sheet pan lined with parchment, reserving the butter and spices in the skillet.

REDUCE THE WINE: Add the remaining 2 tablespoons butter, the shallots, and a pinch of salt. Cook, stirring often, until the shallots are translucent, 3 to 5 minutes, and then add the wine. Cook until the wine has reduced by about half, around 8 minutes. Add the apple juice and raisins, then remove from the heat and pour this mixture over the cabbage halves.

COOK THE CABBAGE: Place the sheet pan in the center of the oven. Bake the cabbage steaks until they are slightly tender and yielding at the edges, about 20 minutes. Using tongs or a spatula, flip them over and cook until the cabbage is tender and yielding when you insert a knife into the center of a steak, about 20 minutes. If it isn't tender yet, cook for 10 to 15 minutes more.

Transfer the cabbage to a serving platter and spoon any remaining liquid from the pan over the top. Season with salt. Top with the halved grapes and toasted walnuts, and serve.

Broiled Cauliflower Steaks

WITH COCONUT MILK AND PARSLEY-LEMON GREMOLATA

A stunning browned and tender cauliflower steak (really just a cross-section slice of a head of cauliflower) could be the centerpiece for a vegetarian Thanksgiving table. It makes a great companion to the heavier traditional sides we know and love, like mashed potatoes and stuffing. Here the cauliflower gets the full spa treatment before it's served: First, it's partially cooked in water to hydrate it; this adds moisture to the steaks. Next, it's marinated in spiced coconut milk to tenderize it and add richness. The marinade also removes some of that powerful raw cauliflower "funk" that we don't want here. When you grate the lemon for the gremolata, do so deeply, pulling up the floral outer yellow zest and the pleasantly bitter white pith beneath as well. We want both flavors in this dish.

SERVES 4 TO 6

- 2 large heads cauliflower (2 to 2½ pounds total)
- Kosher salt
- 2 (13.5-ounce) cans unsweetened coconut milk
- 2 tablespoons coriander seeds, lightly crushed
- 1 teaspoon dried red pepper flakes
- 2 tablespoons Dijon mustard
- Grated zest and juice of 1 large lemon
- 2 tablespoons red wine vinegar
- ¼ cup extra-virgin olive oil
- 1 cup fresh flat-leaf parsley leaves, chopped
- 2 large garlic cloves, minced

PREPARE THE CAULIFLOWER: Place one head of cauliflower upright (stem-side down) on a flat surface. Using a large knife and visualizing that you are creating two large steaks from the head of cauliflower, trim a little off each side so that when you split the cauliflower in half, each half will lie flat. Cut the cauliflower in half. You should end up with two "steaks," each weighing 8 to 10 ounces. Repeat with the other cauliflower. (Save the trimmed bits for nibbling raw or adding to soup or a salad.)

BLANCH THE CAULIFLOWER: In a pot large enough to hold the steaks, bring 6 quarts of water to a rolling boil. Add salt until the water tastes like mild seawater. (How will you know? Taste a drop of it on a spoon.) Line a sheet pan with a kitchen towel. Add the cauliflower to the boiling water and cook until the core is slightly tender when pierced with the tip of a knife, 6 to 8 minutes. Use a large slotted spoon to carefully transfer the steaks to the lined sheet pan.

MARINATE: In a roasting pan that will fit the cauliflower steaks snugly in a single layer, whisk the coconut milk with the coriander seeds, red pepper flakes, and a generous pinch of salt. Submerge the steaks in the marinade, cover the pan with plastic wrap, and refrigerate for at least 4 hours or up to 24 hours.

Preheat the oven to 375°F.

MAKE THE VINAIGRETTE: In a medium bowl, whisk together the Dijon mustard, lemon juice, and red wine vinegar. Slowly whisk in the olive oil. Set aside.

MAKE THE GREMOLATA: In a small bowl, combine the parsley, lemon zest, and garlic. Set aside.

COOK AND SERVE: Remove the cauliflower steaks from the marinade and arrange them in a single layer on a sheet pan lined with parchment paper. Season with salt. Place in the oven and cook until they are completely tender when pierced with a knife, 15 to 20 minutes. Meanwhile, in a medium pot on the stove, simmer and reduce the marinade over medium heat until it becomes glossy and thick, 10 to 15 minutes, stirring occasionally.

Place an oven rack in the upper-middle position and heat the broiler to high. Move the sheet pan to this rack and broil until the tops of the steaks are charred, 2 to 3 minutes. Transfer the steaks to a serving platter. Glaze each steak with a few spoonfuls of the reduced marinade, drizzle with the vinaigrette, and sprinkle with the gremolata. Serve hot.

Whole Broiled Cauliflower

WITH BUTTER-TOASTED QUINOA

I am not a vegetarian by any means, and that's why this dish gets me every time. The quinoa obviously adds protein to the equation, but it also provides a satisfying crunch and a great toasty flavor. The presentation is dramatic, too. The whole "roast" in the center of the table, coated in scallions and crisped red quinoa, encourages people to eat with their hands, which I love. My mother and father always enjoyed communal dishes that were eaten almost like street food. It creates a certain intimacy with food that's exciting. Serving and eating the cauliflower requires a mixture of slicing and tearing, which makes this dish feel so communal and even primal. Be sure to sprinkle the interior with salt as you break it apart.

SERVES 2 OR 3

QUINOA

4 tablespoons (½ stick) unsalted butter

¾ cup red quinoa, rinsed and drained

Kosher salt

CAULIFLOWER

1 large head cauliflower (1 to 1½ pounds), bottom trimmed so it can sit upright (remove any leaves)

¼ cup extra-virgin olive oil

Kosher salt and freshly ground black pepper

Juice of 1 large lemon

4 scallions (green parts only), thinly sliced

Preheat the oven to 400°F.

COOK THE QUINOA: Melt 1 tablespoon of the butter in a medium sauté pan set over medium heat. Add the quinoa, season it with salt, and cook, stirring, until it crackles and smells nutty, 2 to 3 minutes. Gently stir in 2 cups of water. Simmer, uncovered, until the quinoa has unspiraled and is fully cooked, 12 to 15 minutes. (Flake a few grains off the top and taste for doneness—they should be tender with a little pop at the core. The quinoa may need another few minutes to fully cook.) Remove the pan from the heat, drain off any remaining liquid, and stir in 1½ tablespoons of the butter. Spread the quinoa out on a sheet pan to cool.

COOK THE CAULIFLOWER: Place the cauliflower upright (stem-side down) on a sheet pan. Drizzle it with the olive oil and sprinkle it generously with salt and a few generous grinds of black pepper. Roast the cauliflower until the tip of a knife easily pierces through to the center, 45 to 50 minutes.

MEANWHILE, TOAST THE QUINOA: In a medium skillet, melt the remaining 1½ tablespoons butter over medium heat. Add ½ cup of the cooked quinoa and cook until it is toasted and crispy, 3 to 5 minutes. It will crackle and pop almost like small popcorn kernels as it crisps. Season with salt and set aside.

SERVE: Spoon the remaining untoasted quinoa across a large serving platter and place the head of cauliflower on it. Top it with the lemon juice, crisped quinoa, and scallion greens, and serve with extra salt in a dish on the table for seasoning the interior of the cauliflower. I put this on the table as is and bring a large knife as if I were about to carve a roast chicken. Quarter the cauliflower through the center and watch as the pieces fall onto the sides of the dish, then cut them into smaller pieces and let people serve themselves.

Roasted Broccoli

WITH GARLIC AND TAMARI

Roasting broccoli draws out its natural water content, so you end up with a meaty vegetable that is nutty with a soft natural sweetness and a pleasing crunch. Add flavorful garlic, a little heat from red pepper, and the saltiness of tamari sauce, and you've got a dish that will convert any broccoli skeptic.

I actually have a broccoli skeptic in my own family: My daughter is an adventurous eater, but getting her to eat broccoli used to be a real struggle. I read in a parenting book that you have to have your child witness you cooking and/or eating a food at least twenty (twenty!!) times before giving up on it. So I did. I would say around moment number twelve she ate some, and then a little more. This was a real victory for a parent! My parents had a different style: they would put dinner on the table and I either ate it or I didn't eat. I am trying a slightly gentler approach. Now Ava eats broccoli and enjoys it. Would she rather have potatoes or corn? Of course. But broccoli can at least be in the mix.

SERVES 2 TO 4

- 2 large heads broccoli (crowns with stems, about 1½ pounds each)
- ¼ cup extra-virgin olive oil
- 8 large garlic cloves, thinly sliced
- ¼ teaspoon cayenne pepper
- Kosher salt
- ¼ cup tamari
- 2 tablespoons unsalted butter
- Sugar (optional)

Preheat the oven to 450°F.

PREPARE THE BROCCOLI: Place the broccoli on a flat surface. Peel the stems with a vegetable peeler, then slice the broccoli heads in half lengthwise. In a medium bowl, lightly combine the olive oil, garlic, and cayenne with 2 teaspoons salt. Arrange the broccoli halves, cut-side down, on a sheet pan and drizzle with the oil mixture, making sure that the broccoli is lightly and evenly coated with oil.

COOK THE BROCCOLI: Place the pan in the oven and pour ½ cup of water into the pan (this helps keep the broccoli tender). Roast the broccoli until the edges begin to brown and the tip of a knife easily slips into the center part of the stem, 15 to 20 minutes. If the broccoli isn't quite tender enough, roast for another 5 to 10 minutes.

MAKE THE SAUCE: In a medium sauté pan, bring the tamari to a simmer over medium heat and whisk in the butter. Taste for seasoning and add a pinch of salt or sugar if needed to balance the flavors.

SERVE THE BROCCOLI: Remove the broccoli from the oven and transfer it to a serving platter. Spoon the sauce over the top and serve.

Steamed Spaghetti Squash

WITH BLACK PEPPER, HONEY, AND ALMONDS

Sometimes my daughter wants steak or pork chops for dinner—you know, a real protein-rich meal. The day after, I often crave a meatless dinner to balance the week's choices. Many people turn to spaghetti squash in these moments, but I always had trouble coming around to it. Spaghetti? Nope, this squash has nothing to do with pasta (and don't even try to convince me otherwise). Squash? Nope, not like any other squash I know. I tried oven-roasting it until browned and tender, but I still didn't know what to do with it. But I didn't give up. One night, as I stared at the two spaghetti squash in the middle of my fridge (I do love a challenge), I thought: *This is it—I am going to conquer this vegetable.* I created this recipe and fell in love with the squash's grassy sweetness, the almost hydrating juiciness made so much more interesting by honey and cider vinegar. You can microwave these, split, skin-side up, in a baking dish for 12 to 15 minutes until tender, but I prefer roasting them, flesh-side up. I think the squash develops more flavor that way—and it takes the same amount of time.

SERVES 2 TO 4

- 2 medium spaghetti squash (about 2½ pounds each), split lengthwise, and seeded
- 2 tablespoons kosher salt, plus more if needed
- 2 teaspoons freshly ground black pepper, plus more if needed
- 3 tablespoons honey
- 5 tablespoons extra-virgin olive oil
- ½ cup sliced almonds
- 2 tablespoons apple cider vinegar

Preheat the oven to 400°F. Line a sheet pan with foil.

COOK THE SQUASH: Arrange the squash halves, cut-side up, on the foil-lined sheet pan and season them with the salt and pepper. In a small bowl, whisk together 2 tablespoons of the honey and half of the olive oil; drizzle this over the squash. Add 1 cup of water to the sheet pan and cover it tightly with foil, crimping the edges around the rim to seal it. Roast until the tip of a small knife slides easily into the center of the squash, 20 to 25 minutes. Remove the pan from the oven, carefully remove the foil, and set aside to cool.

TOAST THE ALMONDS: While the squash is roasting, scatter the almonds in a quarter sheet pan and toast them in the oven until golden brown, 3 to 5 minutes.

FINISH THE DISH: In a small bowl, combine the remaining 2½ tablespoons olive oil with the vinegar and the remaining 1 tablespoon honey. Use a fork to scrape the flesh from the squash halves onto a medium platter. Drizzle with the vinaigrette, taste for seasoning, and add salt and pepper if needed. Top with the toasted almonds and serve.

Twice-Baked Honeynut Squash

WITH BROWN BUTTER AND ORANGE

From the moment I first saw a small Honeynut squash at the market, I imagined it halved, stuffed, and boosted with a little roasted sweet potato, brown butter, and orange. This is such a satisfying main course—a wonderfully hearty stuffed vegetable always feels like a complete thought to me. Honeynut is a relatively new variety, so if you don't see any in your market, sub in small Hokkaido or smaller butternut squash for this recipe. As squash can vary in size, you may have to alter your cooking time based on the variety and exact size of your squash. Most important, and no matter what kind of squash you choose, don't undercook it—it's better to judge its tenderness by how easily a fork slides into the flesh than by timing alone since the cooking time for squash can differ so much. Be patient and wait until it's perfectly tender. It's worth it, I promise.

SERVES 4

- 4 small Honeynut squash, halved and seeded (see above for other varieties)
- 1 cup (2 sticks) unsalted butter
- 3 tablespoons blackstrap molasses
- ½ cup packed dark brown sugar
- Kosher salt
- 2 teaspoons ground ginger
- 2 teaspoons ground cinnamon
- 2 small sweet potatoes
- Grated zest and juice of 1 medium orange
- 1 tablespoon grated fresh ginger
- ½ cup finely grated Pecorino Romano cheese
- ½ cup pepitas (hulled pumpkin seeds), toasted and salted
- 1 large lemon, cut into wedges

Preheat the oven to 375°F. Set one oven rack in the middle position and a second rack in the lower-middle position.

PREPARE THE SQUASH: Arrange the squash halves, cut-side up, in a single layer on a sheet pan. In a medium skillet set over medium heat, melt 1½ sticks of the butter, swirling it often, until the butter solids turn from white to light brown and the butter smells nutty, 5 to 6 minutes. Pour the brown butter over the squash and follow it with the molasses. Sprinkle with the brown sugar, salt to taste, the ground ginger, and cinnamon. Fill the bottom of the pan with about ½ inch of water and cover the pan with foil, crimping the edges around the rim to tightly seal it.

COOK THE SQUASH AND SWEET POTATOES: Place the sheet pan in the oven on the center rack and set the sweet potatoes on another sheet pan on the rack below the squash. Bake until the tip of a small knife easily slides into one of the squash halves (and a potato), meeting no resistance, about 1 hour (the sweet potatoes may be tender before or after the squash, depending on their size). If either is too firm, continue to bake until tender, checking every 15 minutes. Remove both the squash and the sweet potatoes from the oven and set them aside to cool. Leave the oven on.

SEASON THE DISH: In a small saucepan, simmer the orange zest and juice over medium heat until reduced by about half, 2 to 3 minutes. Turn off the heat and use a spoon or a fine-mesh skimmer to remove the zest (discard it). Set the reduced juice aside.

recipe continues

Carefully scrape the flesh out of the squash halves, letting it fall into a medium bowl, leaving a thin layer of flesh inside each shell so they somewhat hold their shape. Add the reduced orange juice to the squash flesh. Halve the sweet potatoes and scoop out the flesh, discarding the skins. Add the sweet potato to the squash and stir with a wooden spoon until smooth. Stir in the remaining 4 tablespoons (½ stick) butter, the fresh ginger, and the cheese, and taste for seasoning. Do not overmix or the mixture will become gummy.

FINISH THE DISH: Spoon the seasoned squash mixture back into the squash halves and bake until hot, 15 to 18 minutes. Arrange 2 halves on each plate. Top them with the pepitas and serve with the lemon wedges on the side.

Beet and Brown Rice Burgers

There are a lot of plant-based meat substitutes out there, but I'm just not a fan. When I am eating a vegetable burger, I want it to be made from fresh vegetables. Beets are the obvious choice for their vibrant color and natural sweetness. When you combine the beets and their luscious tops with meaty walnuts, brown rice, the tang of a few golden raisins, and the heat of cayenne pepper, you get a dynamite burger. It tastes fresh and has that made-from-scratch flavor. I like to sandwich them in classic potato buns to give that authentic burger feel.

SERVES 4

BURGERS

1 cup brown rice

Kosher salt

4 tablespoons extra-virgin olive oil

1 medium yellow onion, grated on the large holes of a box grater (about ⅓ cup)

4 medium garlic cloves, grated on a Microplane

½ teaspoon cayenne pepper

2 medium red beets with tops, greens removed and coarsely chopped (about 1 cup), beets peeled and coarsely chopped (about 1½ cups)

1 cup walnut halves

1 tablespoon honey

½ cup golden raisins

1 large egg, lightly beaten

1 tablespoon red wine vinegar

FOR SERVING

4 classic potato buns

1 medium head Boston lettuce, washed

½ cup Thousand Island dressing (page 180)

1 beefsteak tomato, cut into 4 slices

1 to 2 large dill pickles, cut into ½-inch rounds

MAKE THE RICE: In a medium pot set over medium heat, bring 2¼ cups of water to a boil and add the rice and 2 teaspoons salt. Return the water to a boil, reduce the heat to a gentle simmer, cover, and cook until the rice is tender and all of the water is absorbed, 30 to 40 minutes. Transfer the rice to a medium sheet pan and refrigerate to cool. The yield should be about 2 cups.

COOK THE ONION AND GREENS: Heat a large skillet over medium heat and add 2 tablespoons of the oil. Add the onion, garlic, cayenne, and a pinch of salt. Cook until the onion is translucent, 3 to 5 minutes. Stir in the beet greens with another pinch of salt and cook until the greens are wilted, 2 to 3 minutes. Remove from the heat and set aside to cool.

MAKE THE BEET BURGERS: Put the walnuts in a food processor and pulse until they become coarse and powdery, 10 to 12 pulses. Add the brown rice, chopped beets, honey, raisins, and cooked onion mixture to the walnuts, and pulse until it looks similar to ground beef, 10 to 12 pulses. Transfer the mixture to a medium bowl and mix in the egg, vinegar, and a generous pinch of salt. Mix by hand until the mixture is uniform, then scoop out a little less than 1 cup (about 7½ ounces) and form it into a tight patty. Repeat with the remaining mixture to make a total of 4 patties. Place the patties on a plate, cover, and refrigerate for at least 1 hour or up to 4 hours.

Preheat the oven to 350°F.

recipe continues

COOK THE BURGERS: Heat a large cast-iron skillet over medium heat and add the remaining 2 tablespoons oil. Season both sides of the patties generously with salt. When the oil begins to smoke lightly, after 2 to 3 minutes, remove the pan from the heat and arrange the patties in it with space between them. Sear on the first side until browned, 8 to 10 minutes. Turn them over and brown the second side for 5 to 8 minutes. Place the skillet in the oven and cook until the patties feel firm to the touch, 8 to 10 minutes. Insert a small knife into the center of the burger and leave it there for 10 seconds. Remove the knife and touch the tip to make sure it is warm. If it is cold, cook the patties for an additional 5 to 8 minutes and test again. Transfer the burgers to a plate and let them rest for 5 to 10 minutes.

SERVE: Toast the buns in the oven for a few minutes until they are light brown—you want to take the chill off them and create those crispy bun edges. Add a leaf of Boston lettuce and a dollop of the Thousand Island dressing to each bottom bun. Top with a burger, more dressing, more lettuce, a slice of tomato, 3 or 4 pickle rounds, and the top bun.

ONE & DONE: ONE-PAN DINNERS

The struggle to keep dinner homemade can be real when you get home from work. I watched my dad come home after a long day and get dinner going in spite of his fatigue. Other than roasting a piece of meat or a whole piece of fish, my dad was a big stovetop-type for weeknight meals. He didn't know what a sheet pan dinner looked like—if he had known, I think he would have liked these recipes. Ava and I have adopted different traditions for quick meals, and one of them is a sheet pan dinner. I love the way everything cooks together, with the flavors and aromas melding. While dinner comes to fruition in the oven, I'll set the table, letting the fragrance of dinner become like weeknight aromatherapy. These recipes will help you stay on track because you can get a lot done on a sheet pan or in a skillet, from roasting pork chops with Brussels sprouts to making a fluffy quinoa-turkey pilaf. I admit that I enjoy putting the pan down on the counter or in the center of the table and letting people dig in, serving themselves straight from it. It takes away formality and a lot of dirty dishes, two things anyone could likely do without on weeknights. You can even heat your sheet pan and then use it to get a quick sear, broadening the scope of what can be made on a single pan for dinner. Keep in mind that since one-pan dinners are generally super simple, good ingredients are essential.

Quinoa Pilaf

WITH GROUND TURKEY

This is such a hearty, belly-warming dish that I forget it happens to be healthy, too. The curry powder and ground cumin fill the kitchen with an aroma that makes my stomach growl with hunger. Ground turkey isn't the "cheffiest" of ingredients, but to be honest, it offers comfort to me on regular weeknights when I crave lean protein. I think ground turkey gets a bad rap from being formed into tight patties and overcooked into bland burgers. Here I keep it loose so it can meld with the nutty flavor of the quinoa to create a protein-packed meal that also has a lot of flavor—and honestly, this feels like a whole meal that doesn't skimp anywhere or leave you hungry. I prefer ground thigh or other dark meat because it has some fat and more flavor than breast meat (but for a leaner result, feel free to use ground breast meat). After Thanksgiving, I have been known to stir shredded leftover turkey into this pilaf instead of using ground turkey.

SERVES 6 TO 8

- 4 tablespoons extra-virgin olive oil
- 1 teaspoon sweet curry powder
- 1 teaspoon ground cumin
- 1 medium yellow onion, halved and thinly sliced
- Kosher salt
- 1 cup red quinoa, rinsed and drained
- 1 pound ground turkey, preferably dark meat
- 1 tablespoon red wine vinegar

Preheat the oven to 350°F.

COOK THE QUINOA: Heat a large sauté pan over medium heat and add 2 tablespoons of the olive oil along with the curry powder, cumin, onion, and about 2 teaspoons salt. Cook until the onions become translucent, 3 to 5 minutes. Then stir in the quinoa and cook for 2 minutes, until you hear it crackling. Gently stir in 3½ cups of water and bring it to a simmer over medium heat. Transfer the quinoa mixture to a medium baking dish (you'll use the sauté pan again for the turkey), place it in the oven, and bake until the grains fluff slightly and separate, 20 to 25 minutes. Remove from the oven.

COOK THE TURKEY: Wipe out the sauté pan and add the remaining 2 tablespoons olive oil. Add the ground turkey, season it with salt, and cook over medium-high heat, stirring to brown the turkey evenly, until it's fully cooked, 8 to 10 minutes.

SERVE: Fluff the quinoa with a fork and taste for seasoning. Stir in the turkey and the vinegar, and serve.

Sheet Pan Blackened Salmon

WITH GARLICKY KALE

This is my modified weeknight version of Louisiana chef Paul Prudhomme's classic and legendary blackening technique. Traditionally you dip the protein, typically redfish, in melted butter and then in a mix of spices (a sort of local Louisiana masala) that often includes dry mustard, ground garlic, ginger, and cayenne pepper. When the protein is seared in a roaring-hot (usually cast-iron) pan, the butter and spices almost form a crust, giving the fish a charred and spicy exterior. To save some steps and make this a complete meal, I sift the spices evenly over olive oil–drizzled fish instead (if you don't have a strainer or sieve, sprinkle the spices directly over the fish) and then roast it with some Tuscan kale on a sheet pan. The sturdy kale leaves pack a taste that makes me think of leafy spinach mixed with a stronger mystery cousin. The kale absorbs the olive oil, which makes it tender, and then it is tossed with vinegar and lime juice, a tip I learned from food guru J. Kenji López-Alt.

SERVES 4

½ teaspoon sweet paprika

½ teaspoon cayenne pepper

1 teaspoon garlic powder

1 teaspoon dry mustard

1 teaspoon dried oregano

6 tablespoons extra-virgin olive oil

4 (8-ounce) portions wild salmon, skin on, pin bones removed

Kosher salt

1 large bunch Tuscan kale (about 12 ounces), stems removed, leaves torn into bite-size pieces

4 large garlic cloves, minced

1 tablespoon honey

Grated zest and juice of 1 large lime

Preheat the oven to 400°F. Set an oven rack in the lower-middle position.

PREPARE THE SALMON: In a small bowl, mix together the paprika, cayenne, garlic powder, dry mustard, and oregano and set aside. Use 1 tablespoon of the olive oil to grease a sheet pan. Place the salmon, skin-side down, on a flat surface and season it with salt. Drizzle the salmon with 2 tablespoons of the oil. Transfer the spice mixture to a small fine-mesh sieve or strainer and sift an even layer of the spices over the salmon. Arrange the fillets skin-side down on the prepared sheet pan, leaving space between them.

PREPARE THE KALE: In a medium bowl, massage the kale with the remaining 3 tablespoons olive oil and the minced garlic. The oil will actually tenderize the kale. Arrange it all around (but not covering) the fish on the pan.

COOK THE SALMON: Place the pan on the lower-middle rack and roast for 10 to 12 minutes for medium to medium-rare salmon. (For well-done fish, leave it in the oven for an additional 5 to 8 minutes.) Remove the pan from the oven and drizzle the honey over the fish. Then sprinkle all of the lime zest and juice over the fish. Serve immediately.

Macaroni and Cheese

This is such a classic, and my version highlights a pure, rich, and comforting cheese flavor since I skip the roux (a mixture of butter and flour cooked with milk or cream) as a base and start by melting grated Gruyère, Parmesan, and sharp cheddar directly into warmed cream instead. I've always felt that a roux dulls the other flavors and almost clashes with the floury nature of the macaroni itself. Dijon and a splash of Tabasco add some heat, while Worcestershire offers salt and the umami quality that keeps you coming back for more. Note: Worcestershire contains anchovies, so if you want this to be vegetarian, substitute soy sauce.

SERVES 8 TO 10

Kosher salt

1 pound elbow macaroni (preferably De Cecco brand)

1 quart (4 cups) heavy cream

2 tablespoons Dijon mustard

3 to 3½ cups finely grated Gruyère cheese

Freshly ground black pepper

1 cup finely grated Parmesan cheese (grated on a Microplane)

½ cup finely grated sharp cheddar cheese (grated on a Microplane)

Splash of Worcestershire sauce

Splash of Tabasco

1 large garlic clove, grated on a Microplane

2 tablespoons unsalted butter, melted

1 cup panko bread crumbs, toasted

COOK THE MACARONI: In a large pot, bring 4 quarts of water to a rolling boil over medium heat. Add enough salt to make it taste like seawater (I like to add about 4 tablespoons). Then add the macaroni and use a wooden spoon to stir it, making sure that the macaroni does not stick to the bottom of the pot as it cooks. Cook until the macaroni is still quite firm, generally 6 to 8 minutes (or a few minutes shy of al dente according to the package's instructions). Reserve 1 cup of the pasta water and drain the macaroni in a colander.

Preheat the oven to 350°F.

MAKE THE SAUCE: In the same pot you used to cook the macaroni, bring the cream and the reserved pasta water to a simmer over medium heat. Whisk in the mustard and then stir in 3 cups of the Gruyère. Season with salt and pepper. Simmer gently, stirring constantly, until the cheese is melted and integrated with the cream. Add ½ cup of the Parmesan and the cheddar, and stir until smooth. Add the Worcestershire and Tabasco and the garlic, and stir to blend. Taste for seasoning.

COMBINE: Add the macaroni to the cheese sauce and stir gently to blend. Remove the pot from the heat and set it aside so the macaroni absorbs the flavor of the sauce, 5 to 10 minutes. Taste. If it needs more cheesy flavor, add the remaining ½ cup Gruyère.

FINISH IN THE OVEN: In a medium bowl, mix the butter and the toasted bread crumbs. Season with salt and the remaining ½ cup Parmesan. Transfer the macaroni to a baking dish and top it with an even layer of the bread-crumb mixture. Bake the macaroni and cheese until it is hot and bubbling, 10 to 15 minutes. Remove from the oven, let rest for a few minutes, and serve.

Garlicky Lamb Steaks

WITH BABY RED POTATOES

Imagine: A slab of seared lamb, touched with garlic and mustard, sitting atop some simply roasted baby red potatoes sprinkled with red wine vinegar. Not only is it tasty, it's so achievable. Start with some center-cut lamb steaks. It sounds good when you say it—"center cut." The center-cut steaks on any whole cut of meat tend to be the best for many reasons: they are easy to cook because they are all generally the same size; they are usually free of the tougher, sinewy ends of any cut of meat; and they are the meatiest! My daughter, Ava, loves lamb far more than I do. She's a real carnivore, so this one's for her.

SERVES 4

- 4 (¾- to 1-inch-thick) center-cut lamb steaks (2 to 2½ pounds total)
- Kosher salt and freshly ground black pepper
- 2 tablespoons canola oil
- 1 cup dry red wine
- 16 to 18 baby red potatoes, such as Red Bliss, quartered
- 12 large garlic cloves
- 2 tablespoons grainy mustard
- 2 tablespoons red wine vinegar

Preheat the oven to 375°F. Set an oven rack in the upper-middle position.

SEAR THE LAMB: Season the lamb steaks on both sides with salt and pepper. Heat a heavy-bottomed skillet large enough to hold all of the lamb steaks over high heat. Add the oil to the pan and when it begins to smoke, after 2 to 3 minutes, add the lamb steaks in a single layer and cook until browned on the first side, 3 to 5 minutes. Resist the temptation to move them around. Turn them over and brown on the second side for 3 to 5 minutes. Transfer the lamb steaks to a sheet pan, leaving some space between them.

COOK: In the same skillet, simmer the wine for 2 to 3 minutes. This will deglaze the pan and blend all the good browned drippings into the wine. Pour these pan juices over the meat on the sheet pan. Arrange the potatoes and garlic cloves around the meat.

FINISH: Place the pan in the oven on the upper-middle rack and bake the lamb until an instant-read thermometer reads 125°F to 130°F for medium-rare to medium, 15 to 18 minutes. If you like well-done meat, cook the lamb for 5 to 8 minutes longer. Remove the pan from the oven and put it on a burner on top of the stove. In a small bowl, mix the mustard and vinegar together and spoon it over the meat—the liquid will simmer since the pan is so hot. Simmer for 1 minute, tossing to coat the potatoes and meat with the mustard mixture and the cooking juices. To serve, place the pan, with the bubbling-hot juices, in the center of the table or transfer it all to a serving platter.

Mixed Roasted Mushrooms

WITH MISO DRESSING

This dish could be called the "pot roast" of the vegetarian world. The mushrooms sizzle as they emerge from the oven and then get drizzled with a zingy, salty dressing and sprinkled with nutty sunflower seeds before serving. I love white miso paste (made from fermented soybeans) because it adds deep salt and flavor to a dish without tasting too strong. It contributes a unique richness and umami. It's the ingredient that makes people ask, "Why is this so good?" and "What did you put in here?" Let the miso paste be our little secret.

Using neutral-tasting oil allows the vinegars and miso to come through and meld with the earthy notes from the mushrooms. I suggest a combination of mushrooms that are easy enough to find, but feel free to use whatever varieties you like best. Mushrooms are often quite dirty and require washing, but wait to wash them until just before cooking so they don't sit, soaking wet, in the refrigerator. If the mushrooms are just slightly dirty on the surface, wipe them clean with a damp towel.

SERVES 4, MAKES ¾ CUP MISO DRESSING

- ¾ cup canola oil
- 4 large portobello mushrooms, wiped clean or washed
- 20 medium cremini mushrooms, wiped clean or washed
- 20 medium shiitake mushrooms, stemmed, wiped clean or washed
- 3 medium shallots, minced
- 3 scallions, green and white parts separated, minced
- Kosher salt
- 1 tablespoon plus 1 teaspoon white miso paste (shiro miso)
- ¼ cup red wine vinegar
- 1 tablespoon Japanese rice vinegar
- 2 teaspoons coarsely ground black pepper
- 1 teaspoon sugar
- ¼ cup roasted shelled sunflower seeds

Preheat the oven to 375°F. Position a rack in the center of the oven.

COOK THE MUSHROOMS: Drizzle 1 tablespoon of the oil on a sheet pan. Arrange the mushrooms in a single layer on the pan and sprinkle with the shallots, the scallion whites, and ½ cup plus 1 tablespoon of the oil. Season generously with salt, and roast the mushrooms until they are tender when pierced with the tip of a knife, 15 to 20 minutes.

MAKE THE DRESSING: In a large bowl, whisk the miso and the remaining 2 tablespoons oil together until smooth. Whisk in the red wine vinegar, rice vinegar, pepper, a pinch of salt, and the sugar. Taste for seasoning.

SERVE: Remove the pan from the oven, top the mushrooms with the dressing, the scallion greens, and the sunflower seeds, and serve.

Sheet Pan Pork Chops

WITH SPICY BRUSSELS SPROUTS

This is a weeknight dinner that I often cook up with my daughter—the kind of simple twenty-minute one-pan meal that will save you from the yawning jaws of takeout or prepared foods. Ava and I meet each other at the stove to cook meals together about three nights a week on average, and I always look forward to these cooking experiences. Not only do I get quality time with her and the chance to teach as we go, but we have two people doing the trimming and prep, meaning dinner gets on the table twice as fast. Cooking for a hungry twelve-year-old is no joke; a thirty-minute meal used to sound so reasonable, but Ava now needs more like a three-minute meal! We move like two silent, *hangry* ninjas until the chops are juicy and the Brussels sprouts perfectly tender, then we sit down with the sheet pan on a trivet in the middle of the table and dig in. If you can't find bone-in chops, simply buy thicker boneless ones. I would rather serve one thick, juicy chop per person than a bunch of thinner ones. The pumpkin pie spice and red pepper flakes are great with the Brussels sprouts, and the mustard ties the pork and everything else into the story.

SERVES 3 OR 4

- 16 to 18 Brussels sprouts (about 12 ounces), ends trimmed, quartered
- 2 tablespoons extra-virgin olive oil
- ¼ teaspoon dried red pepper flakes
- ½ teaspoon pumpkin pie spice
- 2 tablespoons sugar
- Kosher salt
- 4 (1½-inch-thick) single-bone pork rib chops (about 2 pounds)
- Freshly ground black pepper
- 2 tablespoons Dijon mustard
- 1 tablespoon balsamic vinegar

Preheat the oven to 425°F. Place a heavy-gauge sheet pan on the center rack in the oven.

PREPARE THE SPROUTS AND CHOPS: In a medium bowl, toss the Brussels sprouts with the olive oil, red pepper flakes, pumpkin pie spice, sugar, and salt to taste. Season the pork chops on both sides with salt and pepper.

COOK: Remove the hot sheet pan from the oven and place it on top of the stove. Use tongs to arrange the pork chops in a single layer on the sheet pan. They will sizzle! Scatter the Brussels sprouts all around the chops (save the bowl—you'll use it again) and return the pan to the oven. Reduce the oven temperature to 375°F and bake until the chops are cooked through, or to an internal temperature of 155°F to 160°F, 18 to 20 minutes.

SERVE: In the same bowl that you used to mix the Brussels sprouts, whisk the mustard and balsamic vinegar with a splash of water. Drizzle the dressing over everything and serve.

TAKE A CHICKEN . . .

Chicken is an entire food group in my house. From little drumsticks to a whole roasted bird, I never get tired of it. In a way, chicken is both universal and nostalgic. In fact, chicken was part of so many great moments of my childhood. It was also something we ate a lot outdoors. I had some great barbecue chicken platters and fried chicken picnics—my mother would pack a whole spread for the beach and we would eat it all, even enjoying the sand in between some bites. My mother made a lot of recipes using drumsticks and thighs, and while I also love the breast meat, some of those drumstick-heavy dishes are the ones that stick with me the most. Like her chicken with barbecue sauce, a sauce she feels is best with *only* chicken or pork, nothing else. Fried chicken, shaken in a flour-filled paper bag, was always a hit. I also love the comforting stews with tomato sauce, like a simple cacciatore, and even just plain roasted thighs and legs. Chicken is deeply delicious to me, and I never get tired of it. In fact, I'm always looking for new ways to cook chicken. Here you will find some of my childhood favorites, like chicken Parm, as well as some more unusual ideas for cooking chicken, like spatchcocking. From a hearty main course dish to a tasty cutlet sandwich, it's all here.

Fried Chicken Wings

WITH GARLICKY RANCH

This is not the classic fried chicken with flour and spices that you shake up in a paper bag. For these wings, I combine cornstarch and flour to make the coating a little crunchier while keeping the breading layer thin and light. I usually make a batch of ranch dressing and keep it hanging around until I need it. (I especially love ranch on very chilled iceberg lettuce or with raw sweet carrots; it gets better when it has a few days to sit in the fridge and develop a more complex flavor.) Don't think of this dish as something you would make instead of the classic Buffalo-sauce-and-blue-cheese-dressing combo; that's spectacular, too. This is just a variation where I enjoy the crunch of the breading with the tang and creaminess of the dressing.

SERVES 4 TO 6

GARLICKY RANCH

1 cup (8 ounces) sour cream

¼ cup mayonnaise

¼ cup buttermilk

1 tablespoon chopped fresh dill

2 teaspoons hot sauce

1 teaspoon garlic powder

1 teaspoon onion powder

CHICKEN WINGS

1½ quarts (6 cups) canola oil

1 cup all-purpose flour

1 cup cornstarch

18 chicken wings (about 3½ pounds total), each wing separated into the flat and drumette

Kosher salt

1 large lemon, sliced into very thin rounds

MAKE THE DRESSING: In a medium bowl, whisk the sour cream, mayonnaise, and buttermilk with the dill, hot sauce, garlic powder, and onion powder. Taste for seasoning and adjust if needed. Cover the bowl with plastic wrap, and refrigerate until the wings are ready.

Preheat the oven to 350°F.

PREPARE THE CHICKEN: Pour the oil into a deep, heavy-bottomed pot and heat it over medium heat until it reaches 350°F on an instant-read thermometer. Line a sheet pan with a clean kitchen towel and place a second sheet pan next to it. In a large bowl, combine the flour and cornstarch. Separate the larger pieces of chicken from the smaller ones. Season all of the chicken with salt and toss it in the flour mixture to coat all sides. Shake off the excess.

FRY THE CHICKEN: Drop half of the larger pieces of chicken into the hot oil and use a slotted spoon to gently swirl the oil as they fry. (This swirling will ensure that they fry more evenly on all sides.) When they are light to medium brown, after 5 to 7 minutes, use the slotted spoon to transfer them to the kitchen towel to drain and cool. Season with salt, place them on the second sheet pan, and keep them warm in the oven while you cook the rest of the chicken in batches, transferring pieces to the sheet pan in the oven until all of the wings are cooked. Leave the chicken in the oven for at least 10 minutes to ensure that all of the wings are cooked through.

SERVE: Arrange the chicken on a serving platter, with the bowl of Garlicky Ranch alongside for dunking.

Whole Roasted Chicken

I used to roast chicken in a fancier way, stuffing the cavity with exotic herbs and wedges of lemon and carefully nestling it into a gleaming, heavy-bottomed roasting pan—like how Beyoncé gets into a Bentley. The results were always great, but what I discovered over time is that I love simplicity when it comes to chicken. I can now guarantee you that four everyday ingredients—chicken, salt, pepper, and lemon—never tasted so good together. My favorite way to roast a chicken is to use a sheet pan or shallow roasting pan with a wire rack set inside to allow for maximum exposure and browning of the chicken skin (let's face it: we all want that chicken skin). One night, I roasted a chicken for my daughter and we ate about half of it for dinner. I put the other half in the fridge. When I came back later, I discovered my daughter had snuck back in and peeled away the crispy sheet of skin on the other half as a snack. Who can blame her? I often make chicken salad from whatever chilled leftovers we have the next day and save the carcass in a resealable bag in the freezer for making stock.

SERVES 4 TO 6

- 1 (3- to 3½-pound) whole chicken
- Kosher salt and freshly ground black pepper
- 1 large lemon, cut into wedges

Preheat the oven to 450°F.

GET READY: Set a wire rack in a shallow roasting pan or on top of a sheet pan. Place the chicken, breast-side up, in the center of the rack. Season the chicken generously all over with salt and pepper.

COOK: Roast the chicken until it is browned and juicy, about 30 minutes. Reduce the oven temperature to 375°F and roast until the juices at the leg/thigh joint run clear or a thermometer inserted into the thickest part of the thigh registers 165°F, 25 to 30 minutes more. (I count 12 to 15 minutes per pound of bird; for a 3½-pound bird, I start checking the juices and temperature after 45 to 50 minutes of cooking, since some chickens cook faster than others.) Remove the pan from the oven and set the chicken aside to rest for 10 minutes.

CARVE AND SERVE: Remove the bird from the pan and place it breast-side down on a cutting board. Let it rest for an additional 10 to 15 minutes so the juices can flow into the breast meat. Then turn the chicken breast-side up and carve it. As you cut the breast and thigh meat, season the meat directly with salt and pepper to deepen the flavor. Transfer the meat to a serving platter. Pour the drippings from the pan over the meat. Serve with the lemon wedges.

Spicy Hacked Chicken

The point of Dad's hacked chicken, one of his signature Chinese dishes (which has the trappings of a classic Thai dish, too), is a whole new way to look at chicken. Served chilled and with a super-spicy heat-packed sauce, this dish offers a lesson in how delicious a canvas an unseasoned poached chicken breast can be when it's mixed with a flavorful sauce. It's also unique because it's chilled. Make no mistake: the peanut sauce is *very* spicy, meaning *this is not for the kids; it's for you,* but if you want to dial back the spice (unlike my dad, who would make it with *double* the spice!), simply omit the cayenne and red pepper flakes and use half the amount of Sichuan peppercorns. When my father would drop this dish on the table, I would take one bite and marvel at the rich notes of peanuts, sesame, and soy playing with the heat. (Remember: these flavors were quite unusual in the 1980s, when you couldn't get Thai or Sichuan food delivered to your door on demand. The flavors spoke to me.) One bite was really all I could handle before the floral peppercorn notes and the delicate flavor of the chicken were buried by the heat! Dad would often make the sauce in advance and then cook and serve the chicken day-of with piping-hot steamed rice, which would have an almost cooling effect and get me to a second bite of the chicken . . . sometimes.

SERVES 4 TO 6

- 2 tablespoons peanut oil
- 2 tablespoons Sichuan peppercorns
- 3 cups chicken stock, store-bought or homemade (page 107)
- 4 (8-ounce) boneless, skinless chicken breasts (about 2 pounds total)
- ½ cup smooth peanut butter
- 4 large garlic cloves, minced
- 3 tablespoons grated fresh ginger
- 3 tablespoons low-sodium soy sauce
- 3 tablespoons distilled white vinegar
- 2 tablespoons Asian sesame oil
- 1 teaspoon cayenne pepper
- 1 teaspoon dried red pepper flakes
- ¼ cup fresh cilantro leaves
- 4 scallions (green and white parts), minced

COOK THE PEPPERCORNS: Add the peanut oil and Sichuan peppercorns to a medium skillet set over low heat. Cook the peppercorns until they start to crackle and release a floral, spicy aroma, 2 to 3 minutes. Use a slotted spoon to transfer the peppercorns to a flat surface and lightly crush them with the bottom of a cool skillet or pot; then transfer them to a medium bowl and set aside. Discard the oil in the skillet (you will use the pan again in the next step).

COOK THE CHICKEN: Pour the chicken stock into the skillet and bring it to a simmer over medium heat. Lower the heat and submerge the chicken breasts in the warm stock (it should be barely simmering), raise the heat to medium-low, and poach until the thickest part of a breast registers 165°F and is completely cooked through, 12 to 15 minutes. You do not want to boil the meat or even cook it at a high rate. Transfer the chicken breasts to a cutting board and use a sharp knife to cut the meat crosswise into ¼-inch-thick slices (reserve the stock for another use; it has been enriched from poaching the chicken and is delicious). Arrange the breast meat on a platter as if the breasts were still whole, cover with plastic wrap, and refrigerate until the chicken is slightly chilled, at least 1 hour or up to 4 hours.

MAKE THE SAUCE: To the bowl containing the Sichuan peppercorns, add the peanut butter, garlic, ginger, soy sauce, vinegar, sesame oil, cayenne, red pepper flakes, and cilantro. Whisk to combine.

SERVE: Spoon the sauce over the chicken and sprinkle the scallions on top. Serve slightly chilled.

Spatchcocked High-Heat Chicken

WITH 20 GARLIC CLOVES

This is a riff on the classic chicken-with-lots-of-garlic dish. Spatchcocking the chicken—meaning removing the chicken's spine with shears and cracking the breastbone so the chicken lies flat on the pan—allows a lot of the skin surface area to be exposed to the direct heat of the oven. Does it cook the chicken a *lot* faster? No. Is it easier to cook this way to get more delicious browned skin and to speed up cutting the cooked meat? Yes. Is it fun and will you look cool in front of your friends and family? Yes.

SERVES 4 TO 6

1 (3½- to 4-pound) whole chicken

Kosher salt

20 large garlic cloves, unpeeled

2 tablespoons extra-virgin olive oil

1 large lemon, halved

Preheat the oven to 500°F.

SPATCHCOCK THE CHICKEN: Place a paper towel on a cutting board or other flat surface (this helps prevent the chicken from sliding around). Place the whole chicken, breast-side down, on the towel. Find the backbone running down the center. Use a pair of sharp poultry shears or scissors to cut down the length of one side of the backbone and then along the other side to remove the backbone (save it in a resealable plastic bag in your freezer and add it to chicken stock for extra flavor). Flip the bird over so it's breast-side up. Press down firmly on the on the center of the breast to crack the breastbone so the chicken lies flat.

PREPARE THE CHICKEN: Place the chicken, breast-side up, on a parchment-paper-lined sheet pan and season it with salt. Toss the garlic cloves with the olive oil in a small bowl and then arrange them all around the chicken.

COOK: Place the pan in the oven and roast for 20 minutes. Then reduce the oven temperature to 400°F and cook until an instant-read thermometer inserted in the thickest part of the bird registers 165°F and the juices at the leg/thigh joint run clear, not pink, 25 to 30 minutes.

RESTING AND CUTTING THE CHICKEN: Remove the chicken from the oven and set it aside to rest for at least 10 to 15 minutes before transferring it to a cutting board for slicing. I find it easiest to cut the chicken using (clean) poultry shears or scissors. Arrange the chicken pieces on a platter and then scatter the roasted garlic cloves over the cut meat. Pour the drippings over it all and squeeze the lemon halves over the top. Season with salt and serve. (If you prefer to serve the chicken cut up into smaller pieces, season each piece with salt individually.)

Chicken Paprikash's Tomatoey Cousin

This is a chicken dish my mother would make from time to time. While not entirely loyal to a classic paprikash, I love that she mixes in some Italian chicken cacciatore vibes with the tomato. I definitely think a good chicken breast, cooked until perfectly juicy, doesn't get enough love. Too often, a boneless, skinless breast cooks up so dry that it resembles shoe leather. Not here. In this dish, the breasts are almost treated like thighs. They are seared skin-down first to get the skin nice and crispy. The cayenne delivers a tingling heat that gets bookended by the sweetness of the paprika and tomatoes on one side and the vinegar on the other. Traditionally, paprikash is served with egg noodles and tossed in a little sour cream, but I love it even more with basmati rice pilaf (see page 213) or a crusty loaf of sourdough bread to soak up all that sauce.

SERVES 4

- 4 (8-ounce) skin-on, bone-in chicken breasts
- Kosher salt
- 2 tablespoons canola oil
- 2 medium yellow onions, halved and thinly sliced
- 4 large garlic cloves, thinly sliced
- 1 large red bell pepper, cored, seeded, and thinly sliced
- 3 tablespoons sweet Hungarian paprika
- ½ teaspoon cayenne pepper
- 2 medium plum tomatoes, cored and coarsely chopped
- 2 cups chicken stock, store-bought or homemade (page 107)
- 1 tablespoon red wine vinegar

Preheat the oven to 350°F. Position a rack in the center of the oven.

BROWN THE CHICKEN BREASTS: Season the chicken breasts with salt. Heat the canola oil in an ovenproof medium sauté pan set over medium heat. When the oil begins to smoke lightly, after 2 to 3 minutes, remove the pan from the heat and add the chicken breasts, skin-side down. Return the pan to the heat and cook until the skin is browned, 5 to 8 minutes. Remove the chicken from the pan (you'll use the pan again), transfer it to a plate, cover with foil, and keep warm.

MAKE THE SAUCE: Add the onions, garlic, bell pepper, paprika, and cayenne to the pan you used to brown the chicken. Cook over medium heat until the onions are translucent, 5 to 8 minutes. Stir in the tomatoes, chicken stock, and vinegar and cook until the sauce comes together, 12 to 15 minutes. Taste for seasoning.

FINISH COOKING THE CHICKEN: Arrange the chicken breasts, skin-side up, in the sauce. Place the pan in the oven on the center rack and bake the chicken until the skin is golden brown and the juices run clear when the thickest part of a breast is pierced with the tip of a knife, 20 to 25 minutes. (Alternatively, an instant-read thermometer should read 165°F when inserted into the thickest part of the breast.) Remove the pan from the oven and let the chicken rest for 10 to 15 minutes in the sauce.

SERVE: Taste the sauce for seasoning. Arrange the chicken breasts on a platter and serve topped with the sauce.

Tomato and Gingery Coconut Milk Chicken

My mother essentially operated her kitchen like a French bistro where the chef had likely worked in a few Michelin-starred joints along the way. With each passing year of my childhood I fell deeper in love with her soufflés, quiches, and mousses. She was, by way of eggs and some advice from the great Julia Child, turning me into a little Francophile. That said, once in a blue moon, she would cook a dish like this one. I was used to richness coming only from buttery, creamy French dishes, so the coconut milk stood out as a real star to me. I remember wondering how a chicken could taste so rich and feel so light and clean at the same time. The answer: Because this is a dish where coconut milk and canned tomatoes live in wedded bliss. The richness of the coconut links up with the acidity and sweetness of the tomatoes. In the middle of it all? The juicy chicken with tasty skin and tender meat. It's not about crispy skin here but rather the true deliciousness of the chicken. I love to spoon this over a bed of rice. It would be equally tasty with some of the potatoes from the Mojo-Marinated Skirt Steak recipe on page 196.

SERVES 6 TO 8

- 6 chicken thighs and 6 drumsticks (3 to 4 pounds total)
- Kosher salt
- 2 tablespoons canola oil
- 2 teaspoons cumin seeds
- 2 large yellow onions, thinly sliced
- 4 medium garlic cloves, pressed through a garlic press
- 1 teaspoon ground cinnamon
- 1 teaspoon dried red pepper flakes
- 2 dried bay leaves
- 1 (15.5-ounce) can unsweetened coconut milk
- 1 (28-ounce) can peeled whole tomatoes
- 1 small knob fresh ginger, peeled and grated

BROWN THE CHICKEN: Arrange the chicken in a single layer on a sheet pan and season with salt. Turn the pieces over and season again. Heat a large skillet over high heat, add the oil, and heat until it begins to lightly smoke, 2 to 3 minutes. Then carefully add enough chicken pieces to fill the skillet without crowding (you will need to cook the chicken in batches). Resist the temptation to move or turn the pieces so they can brown properly on their first side, 5 to 8 minutes. With tongs, turn the chicken pieces over and cook until they are browned on the second side, 3 to 5 minutes. Transfer the chicken pieces to a sheet pan and set aside. Repeat with the remaining chicken pieces.

MAKE THE SAUCE: Drain all but about 2 tablespoons of the fat from the skillet. Return the skillet to medium heat and add the cumin seeds, stirring rapidly to give them a quick 10- to 15-second toast. Add the onions and garlic, season with salt, and cook over medium heat, stirring frequently, until they turn light brown, 5 to 8 minutes. Stir in the cinnamon, red pepper flakes, and bay leaves. Add the coconut milk and the tomatoes, using a wooden spoon to break them up. Cook the sauce until all the flavors come together, 10 to 15 minutes.

FINISH THE CHICKEN: Add ¼ cup of water to the skillet and arrange the chicken pieces, skin-side up, in the sauce. Keeping the heat on medium-low, cook until the pieces are cooked through, 30 to 35 minutes. Stir in the ginger and remove the bay leaves. Taste for seasoning. If the sauce is thin, simmer it for a few more minutes before serving.

Chicken Stir-Fry

WITH RADISH GREENS

"How do I make chicken interesting?" That's what people often ask me. Truth is, chicken *is* interesting, and delicious—we just eat it so much that we crave variety. The tart flavor of sumac, which is zingy and fresh like lemon but more balanced, picks up the sweetness of the radish and radish greens here and brings an exciting flavor to the chicken. Sumac is a spice made from the berries of a bush that grows wild around the Mediterranean. Don't have radish tops? You can use beet tops or Swiss chard leaves instead. Be warned: the leafy green tops from a root vegetable can sometimes be delicious and sometimes not, so taste and evaluate them on a case-by-case basis. Before using any greens, always take care to wash them well so they are not gritty: just one pinch of grit can ruin a whole dish.

SERVES 3 OR 4

1½ pounds boneless, skinless chicken thighs, cut into 1½- to 2-by ½-inch pieces

Kosher salt

1 teaspoon dried red pepper flakes

1 teaspoon ground sumac

2 tablespoons canola oil

3 large garlic cloves, grated on a Microplane

12 to 15 small red radishes, quartered, plus 1 cup loosely packed radish greens, washed and coarsely chopped

1 small knob fresh ginger, peeled and grated

2 tablespoons low-sodium soy sauce

2 tablespoons apple cider vinegar

1 tablespoon grainy Dijon mustard

PREPARE THE CHICKEN: Arrange the chicken pieces in a single layer on a sheet pan. Season on one side with salt, the red pepper flakes, and the sumac. Turn the pieces over and season the other side with just salt.

COOK THE CHICKEN: Heat the oil in a large heavy-bottomed skillet over high heat. When it begins to smoke, after 2 to 3 minutes, remove the skillet from the heat and quickly (and carefully!) add the chicken in a single layer. Return the skillet to high heat and cook, stirring from time to time, until the chicken is cooked through, 3 to 5 minutes.

FINISH THE DISH: Reduce the heat and stir in a few pinches of salt, the garlic, and the radishes and radish greens. Cook, stirring often, until the radish greens wilt, 5 to 8 minutes. Then stir in the ginger, soy sauce, vinegar, and mustard and simmer until the ingredients meld together, 2 to 3 minutes more. Taste for seasoning and serve.

My Mother's Chicken

WITH BARBECUE SAUCE

You can smell how uniquely good this sauce will be the minute you combine all the ingredients and turn the heat on under the pot. When my mother would make barbecue sauce, she'd combine everything in a pot and just let it simmer and then sit, cooling, on the stove for what seemed like forever. I remember the smell would be somewhat acrid at first, like vinegar. Then the ginger, spices, and lemon would take over and create this wonderful aroma. She often made a double batch and kept some in the fridge. This is not an "everywhere" barbecue sauce; it's really best for chicken and pork. But sometimes I'll use it on vegetable steaks, like the cauliflower steaks on page 48, or I might glaze shrimp with it. I'm not one to impose name brands in a recipe, but here they matter to get that exact flavor my mom created.

SERVES 4 TO 6

3 cups Heinz ketchup

2 cups Bragg apple cider vinegar

½ cup Lea & Perrins Worcestershire sauce

½ cup Kikkoman low-sodium soy sauce

2 cups packed dark brown sugar

2 tablespoons Colman's dry mustard powder

2 tablespoons Dijon mustard

¼ cup chili powder

1 (2-inch) knob fresh ginger, peeled and cut crosswise into ¼-inch-thick rounds

6 large garlic cloves, thinly sliced or pressed through a garlic press

2 large lemons, cut crosswise into ½-inch-thick slices

Kosher salt

4 pounds skin-on, bone-in chicken parts, a mixture of light and dark meat, all relatively the same size

MAKE THE SAUCE: In a large pot, whisk together the ketchup, vinegar, Worcestershire, soy sauce, brown sugar, dry mustard, Dijon mustard, and chili powder. Bring everything to a simmer over medium heat and then add the ginger, garlic, and lemon slices. Simmer, stirring from time to time to ensure that nothing sticks to the bottom and burns, until the vinegar mellows slightly and the consistency thickens, 25 to 30 minutes. Remove the pot from the heat and set it aside to cool. Taste for seasoning, adding salt if needed.

Preheat the oven to 350°F. Set oven racks in the lower-middle and middle positions. Line two sheet pans with parchment paper.

PREPARE THE CHICKEN: Season the chicken parts on all sides with salt. Pour about 1½ cups of the barbecue sauce into a medium bowl (reserve the remaining sauce for serving). Submerge the chicken pieces, one at a time, in the sauce and then divide them between the two prepared sheet pans.

COOK AND SERVE THE CHICKEN: Place one sheet pan on the middle rack of the oven and the second on the lower-middle rack and bake the chicken, undisturbed, for 20 minutes. Remove the pans from the oven and turn the pieces over. Use a pastry brush to coat the second side of the chicken with the remaining barbecue sauce (discard any leftover sauce and don't reuse the brush—it touched uncooked chicken; take care to soak the brush in hot, soapy water for a few hours or wash it in the dishwasher).

Return the sheet pans to the oven. Bake for another 15 to 20 minutes, until the chicken juices run clear (they shouldn't be pink) when you poke the meaty party of a thigh with the tip of a small knife, or until the temperature reads 165°F on an instant-read thermometer. Serve with the reserved sauce, warmed up, on the side.

STAINLESS
STEEL

Roasted Chicken Pot Pie

WITH CREAM BISCUIT TOPPING

If there's one cloud in the sky, I get the urge to start rolling biscuit dough! When I crave something belly-warming and comforting, this is the type of dish I immediately gravitate to. For this pot pie, I treat the filling and the sauce almost as two separate recipes. The Worcestershire and red wine vinegar lift the filling up, make it edgy, and take it away from the heavy part of a classic pot pie that we can actually do better without. Another thing about pot pie made entirely from scratch? It can be time-consuming. There's no shame in some tasty shortcuts: use leftover cooked chicken or store-bought rotisserie chicken instead of roasting the chicken yourself; while I love the homemade cream biscuits, you can also use store-bought frozen puff pastry for the topping instead. I like to make this in a 9-inch deep-dish pie pan and place it, bubbling hot, right on the table to let people dig in. This is a great comfort dish, especially on rainy or snowy days.

SERVES 3 OR 4

POT PIE

1 tablespoon canola oil

1½ pounds skin-on, bone-in chicken thighs, cut into roughly 1½- to 2-inch cubes, or about 2½ cups cubed cooked chicken

Kosher salt

2 tablespoons unsalted butter

24 small pearl onions, peeled if fresh, thawed if frozen, halved

3 medium carrots, sliced into ½-inch-thick rounds

3 small celery stalks, sliced into ½-inch pieces

Freshly ground black pepper

1 cup frozen peas, thawed

¼ cup fresh flat-leaf parsley leaves

Preheat the oven to 375°F. Position a rack in the center of the oven.

ROAST THE CHICKEN: In a large ovenproof skillet, heat the oil over medium heat until it begins to smoke lightly, 2 to 3 minutes. Season the chicken pieces generously with salt and place them, skin-side down, in a single layer in the hot oil. Cook until the skin starts to brown around the edges, 5 to 8 minutes. Transfer the skillet to the oven and bake until the juices run clear or until an instant-read thermometer registers 160°F when it is inserted into the center of a piece, 12 to 15 minutes. Remove the chicken pieces from the skillet (you'll use the skillet again), put them in a medium bowl, and refrigerate.

MAKE THE FILLING: In the same skillet, melt the butter over medium heat. Add the onions, carrots, and celery, season with salt and pepper, and cook, stirring, until the vegetables are tender, 8 to 10 minutes. Transfer the vegetables to a large bowl and stir in the chicken, peas, and half of the parsley. Refrigerate.

MAKE THE SAUCE: In a medium pot, bring the chicken stock to a simmer over medium heat. Add the cream, Worcestershire, vinegar, and a generous pinch each of salt and pepper. Simmer gently until the mixture is as thick as a light cream soup, 15 to 18 minutes. Taste for seasoning and add salt if needed. Remove the pot from the heat and set it aside to cool. (The filling needs to cool so the biscuit dough doesn't sit on top of piping-hot filling. The biscuits will brown better if both the filling and the dough are cool.)

2½ cups chicken stock, store-bought or homemade (page 107)

2½ cups heavy cream

1 tablespoon Worcestershire sauce

1 tablespoon red wine vinegar

CREAM BISCUITS

1½ cups all-purpose flour, plus extra for shaping

2½ teaspoons baking powder

2 teaspoons sugar

2 teaspoons kosher salt

1¼ cups heavy cream

MAKE THE BISCUIT DOUGH: In a large bowl, sift together the flour, baking powder, and sugar. Add the salt and the cream to the dry ingredients. Use your hands to mix the dough. It will look slightly wet and will be somewhat elastic. Do not overmix. Turn the dough out onto a lightly floured surface and, with floured hands, shape it into a 9-inch round. Transfer the biscuit round to a sheet pan lined with parchment paper. Chill it in the freezer for at least 30 minutes or up to 2 hours.

ASSEMBLE: Transfer the filling and sauce to a 9-inch deep-dish pie pan and top it precisely with the biscuit round.

BAKE: Place a rimmed sheet pan on the middle oven rack and set the pie plate on the sheet pan (this will prevent any liquid that might overflow from burning on the bottom of your oven). Bake until the biscuit is golden brown and the filling is hot, 30 to 35 minutes. (Even if the biscuit is browned on top, it could still be undercooked and the filling not hot enough. Test it by inserting a small knife into the center and letting it sit for 10 to 15 seconds. When you remove the knife, the blade should feel hot to the touch.)

SERVE: Top the biscuit with the remaining parsley leaves and place the dish in the center of the table with a few large spoons for everyone to serve themselves.

Chicken and Ginger Pad Thai

Here is a dish that became a part of our family repertoire because Ava once had great Thai food at a birthday party. "Make pad thai, Mom!" She looked up at me as I panicked. "You're a chef, Ma." She paused. "You know how to make anything, right?" I have to be Wonder Woman if only for a few more years, and it starts with this tasty dish, a textural and flavorful wonderland of crunchy bean sprouts, chicken bolstered by eggs, the bite of scallions and ginger with salty soy sauce, and the chew of rice noodles. The leftovers are also so tasty after they sit in the fridge overnight! A note about peanut butter: I love Jif brand and proudly use it here.

SERVES 3 OR 4

8 ounces pad thai rice noodles

Boiling water

3 tablespoons peanut oil

1 tablespoon honey

1 tablespoon fresh lime juice

¼ cup smooth peanut butter, preferably Jif

¼ cup low-sodium soy sauce

6 large garlic cloves, minced

2 large eggs

1 boneless, skinless chicken breast (about 8 ounces), cut into ½-inch pieces

Kosher salt

2 tablespoons grated fresh ginger

1 cup bean sprouts

4 scallions (green and white parts), sliced

¼ cup fresh cilantro leaves

PREPARE THE NOODLES: Place the noodles in a large heatproof bowl and cover them with boiling water. Add 1 tablespoon of the peanut oil and set aside until the noodles are tender, 5 to 8 minutes. Drain the noodles in a colander and set them aside.

MAKE THE SAUCE: In a medium saucepan, stir together the honey, lime juice, peanut butter, soy sauce, and two-thirds of the garlic with ½ cup of water. Bring the mixture to a boil over medium heat and cook until the sauce reduces and thickens slightly, 3 to 4 minutes. Set it aside.

COOK THE EGGS: In a large nonstick skillet, heat 1 tablespoon of the peanut oil over medium heat. Crack the eggs into the skillet and use a heatproof rubber or silicone spatula or a spoon to scramble the eggs gently until they are firm but not overcooked, 1 to 2 minutes. Set the eggs aside on a plate.

FINISH AND ASSEMBLE: In the same skillet, heat the remaining 1 tablespoon peanut oil over medium heat. When the oil begins to smoke lightly, after 2 to 3 minutes, add the chicken and the remaining garlic along with a pinch of salt. Cook, stirring often, until the chicken is fully cooked, 4 to 5 minutes. Stir in the ginger, bean sprouts, sauce, noodles, and eggs, and toss gently to combine. Taste for seasoning. Serve topped with the scallions and cilantro.

SABATIER

Fried Chicken Cutlet Sandwiches

The fun in this dish lies in gathering and making all of the components and then building the tasty sandwiches. Using grassy sage instead of more classic choices like oregano or basil makes the breaded chicken unique, and it melds well with the mayonnaise touched with the two flavors I remember most from my childhood: garlic powder and red wine vinegar. When my dad took the bottle of vinegar and the jar of garlic powder out of the kitchen cabinet, he meant business! Most of his salad dressings began and ended there. The other secret to this dish is to make sure the chicken is pounded really thin. If you buy chicken breasts, butterfly them so you begin with pieces that are already half as thick, then place them between two pieces of plastic wrap and pound them gently with the flat side of a cleaver or a mallet. (You can also ask your butcher to do it for you.) I mix two types of bread crumbs, panko and fresh, so the breading has lots of texture. The mixed bread crumbs also help the breading stick to the chicken. A better coating leads to better texture in the final product. It's important to let the breaded cutlets rest and chill in the refrigerator before cooking them. The breading will adhere better that way.

SERVES 4

1 cup canola oil, for frying

20 to 24 fresh sage leaves

Kosher salt

3 large eggs

2 cups plain fresh bread crumbs, toasted

2 cups panko bread crumbs

1 pound chicken cutlets, butterflied and pounded very thin (about ¼ inch thick)

½ cup mayonnaise

2 tablespoons red wine vinegar

1 teaspoon garlic powder

2 romaine lettuce hearts, left whole or cut lengthwise into 1-inch pieces

Juice of 1 large lemon

4 seeded kaiser or Italian rolls

¼ cup finely grated Parmesan cheese

FRY THE SAGE: In a large skillet, heat the oil to 340°F on an instant-read or deep-frying thermometer. Add the sage leaves and cook until they turn pale in color and become crisp, 1 to 2 minutes. Using a slotted spoon, transfer the leaves to a plate lined with paper towels and season them with salt. Set aside. Remove the skillet, with the oil, from the heat and reserve it.

PREPARE THE CHICKEN: Crack the eggs and separate them, dropping the yolks into a small bowl. Save the whites for another use, like a Pavlova, meringue cookies, or my egg white omelet (page 115). Add a splash of cold water to the yolks and whisk to blend. In another bowl, combine the two types of bread crumbs. Season the chicken pieces on both sides with salt and dip each one thoroughly in the eggs and then thoroughly in the bread crumbs. Place the chicken in a single layer on a sheet pan lined with parchment paper. Refrigerate.

COOK THE CHICKEN CUTLETS: Reheat the oil you used to fry the sage to 350°F. In two batches, add the chicken cutlets and fry them until they are golden brown on both sides and cooked through, 5 to 8 minutes. Drain the chicken on a paper towel and immediately season with salt.

MAKE THE DRESSING: In a medium bowl, whisk together the mayonnaise, red wine vinegar, and garlic powder.

MAKE THE SANDWICHES: Arrange the romaine leaves on a flat surface and drizzle them with the lemon juice and then the dressing. Split the rolls and add the chicken, dressed romaine, crispy sage leaves, and Parmesan to the bottom halves. Place the tops on and serve.

Grilled Spatchcocked Chicken

WITH HONEY GLAZE

I love what the yogurt in the marinade does to tenderize and add richness to the chicken, and the honey-vinegar sauce at the end leaves people wanting more. Don't bother peeling the ginger; leaving the skin gives the marinade more flavor. Why add both lemon and vinegar here? The vinegar teases out the tang of the yogurt, and the lemon adds a floral note as well as additional acidity—and combined with the smoky and charred flavor from the grill, they make a chicken dinner that people go crazy for. (See page 82 for more about the technique of spatchcocking chicken.)

SERVES 4 TO 6

1 (4- to 4½-pound) whole chicken

1 cup plain whole-milk yogurt

1 (2-inch) knob fresh ginger, grated

1 teaspoon ground cumin

1 teaspoon dried red pepper flakes

Kosher salt

½ cup honey

2 tablespoons red wine vinegar

2 teaspoons coarsely ground black pepper

4 scallions (green and white parts), thinly sliced

Juice of 1 large lemon

SPATCHCOCK THE CHICKEN: Place a kitchen towel on a flat surface (this will prevent the chicken from sliding around) and set the chicken, breast-side down, on the towel. Find the backbone running down the center. Use a pair of sharp poultry shears or scissors to cut down the length of one side of the backbone and then along the other side to remove the backbone. Flip the bird over so it's breast-side up. Press down firmly on the center of the breast to crack the breastbone so the chicken lies flat.

MARINATE: In a large bowl, combine the yogurt, ginger, cumin, red pepper flakes, and several pinches of salt. Whisk until smooth. Place the chicken in the bowl and slather it with the yogurt mixture. Cover the bowl with plastic wrap and refrigerate for at least 4 hours or up to 12 hours.

MAKE THE HONEY GLAZE: In a small skillet, bring the honey to a simmer over medium heat. When the honey starts to foam and turn light brown, remove the skillet from the heat and stir in the vinegar. Return the skillet to the heat and simmer for 2 to 3 minutes to let the vinegar meld with the honey. Then stir in the black pepper and the scallions. Set aside.

Preheat a grill to medium-high.

COOK THE CHICKEN: Place a large double layer of foil on a rimmed sheet pan. Remove the chicken from the yogurt marinade, leaving any excess marinade behind, and lay it out on the foil, breast-side up. Place the sheet pan in the center of the grill and close the lid. Cook the chicken until an instant-read thermometer inserted into the thigh meat registers 150°F, 30 to 35 minutes.

CHAR THE CHICKEN: Use two pairs of tongs or two large spatulas to lift the chicken off the sheet pan and place it directly on the grill rack. Char it, breast-side up, on the grill for 5 to 10 minutes, until it reaches an internal temperature of 165°F.

SERVE: Transfer the chicken to a platter or cutting board. Use a clean pair of poultry shears to cut the chicken into smaller pieces. Sprinkle the pieces with the lemon juice, and then pour the honey glaze over the chicken. Serve immediately.

Waldorf Salad

I grew up blocks away from the Waldorf Astoria hotel in New York City. I remember walking by the heralded building as kid and wondering if all the guests inside were eating nothing but Waldorf salad. I imagined the hotel must have needed a lot of grapes, walnuts, and mayonnaise! When I first made the salad as a young chef in Larry Forgione's kitchen decades later, I marveled at how good this salad can be when it's treated with care. A small cheffy note: The confectioners' sugar on the grapes brings out more of their vibrant color when you roast them, making for a tasty, delicate balancing act between them and the lettuce on one side and the roasted chicken, crunchy walnuts, and mayonnaise-style dressing on the other. I like to mix this salad together at the very last minute so the flavors are all still independently delicious and therefore even better when eaten all together.

SERVES 4 TO 6

1 cup walnut pieces

1½ cups seedless red grapes

1 tablespoon confectioners' sugar

Kosher salt

6 tablespoons extra-virgin olive oil

Grated zest and juice of 1 large lemon

3 tablespoons white wine vinegar, plus extra if needed

1 tablespoon Dijon mustard

2 teaspoons granulated sugar

4 or 5 small inner celery stalks with leaves (use the very tender yellowish stalks), cut crosswise into ½-inch-thick pieces

Freshly ground black pepper

1 (3½-pound) fully cooked whole chicken, meat torn into bite-size pieces (about 4 cups)

2 medium heads Boston lettuce, leaves separated

1 large Granny Smith apple, cored, halved, and thinly sliced

Preheat the oven to 350°F.

TOAST THE WALNUTS: Place the walnuts on a rimmed quarter sheet pan and toast them in the oven until they are fragrant and browned, 5 to 8 minutes. Set aside to cool.

ROAST THE GRAPES: In a medium bowl, toss the grapes with the confectioners' sugar, a pinch of salt, and 1 tablespoon of the olive oil. Arrange the grapes in a single layer on a rimmed sheet pan and bake until their skins start to wrinkle, 12 to 15 minutes. Remove the grapes from the oven and set them aside to cool.

MAKE THE DRESSING: To a blender, add the lemon zest and juice, vinegar, mustard, granulated sugar, and a generous pinch of salt. Blend until smooth and, with the blender running, slowly and steadily add the remaining 5 tablespoons olive oil. Taste for seasoning, adding more vinegar or salt if needed. If the flavor is too strong or the dressing is too thick (or separates a little), blend in a splash of cool water.

ASSEMBLE THE SALAD: Toss the toasted walnuts, celery, and roasted grapes in a large bowl with a pinch each of salt and pepper. Add some of the dressing and toss to coat. Then add the chicken and drizzle with some more of the dressing. Arrange some lettuce leaves on a serving platter and scatter the apple slices over the lettuce. Drizzle the apples and lettuce with dressing. Arrange the chicken mixture in the center.

Classic Cobb Salad

This was one of the first salads I ever made (and ate) in a professional kitchen, and it also represents the moment when I realized that while salad seemed like a pretty casual tossing of varied greens in some dressing in a bowl, it might actually be a whole food group. The textures and tastes of the bacon, eggs, and blue cheese are sublime, making the Cobb an American classic for good reason. It's that contrast of freshly cooked, still-warm ingredients on juicy iceberg lettuce (so underrated) that takes this salad over the top (when you bite into the warm bacon and then a chilled cherry tomato, it brings a BLT sandwich to mind). I assemble all the cold parts and then add the warm right before serving. Feel free to use leftover cooked chicken instead of preparing chicken specifically for the salad. For the blue cheese, try a mild, creamy type like Cabrales, St. Agur, or Gorgonzola.

SERVES 4

- 6 tablespoons red wine vinegar
- 1 tablespoon Dijon mustard
- 1¼ cups extra-virgin olive oil
- 1 tablespoon dried oregano
- 2 tablespoons canola oil
- 2 (8-ounce) skin-on, bone-in chicken breasts
- Kosher salt
- 8 bacon strips, cut crosswise into 1-inch pieces
- 2 medium heads iceberg lettuce, cored and halved
- 1 large avocado, halved, pitted, and cut into 1-inch cubes
- 1 pint cherry tomatoes, halved
- 4 large hard-boiled eggs, peeled and coarsely chopped
- 4 ounces blue cheese, crumbled

Preheat the oven to 350°F.

MAKE THE DRESSING: In a medium bowl, whisk together the red wine vinegar, mustard, olive oil, and oregano until combined. Taste for seasoning and set aside.

COOK THE CHICKEN BREASTS: Set an ovenproof medium skillet over medium heat and add the canola oil. When the oil begins to smoke lightly, season the chicken breasts with salt and add them, skin-side down, to the skillet and then place the skillet in the oven. Bake until the chicken breasts are cooked through but still juicy, 18 to 20 minutes. Remove the skillet from the oven and transfer the chicken to a cutting board to rest. Drain off and discard the fat from the skillet.

COOK THE BACON: In the same skillet that you used for the chicken, arrange the bacon pieces in a single layer. Cook the bacon over medium heat until it is crisp, 5 to 8 minutes. Transfer the bacon to the cutting board holding the chicken, and tent both with foil to keep them warm. Reserve the bacon fat.

ASSEMBLE THE SALADS: Place each iceberg half on a plate, cut-side up. Season the lettuce with a sprinkle of salt and a generous spoonful of the dressing. Drizzle with a little bacon fat as well, if desired. Slice the chicken and arrange a few slices in a row on each of the four plates. Arrange side-by-side rows of avocado, tomato, chopped egg, and blue cheese on each plate. Add the bacon and top with any remaining dressing.

Chicken Salad

As a young cook, I worked for years in a famous and fancy Parisian restaurant. I was also flat broke, surviving on leftovers from the restaurant's cheese platter, bags of potato chips, and French fries. I would graze in the pastry department (wouldn't you?), eating the trimmed-away edges of layer cakes and puff pastry mille-feuilles. Occasionally, however, I needed a real meal; so on Sundays, I'd sometimes duck into a random tiny bistro in search of a salad like this one: chicken, tarragon, tomatoes. This screams "France" to me. Even the pop of texture from the grainy mustard in the dressing takes me straight back to the 16th arrondissement.

You can eat the chicken on a bed of lettuce, as it appears here, or it can become the filling for a sandwich on potato bread, sourdough, or a seedy rye. You can also serve it in individual lettuce cups for snacking (Boston or Gem lettuce works great for that). I use roasted white-meat chicken, but feel free to use this recipe as a place to park any kind of leftover cooked chicken.

SERVES 2 OR 3

- 2 (10-ounce) skin-on, boneless chicken breasts, or about 2½ cups shredded cooked chicken
- Kosher salt and freshly ground black pepper
- 3 tablespoons extra-virgin olive oil
- 1 tablespoon mayonnaise
- 1 tablespoon grainy mustard
- 1 tablespoon balsamic vinegar
- 1 large head romaine lettuce, leaves separated
- Leaves from 4 sprigs fresh tarragon
- 1 pint cherry tomatoes, halved

Preheat the oven to 375°F. Position a rack in the center of the oven.

COOK THE CHICKEN: Place the chicken breasts, skin-side up, on a rimmed sheet pan lined with parchment paper, making sure to leave space between them. Season them with salt and pepper, and drizzle with 1 tablespoon of the olive oil. Place the sheet pan in the oven on the center rack and roast until the breasts are cooked through and an instant-read thermometer reads 165°F at the meatiest part, 25 to 30 minutes. Transfer the chicken to a flat surface (reserving the sheet pan with the drippings) and cut it into cubes. Set aside.

MAKE THE DRESSING: In a medium bowl, whisk together the mayonnaise, mustard, balsamic vinegar, and the remaining 2 tablespoons olive oil. Stir in the reserved pan drippings from roasting the chicken. Taste for seasoning and add a pinch of salt if needed.

SERVE: Arrange all the romaine leaves in a row on a serving platter. Drizzle with some of the dressing and season with salt. Toss the chicken, tarragon leaves, and cherry tomatoes in the remaining dressing, and spoon the chicken salad on top of each lettuce leaf, nestling it down the center of the leaf.

MAKING YOUR SLOW COOKER WORK FOR YOU

(WITH A FEW NOTES FOR THE INSTANT POT, TOO)

At the restaurant, slow cooking is something we do for braised meats and stocks. We also slow-cook some soups in the back part of the kitchen. I love coming in to a busy lunch service and seeing a pot of chicken soup simmering its way through the chaos around it. The flavors that come with long cooking are irreplaceable in some recipes. At home when I was growing up, my parents never used a slow cooker. I think they regarded it as a fancy gadget that could be replaced with waiting by the stove for food to cook! I have one and have been playing around with it at home. A slow cooker removes that impatience I used to feel, like hoping a stock was cooked enough to put away so I could go to bed or leave for work in the morning. Now I just gently cook chicken stock in the slow cooker while we eat dinner. A beef stock or lentil soup can be bubbling away while you write emails or sweep the floor. There are a couple of wild cards here, like the brownies. What's wrong with a little chocolate dessert in the slow cooker?

Slow Cooker Chili

I like making chili, and decided I wanted to make a slow cooker version for the days when I want to just come home, open the cooker, add a pinch of salt or a dash of hot sauce, and dig in. While this happens in a slow cooker, browning the meat first on the stovetop adds great depth of flavor and is worth the extra step since the flavor of the beef bridges all of the other flavors. If you have an Instant Pot, you can do the browning right in the pot before adding the liquid and slow cooking.

While developing the flavor of the chili is critical, so is how you finish it. (We chefs can be moody.) I usually serve the chili alongside bowls of sour cream, grated Monterey Jack or cheddar cheese, slivered pickled jalapeños, tortilla chips, avocado (or guacamole), and some chilled chopped tomatoes splashed with a squeeze of lime juice. If you have the luxury of advance planning (or the patience), make the chili the day before, refrigerate it overnight, and warm it up the next day. It always tastes better that way, right?

SERVES 6 TO 8

3 tablespoons canola oil

2 pounds ground beef chuck (80% lean)

Kosher salt

2 medium yellow onions, finely chopped

1 red bell pepper, halved, seeded, and cut into ½-inch-wide slices

1 Fresno chile, halved, seeded, and cut into ½-inch-thick half-moons

8 medium garlic cloves, minced

3 tablespoons tomato paste

1 dried bay leaf

2 teaspoons dried red pepper flakes

2 tablespoons chili powder

½ teaspoon ground allspice

½ teaspoon ground cumin

1 (28-ounce) can peeled whole tomatoes

2 tablespoons apple cider vinegar

1 (15.5-ounce) can black beans, drained and rinsed

5 scallions (green and white parts), thinly sliced

Optional garnishes: 2 cups shredded Monterey Jack or cheddar cheese; 1 large avocado, peeled and sliced; sour cream; tortilla chips; chilled chopped tomatoes seasoned with a little lime juice

BROWN THE MEAT: Heat 1 tablespoon of the oil in a large sauté pan set over medium heat. When the oil begins to smoke lightly, crumble about half of the ground beef into the pan, adding it in a thin layer (you'll need to cook it in two batches—don't crowd the pan or it will steam rather than brown), and season it with salt. Cook over medium heat, stirring with a wooden spoon, until the meat browns, 3 to 5 minutes. Transfer the meat to a sheet pan to cool, drain off some of the excess fat, and repeat the process with the remaining meat.

BROWN THE VEGETABLES: In the same sauté pan, heat the remaining 2 tablespoons oil over medium heat. Stir in the onions, bell pepper, Fresno chile, garlic, and a generous pinch of salt. Cook until the vegetables start to brown, 5 to 8 minutes. Stir in the tomato paste and cook for an additional 2 to 3 minutes.

COOK THE CHILI: Place the browned meat and vegetables in the slow cooker. Add the bay leaf, red pepper flakes, chili powder, allspice, cumin, tomatoes, vinegar, and 2 cups of water. Cover, set the cooker on low, and cook for about 8 hours. After a couple of hours, stir and taste for seasoning. About 45 minutes before serving, turn the slow cooker to high and stir in the black beans; cover and cook for 30 minutes.

SERVE: Allow the chili to rest for about 15 minutes before serving. Then stir in the scallions, taste for seasoning, and serve it in a bowl with your choice of (or all of) the garnishes.

Slow Cooker Beef Stock

People ask me all the time what the difference is between a stock and a broth. The general rule is that a stock is made from bones and a broth is made from meat (usually meat scraps); bone broth is a hybrid of the two. Bottom line, if you are cooking with bones for flavor, there is always meat on those bones, so the lines blur between the two types of fortified, meaty liquid. The ultimate goal is the same: making a stock or broth that tastes delicious! I use beef stock when I want the flavor of beef in my soup, like for French onion soup or beef-barley soup—that's where I love it most. A pot roast or brisket that has been loved by a good beef stock is delicious, too. That said, if I have beef scraps, I put them in my stock. What I *don't* add is lots of beef fat or fatty scraps, and I don't put lots of herbs in the base. The only flavor I like besides the meat itself comes from roasting the vegetables. By roasting them, you draw out their water before you even start building the stock. This means you begin with vegetables that already taste delicious in their own right. If you have an Instant Pot, you can begin by browning the vegetables directly in the pot and then layer the other ingredients on top. We want a good, round beef flavor, and this recipe gets you there.

MAKES 2 TO 2½ QUARTS
(8 TO 10 CUPS)

- 2 large leeks, green tops removed, white stalks halved lengthwise and sliced crosswise into ½-inch-wide pieces (about 3 cups), then washed well
- 5 medium carrots, peeled and cut into ½-inch-thick rounds (about 2 heaping cups)
- 4 large garlic cloves, lightly crushed
- 1 tablespoon canola oil
- 2 dried bay leaves
- 16 to 20 whole black peppercorns
- 10 to 12 sprigs fresh flat-leaf parsley
- 5 pounds (2-inch-thick) beef bones (preferably shank bones)
- 6 to 8 sprigs fresh thyme
- Kosher salt

Preheat the oven to 350°F.

PREPARE THE VEGETABLES: In a large bowl, toss the leeks, carrots, and garlic with the oil, bay leaves, peppercorns, and parsley. Arrange the vegetables and seasonings in a single layer on a rimmed sheet pan and place the pan in the oven. Roast until the vegetables are slightly tender and lightly browned, 15 to 18 minutes.

MAKE THE STOCK: Place all of the beef bones and the roasted vegetables in the slow cooker and fill it with 8 to 10 cups of water. Cover, set the cooker on high, and cook for 3 hours.

After 3 hours, skim any impurities from the surface of the stock and add the thyme sprigs and a pinch of salt. (It's not enough salt to season the stock but just enough to elevate the meat flavors as they develop.) Then set the cooker on low, cover, and cook for 5 hours more.

Strain the finished stock through a fine-mesh sieve into a large bowl, pressing down on the bones and vegetables to extract as much liquid as possible.

STORAGE: I often make a batch of stock because I need it right away to make soups or braises. If you're thinking ahead and making stock for another time, cool it and then freeze it in whatever increments suit you. It can be stored in small plastic freezer bags or in a large sealed container.

Slow Cooker Chicken Stock

Here's the thing about a slow cooker: it's really like a babysitter for the long-term cooking we want to do but don't want to monitor. Although I am a professional chef, I use very little chicken stock. I often use water to cook rice and other grains, and even as the base of many soups. However, there are other times, like when I make chicken soup or braised chicken dishes, where a stock to match the meat in the dish makes all the difference. This is my chicken stock and I love it.

You can save the carcasses from roasting chickens (page 76) and spatchcocking chickens (pages 82 and 96) in the freezer, and when you have five or six whole carcasses, make a roasted chicken stock from those bones. Or just ask your butcher for chicken bones—they often have some tucked away exactly for this purpose. Don't be surprised at having to use the oven before you turn on your slow cooker—roasting vegetables draws out their water and concentrates their flavor before you even start building the stock. If you have an Instant Pot, you can begin by browning the vegetables directly in the pot, and then layer the other ingredients on top.

MAKES 2½ TO 3 QUARTS
(10 TO 12 CUPS)

- 2 medium yellow onions, halved and sliced ¼ inch thick (about 1½ cups)
- 3 medium carrots, peeled and cut into ½-inch-thick rounds (about 1½ cups)
- 2 large celery stalks, peeled and cut into 1-inch-thick pieces
- 1 tablespoon canola oil
- 1 dried bay leaf
- 16 to 20 whole black peppercorns
- 6 to 8 sprigs fresh flat-leaf parsley
- 5 pounds chicken bones
- 6 to 8 sprigs fresh thyme
- Kosher salt

Preheat the oven to 350°F.

PREPARE THE VEGETABLES: In a large bowl, toss the onions, carrots, and celery with the oil, bay leaf, peppercorns, and parsley. Arrange the vegetables in a single layer on a rimmed sheet pan and place the pan in the oven. Roast until the vegetables are slightly tender and lightly browned, 18 to 20 minutes.

MAKE THE STOCK: Place all of the chicken bones and the roasted vegetables in the slow cooker and fill it with 8 to 10 cups of water. Cover, set the cooker on high, and cook for 3 hours.

After 3 hours, skim any impurities from the surface of the stock and add the thyme and a pinch of salt. (It's not enough salt to season the stock but just enough to elevate the meat flavors as they develop.) Then set the slow cooker on low, cover, and cook for 4 hours more.

Strain the finished stock through a fine-mesh sieve into a large bowl, pressing down on the bones and vegetables to extract as much liquid as possible.

STORAGE: I often make a batch of stock because I need it right away to make soups or braises. If you're making yours ahead of time, cool it and then freeze it in whatever increments suit you. It can be stored in small plastic freezer bags or in a large sealed container.

Spiral Ham in the Slow Cooker

It seems funny to me, after all these years of professional cooking, to buy something already cooked just to have to "cook" it again. When it comes to a spiral ham, this process is really more about imparting flavor than about cooking the ham (which comes already cooked). When it's finished, the meat should be tender and almost falling off the bone, *and* you'll have a great cooking liquid that can be sopped up with rice, tortillas, potatoes, bread . . . or egg noodles tossed with a little salt and sour cream. When the maple syrup and brown sugar, each with its own deep, sulfur-y, molasses-y flavor, combine with the cider vinegar and the mustards, they create a tangy liquid to serve with this ham. I like to think of it as a marinade that comes at the end instead of the beginning. Sign me up! I love to serve a bed of braised cabbage here, too.

SERVES 8 TO 10

1 (6- to 7-pound) bone-in, hickory-smoked, uncured fully cooked ham

5 medium parsnips, peeled and halved lengthwise

5 medium carrots, peeled and halved lengthwise

1 cup maple syrup

2 cups unsweetened apple juice

½ cup packed dark brown sugar

½ cup smooth Dijon mustard

½ cup grainy Dijon mustard

2 tablespoons apple cider vinegar

Kosher salt (if needed)

COOK THE HAM: Pour 3 cups of water into a 7-quart slow cooker. Add the ham, cut-side up, as well as the parsnips and carrots. Pour the maple syrup and apple juice over the ham, and sprinkle the brown sugar over the top. Cook on high, uncovered, for 30 to 45 minutes, then cover the slow cooker and cook on low until the ham is tender, 3 to 4 hours. Hams vary in size and tenderness, so be patient. When it's tender, the meat should come off the bone with very little resistance. Taste a small piece for tenderness.

FINISH AND SERVE: Transfer the ham and vegetables to a deep serving platter (reserve the liquid in the pot). Use a pair of kitchen shears or scissors to cut the slices of ham off the bone and let them fall onto the platter. Stir both kinds of mustard and the vinegar into the cooking liquid left in the slow cooker and taste for seasoning—the sauce may or may not need salt. Pour the liquid over the ham and vegetables, and serve.

Lentil Soup

Lentils need only a few things to be really happy: black pepper, balsamic vinegar, and brown sugar. In essence, their earthy heart begs for spice, acid, and sweetness as backup dancers. Do not salt the lentils until they are cooked—lentils actually cook more evenly and tenderize better in the absence of salt. The method here is to slow-cook the lentils separately from the vegetables and then add the caramelized vegetables at the end (with the salt). Make this dairy-free by subbing in a flavorful stock—either beef, chicken, or vegetable—for the cream. If it's easier for you, you can precook everything—the lentils and the vegetables—and stir them together just before serving.

SERVES 4 TO 6

1 pound dried brown du Puy lentils, rinsed and drained

1 dried bay leaf

2 tablespoons extra-virgin olive oil

1 large red onion, halved and finely chopped

½ teaspoon cumin seeds

½ teaspoon ground coriander

Kosher salt

2 medium carrots, cut into ¼-inch-thick rounds

3 celery stalks, peeled and sliced into ½-inch-thick pieces

2 teaspoons dark brown sugar

2 teaspoons freshly ground black pepper

1 tablespoon balsamic vinegar

2 tablespoons Dijon mustard

2 tablespoons low-sodium soy sauce

1 cup heavy cream (or beef, chicken, or vegetable stock)

COOK THE LENTILS: Place the lentils and the bay leaf in a slow cooker and add 6 cups of water. Cover and cook on low for 2 hours. Then raise the setting to high and cook for an additional 4 hours. The goal is to finish with cooked, tender lentils and sufficient flavorful liquid to make the soup.

COOK THE VEGETABLES: Heat the oil in a large skillet over medium heat. When the oil begins to smoke lightly, add the onions, cumin seeds, coriander, and a generous pinch of salt. Stir to blend and cook over medium to high heat, stirring constantly, until the onions begin to brown around the edges, 2 to 3 minutes. Add the carrots, celery, brown sugar, pepper, and another pinch of salt, and cook until the vegetables become completely tender but not mushy, 10 to 12 minutes. Shut off the heat.

FINISH THE SOUP: Check the lentils: they should be tender but not mushy. Remove the bay leaf, season the lentils with a generous pinch of salt, and stir in the cooked vegetables. Remember that the lentils will need a good amount of seasoning because they were cooked without any salt, so the amount of salt you add may surprise you. Stir in the balsamic, mustard, soy sauce, and cream, and let the soup rest for 10 minutes. Taste again for seasoning before serving.

Chickpea and Tomato Chili

This chili honestly snuck up on me. I have to admit that a meaty chili is dynamite, but so are all of the flavors that build in this vegetarian (or vegan, without the sour cream) version. I used to always cook chili on the stove, layering each ingredient in as I was taught in cooking school. The idea that chili can come together so beautifully after a mostly hands-off low, slow cooking time astonished me. I worried the flavors would be dulled and the vegetables uninspired from waiting around too long. I was wrong.

Toasted almonds add great crunch and a toasty flavor, but if you don't want to add them, substitute cooked quinoa or sunflower seeds for a nutty note. If you like your chili less spicy, simply remove the seeds and ribs from the jalapeño before using it. If you don't have time to soak the chickpeas the night before, you can use three (15.5-ounce) cans of low-sodium chickpeas instead, adding them after the tomatoes and spices have cooked. How great is it to have a comforting, healthy meal cooking away all day! All you have to do is come home and dig in.

SERVES 4 TO 6

- 1 (16-ounce) bag dried chickpeas
- 1 (28-ounce) can peeled whole tomatoes, crushed, with their juices
- 1 tablespoon chili powder
- 2 teaspoons hot paprika
- 1 teaspoon ground cumin
- 3 tablespoons extra-virgin olive oil
- 2 medium red onions, finely chopped
- 1 large red bell pepper, halved, seeded, and sliced into ½-inch-wide strips
- 5 large garlic cloves, grated on a Microplane
- 1 small jalapeño, sliced into thin rounds
- Kosher salt
- 2 cups cooked fresh or thawed if frozen corn kernels
- 6 scallions (green and white parts), thinly sliced
- ¼ cup slivered almonds, toasted
- 1 cup (8 ounces) sour cream (optional)

SOAK THE CHICKPEAS: Place the dried chickpeas in a large bowl and add cold water to cover. Cover the bowl with plastic wrap, place it in the refrigerator, and let the chickpeas soak for 8 hours or up to overnight.

START THE CHILI: Drain the chickpeas and place them in a slow cooker. Add the tomatoes, then fill the tomato can with water and add that to the pot. Stir in the chili powder, paprika, and cumin. Cover with the lid, set the slow cooker on low, and cook for 6 hours. After that time, the chickpeas should be completely tender. (If you're using canned chickpeas, add them at this point.)

In a large sauté pan, heat 2 tablespoons of the olive oil over medium heat. When the oil begins to smoke, after 2 to 3 minutes, add the onions, bell pepper, garlic, and jalapeño. Season with salt and cook, stirring from time to time, until the onions soften slightly, 3 to 5 minutes.

FINISH THE CHILI: Transfer the sautéed vegetables to the slow cooker and stir gently to combine. Set the slow cooker on high and cook for 30 minutes.

SERVE: Stir the corn and scallions into the chili and taste for seasoning. Ladle the chili into individual bowls and top with the almonds. Serve with sour cream, if desired.

Slow Cooker Brownies

This is an odd place in the book to insert a dessert, but I fell in love with the idea of having a sweet treat like brownies, which are so good eaten warm just as they finish cooking, come out of a slow cooker! This recipe yields a tasty brownie with chewy edges and a very gooey center. Gooier than your classic oven-baked versions. I like to spoon it out and into a bowl, and then drop a scoop of vanilla ice cream right out of the freezer on top. The warm brownies with ice cream melting over them? The best of both worlds. Don't like nuts? Simply omit. It's refreshing not to need your oven to make dessert. This is also a fun dish to have at a dinner party because when your guests look around for dessert, they'll never guess it's waiting in your slow cooker!

MAKES ABOUT 12 BROWNIES

- 8 tablespoons (1 stick) unsalted butter, cut into 8 equal pieces, plus 1 to 2 tablespoons at room temperature for greasing the slow cooker
- 1¼ cups all-purpose flour
- ¼ cup unsweetened Dutch-process cocoa powder
- ¾ teaspoon baking powder
- 1 teaspoon kosher salt
- 1½ cups walnut halves, coarsely chopped
- 9 ounces (about 1½ cups) semisweet chocolate chips
- 8 ounces bittersweet chocolate, chopped (about 1¼ cups)
- 1 cup sugar
- 3 large eggs, lightly beaten
- 2 teaspoons vanilla extract

PREPARE THE SLOW COOKER: Grease the bottom and sides of the ceramic insert of a slow cooker with the softened butter, and then line the bottom and sides of the insert with buttered parchment paper. Don't worry if the paper bunches a little when you fit it into the round (or oval) pot. It's unavoidable. What you want is to create a protective layer between the cooker and the batter. (And later, you'll be able to grab the sides of the parchment to lift the whole brownie out once it is cooked.)

MAKE THE BATTER: In a large bowl, whisk together the flour, cocoa powder, baking powder, salt, walnuts, and semisweet chocolate chips. Set aside.

Fill a medium saucepan with about 3 inches of water and bring it to a simmer over medium heat. Put the 8 tablespoons butter and the bittersweet chocolate in a medium heatproof bowl and set it over the simmering water (the bottom of the bowl shouldn't touch the water). Reduce the heat to low. Stir the mixture with a spatula until the chocolate and butter melt together, 3 to 5 minutes. Remove the bowl from the heat and gently whisk in the sugar, eggs, and vanilla. Stir the chocolate mixture into the flour mixture until thoroughly blended. Transfer the batter to the slow cooker, using the spatula to level it.

COOK: Cover the cooker and cook on low for 1½ hours. Then remove the cover and cook for an additional 30 minutes to develop a slight crust on top. (Every slow cooker is different and the timing can vary. If the brownies are still not done at this point, cook until they feel firm around the edges, another 15 to 30 minutes.)

Gently run a rubber spatula around the edges to loosen the brownie from the parchment. For a rustic effect, scoop portions of brownie right out of the slow cooker and serve warm. For classic brownie squares, let the brownie cool in the slow cooker for about 1 hour; then use the parchment paper to lift the brownie out of the cooker and onto a cake plate. Cut it into 12 equal pieces for serving.

EGG DISHES FOR ALL THE MOMENTS

Eggs are the best food to start cooking with your kids. Scrambling, frying, soft-boiling. Eventually you graduate to the complex and exciting world of poached eggs, quiche, and béarnaise sauce. Ironically, my mother was always the one to scramble or fry the eggs in the morning. She would melt butter and pour in the eggs, stirring methodically, and always added a few dashes of Worcestershire and Tabasco along with a pinch of salt. I was a spectator to this until I became an adult. My dad would time the toast to her stirring so it would pop out in time for him to run to the table with it as she arrived with the eggs. My first glimpse into the timing that would help me so much with restaurant cooking. Hot toast with freshly scrambled eggs. I think I was twenty-two and cooking at my first restaurant job when my mom finally gave me the okay to scramble the eggs for family breakfast. Maybe that's also where I learned the respect it takes to cook something so simple so well. My own egg repertoire is ever-growing—I could eat eggs every day of my life. These are a selection of my favorite recipes to make at home, from a sandwich to a great sauce. Buy the best eggs your budget can manage. It's an ingredient that goes into so many things that it's worth investing in the best. Buy organic, buy local. Buy what tastes good to you.

Egg White Omelet

WITH PARMESAN AND TARRAGON

I realize that most people who avoid egg yolks, eating only the whites, are looking to conserve calories and eat healthfully. I make egg white omelets for a different reason: egg whites are a blank canvas and leave room for the flavors and textures of herbs and cheese to truly shine. Be sure to use the freshest eggs you can find, because fresh egg whites are denser and cook up heartier than thin older whites. In this omelet, the egg white takes the tarragon and Parmesan and runs with them. By the way, this omelet can easily be made without the cheese and with the addition of roasted mushrooms or cherry tomatoes. I like the "lean" egg white mingling with the rich cheese.

SERVES 2

6 large egg whites

2 teaspoons kosher salt

Freshly ground black pepper

1 tablespoon unsalted butter

1 tablespoon fresh tarragon leaves

¼ cup finely grated Parmesan cheese

1 lemon wedge

PREPARE THE EGG WHITES: In a bowl, whisk the egg whites with the salt and a pinch of pepper. Whisk only enough to integrate the eggs. You don't want to whip too much air into them or make them frothy.

COOK THE OMELET: Place a 6-inch nonstick skillet over medium heat and add the butter. Swirl the butter around as it melts so it coats the whole surface of the pan. When the butter is melted (but not browned), reduce the heat and pour in the egg whites. Use a fork to stir the eggs slightly, as if you were scrambling them. Then allow the eggs to cook undisturbed for 1 to 2 minutes. Sprinkle the tarragon and cheese over the eggs, and then squeeze a little juice from the lemon wedge over the top.

FINISH: Lift the handle of the pan up, tilting the pan away from you and toward the heat. Fold the edge of the omelet closest to you toward the center. Fold the other edge toward the center and tilt the pan over the center of a plate so it lands seam-side down.

Sage, Thyme, and Melty Gruyère Omelet

My omelet education began when my mother taught me that with just slight adjustments, omelets can be infinitely variable—for a fluffy omelet, whisk a splash of cool water into the eggs. For a richer, heartier omelet, whisk in a splash of whole milk or heavy cream. You can use a lot of herb combinations and various cheeses, too—really, whatever you happen to have on hand. Here I include my personal favorite combination: sage and thyme—two herbs that I feel bring the flavors of the eggs and cheese (Gruyère) to life. While I scatter the sage leaves and flake the thyme inside the omelet, you can also serve the herbs sprinkled on the exterior. The last-minute "butter gloss" is something I learned from my friend and fellow Iron Chef Geoffrey Zakarian.

SERVES 2

- 2 tablespoons canola oil
- 8 to 10 fresh sage leaves
- 8 sprigs fresh thyme
- Kosher salt
- 3 large eggs
- 2 tablespoons unsalted butter, chilled
- ½ cup grated Gruyère cheese

COOK THE SAGE AND THYME: Heat a 6-inch nonstick skillet over medium heat and add the oil. When it begins to smoke lightly, after 2 to 3 minutes, turn off the heat and add the sage leaves and thyme sprigs. Stir the herbs to coat them with the oil and cook, stirring constantly, until the leaves pale a bit in color and get slightly crisp, 2 to 3 minutes. Use a slotted spoon to transfer the herbs to a plate lined with a paper towel, season with salt, and set aside to cool. Discard the oil and set the pan aside.

BLEND THE EGGS: In a bowl, combine the eggs with a splash of cool water and a pinch of salt. Whisk until the eggs are well combined.

COOK THE EGGS: Place the skillet you used to fry the herbs over medium heat and add 1 tablespoon of the butter. Swirl the butter around as it melts so it coats the whole surface of the pan. When the butter is melted (but not browned), reduce the heat to medium-low and pour in the eggs. Use a heatproof rubber or silicone spatula to stir the eggs slightly, as if you were scrambling them. Then allow the eggs to cook, undisturbed, until they start to stick to the bottom, 1 to 2 minutes. Now, stir the eggs gently once more so they don't stick. Once the eggs are almost cooked, after 1 to 2 minutes more, sprinkle the cheese and the sage leaves over them. Stem and flake the thyme leaves over the eggs, too. Add a sprinkle of salt.

SERVE: Lift the handle of the pan up, tilting the pan away from you and toward the heat. This tilting should cause the omelet to slide down in the pan a little. Fold the edge of the omelet closest to you toward the center. Fold the other edge toward the center, and then tilt the pan over the center of a plate so the omelet lands seam-side down. Spear the remaining tablespoon of butter with a fork and run the butter over the top of the omelet to gloss the exterior and give it some extra buttery flavor. Serve immediately.

Exceptional Scrambled Eggs

With so few ingredients, this simple dish counts on technique (and great eggs) to make the scrambled eggs exceptional. The water makes the eggs fluffy and light, while a touch of soy sauce adds that "cooked-in" pinch of salt. Salting the eggs before you scramble them adds the potential for tenderer and tastier eggs, too. Can't find crème fraîche at the store? Substitute 2 tablespoons cream cheese (the crème fraîche is worth hunting down, though, as it contributes a deeply creamy note to the eggs). Serve these with deliberately thick slices of buttered and lightly salted sourdough toast. I usually side my scramble with toast swiped with grape or strawberry jam because those flavors are nostalgic and make me feel like I'm at a great diner in my own home.

SERVES 2

- 4 large eggs
- 2 teaspoons kosher salt, plus extra for finishing
- ½ teaspoon freshly ground black pepper
- 2 teaspoons low-sodium soy sauce
- 1 tablespoon unsalted butter
- 2 tablespoons crème fraîche (or 2 more tablespoons unsalted butter)

PREPARE THE EGGS: In a bowl, whisk together the eggs, salt, pepper, soy sauce, and a scant tablespoon of water. Whisk only enough to mix. You don't want to whip too much air into them or make them frothy.

COOK THE EGGS: Place a 6-inch nonstick skillet over medium heat and add the butter. Swirl the butter around as it melts so it coats the whole surface of the pan. Reduce the heat to medium-low and pour in the egg mixture. Use a heatproof rubber or silicone spatula to stir the eggs gently and constantly until they start to stick to the bottom of the pan and take shape, 1 to 2 minutes. Stir the eggs again, scraping the sides and bottom of the pan to keep the eggs moving, until they are cooked but still somewhat soft, 2 to 3 minutes.

FINISH: Quickly dot the top of the scramble with the crème fraîche and sprinkle it with a touch more salt. Stir and quickly transfer the scrambled eggs to a serving dish so they don't continue to cook in the hot pan.

Deviled Eggs

WITH CAYENNE AND A TOUCH OF CURRY

I have a vivid memory of my mother making deviled eggs. The flavor of eggs and mayonnaise was familiar because she often made egg salad. That's where the recipe took a great left turn. Cayenne? Apple cider vinegar? I bit into the egg, and the white was still somewhat warm. It was the first time I remember feeling the power of cayenne pepper, and the vinegar lifted the spice to another level. I was just a kid, so all I knew was that I wanted more. Using whipped cream to lighten the yolk mixture is a trick that my mother taught me—I think it was handed down from a Julia Child recipe. While smoky paprika is always the classic here, I love the heat of cayenne pepper. I also take issue with the fact that we pour so much effort into the yolks but ignore the whites. An unseasoned egg white dilutes the intensity of the yolk filling. So . . . season them!

MAKES 24 DEVILED EGGS

12 large eggs
½ cup mayonnaise
1 teaspoon Tabasco
1 tablespoon Dijon mustard
1 tablespoon Worcestershire sauce
½ teaspoon cayenne pepper, plus extra for dusting
1 tablespoon apple cider vinegar
Juice of 1 large lemon (3½ to 4 tablespoons)
Kosher salt
½ cup heavy cream
1½ teaspoons sweet curry powder

COOK THE EGGS: Gently place the eggs in a medium pot and add cold water to cover them by 2 inches. Bring the water to a rolling boil over high heat. When the water comes to a boil, remove the pot from the heat, cover it, and let the eggs stand for 10 minutes. Then drain and transfer them to a bowl of cool water.

PREPARE THE EGGS: Once the eggs are cool enough to handle, gently crack the eggshells on a flat surface for easier peeling. Peel the eggs (if necessary, rinse them quickly under cool water to remove any small shell bits and then dry them thoroughly) and halve them lengthwise. Remove the yolks, place them in a sieve set over a medium bowl, and use a silicone spatula to push them through the strainer. Arrange the egg white halves on a platter.

MAKE THE FILLING: Add the mayonnaise, Tabasco, mustard, Worcestershire, cayenne, vinegar, and about 2 tablespoons of the lemon juice to the yolks and whisk to combine. Season with salt to taste.

ADD THE CREAM: In a separate bowl, use a whisk to whip the cream until it forms medium (but still fairly soft) peaks. Using a silicone spatula, gently fold the whipped cream into the yolk mixture. Fill a pastry bag fitted with a fluted tip with the egg yolk mixture (alternatively, use a plastic sandwich bag with one of the bottom corners cut off).

FINISH THE EGGS: Season the egg whites with salt. Fill a tea strainer with some cayenne and use it to lightly dust the whites. Fill the cavities of the egg whites with the yolk mixture. Dust the tops lightly with the curry powder.

Beet Deviled Eggs

Pickling the egg whites in borscht, a chilled beet juice–based soup, creates an absolutely stunning effect for these deviled eggs. I first tried it with the juice from canned beets and pickled beets, with perfectly decent results. Then I bought a jar of borscht at the supermarket and used that as the marinating liquid. The taste was next-level delicious. You can get the color on the egg whites with any beet juice, but the taste is not quite the same. The fluffy filling, made with whipped cream, has a great velvety texture. The surprise in this deviled egg comes from the cooling sweetness of the beet-flavored egg whites against the heat of the paprika and the bluntly acidic vinegar. For serving, I like to use a "cool" marble-like serving platter or anything with a darker hue so the eggs really pop visually when you put them on the table.

MAKES 24 DEVILED EGGS

12 large eggs

24 ounces (3 cups) borscht, store-bought or homemade, chilled

½ cup mayonnaise

1 teaspoon Tabasco

1 tablespoon Dijon mustard

1 tablespoon Worcestershire sauce

½ teaspoon hot paprika

1 tablespoon white wine vinegar

Juice of 1 large lemon

Kosher salt

⅓ cup heavy cream

1 small bunch chives, snipped with scissors or sliced

COOK THE EGGS: Gently place the eggs in a medium pot and add enough cold water to cover them by 2 inches. Bring the water to a rolling boil over high heat, remove the pot from the heat, cover the pot, and let the eggs stand for 10 minutes. Then drain and transfer them to a bowl of cool water.

PEEL AND PICKLE THE EGG WHITES: Pour the borscht into a plastic container or glass bowl that's large enough to hold the eggs. Once the eggs are cool enough to handle, gently crack them on a flat surface for easier peeling. Peel the eggs (if necessary, rinse them quickly under cool water to remove any small shell bits, and dry them thoroughly) and then halve them lengthwise. Remove the yolks, collect them in a medium bowl, cover with plastic wrap, and refrigerate. Submerge the egg whites, cavity-side down, in the borscht and refrigerate for at least 30 minutes or up to 4 hours.

MAKE THE FILLING: Press the yolks through a fine-mesh strainer into a medium bowl. Add the mayonnaise, Tabasco, mustard, Worcestershire, paprika, vinegar, and lemon juice, and whisk to combine. Season with salt.

ADD THE CREAM: In a separate medium bowl, whip the cream until it forms medium (but still fairly soft) peaks. Using a rubber spatula, gently fold the whipped cream into the yolk mixture. Fill a pastry bag fitted with a fluted tip with the egg yolk mixture (alternatively, use a plastic sandwich bag with one of the bottom corners cut off) .

SERVE: Remove the pickled egg whites from the borscht and drain them on a plate lined with paper towels. Arrange the whites, cavity-side up, on a serving platter. Pipe the yolk mixture into the cavity of each egg white. Finish with a sprinkling of chives.

Poached Eggs on Cheddar Biscuits

WITH BACON AND SAGE

There are all these little ways the ingredients connect here: the bacon and the sage are great with the egg, and when the poached egg breaks and links up with the sharp cheddar in the biscuit, it's magic. These particular relationships are what turn a sandwich into a "SANDWICH." I admit, this is a lot of work for a sandwich. If you want to use a store-bought biscuit, go for it—I'll never know. But if you make them from scratch, you'll be rewarded with a few extra biscuits to eat with some butter or jam. You can also eat them for breakfast the next day. I always end up devouring one, piping hot, with some strawberry jam while the eggs poach.

MAKES 4 SANDWICHES, WITH 2 BISCUITS LEFT OVER

BISCUITS

- 3 cups all-purpose flour, plus extra for shaping
- ½ teaspoon sweet curry powder
- 1½ tablespoons baking powder
- 2 teaspoons sugar
- 2 teaspoons kosher salt
- 2½ cups heavy cream
- 1 cup coarsely grated sharp cheddar cheese (preferably yellow cheddar)
- 1 tablespoon unsalted butter, at room temperature (optional)

SANDWICH

- 12 thin bacon strips
- 20 fresh medium sage leaves
- 2 teaspoons red wine vinegar
- 4 large eggs
- Kosher salt and freshly ground black pepper
- 1 tablespoon sherry vinegar

Preheat the oven to 350°F.

MAKE THE BISCUIT DOUGH: In a large bowl, sift together the flour, curry powder, baking powder, and sugar. (Sifting not only ensures that the dry ingredients will be free of lumps but also mixes them together in advance of adding the cream. The less you mix your biscuit dough once liquid is introduced, the tenderer your biscuit will be.)

Using your hands, gently work the salt, cream, and cheese into the dry ingredients just until all of the flour is mixed in with the cream. Do not overmix. Turn the biscuit dough out onto a lightly floured surface, and with floured hands, pat the dough into a 9 by 6-inch rectangle that's 1 to 1½ inches thick. If the outside edges of the dough start to show cracks, cup the edges with your hands while pushing the dough toward its center to compress it. Lightly flour a knife and slice the rectangle into 1½- to 2-inch squares. You should have about 6 biscuits.

BAKE: Grease a nonstick sheet pan with the butter (or use parchment paper). Arrange the biscuits on the prepared pan, leaving some distance between them. Bake until they start to brown lightly, 15 to 18 minutes. Remove from the oven and set aside.

COOK THE BACON: Place the bacon strips in a large skillet (overlapping slightly if needed), add ¼ cup of water, and cook over low heat until the water cooks out and the bacon is crisp, 12 to 15 minutes. Just as the bacon is finishing cooking, add the sage leaves to the skillet and cook, stirring constantly, until the sage pales and crisps, 2 to 3 minutes. Transfer the bacon and sage to a plate lined with paper towels to drain, reserving the fat from the pan.

POACH THE EGGS: Fill a medium-size shallow pot with about 3 inches of water and bring it to a simmer over medium heat. Add the red wine vinegar. (This will help the eggs to take shape more easily as you poach them.) Crack an egg into a small bowl and then gently drop it into the water. Repeat with another egg, leaving some distance between it and the first. Repeat until all of the eggs are added. Reduce the heat to medium-low and allow the eggs to cook until the whites are firm and completely opaque, 2 to 3 minutes. Use a slotted spoon to gently transfer the poached eggs to a kitchen towel to drain. Season them with salt and pepper.

ASSEMBLE THE SANDWICHES: Use a knife to split 4 biscuits in half and place each bottom half on its own plate. Set a poached egg on each bottom half. Stir the sherry vinegar into the reserved bacon fat and drizzle a little of this mixture over each egg. Season with salt. Top each egg with 3 strips of bacon and some of the sage leaves. Cover with the top of the biscuits and serve right away.

That's Ava's hand! She couldn't wait for the quiche to cool before digging in.

Quiche Lorraine

Every time I take a bite of hot quiche Lorraine, I'm reminded that it's one of the rare dishes where the smoky flavor of bacon runs through it seamlessly. The *lardons*, which are thick matchstick-like pieces of bacon, are called this because they were originally threaded (or "larded") through bigger cuts of meat with a needle to add richness and flavor. In this quiche, the flavor of the bacon is so pronounced and satisfying that I don't even mind that I am not eating slices of it, crispy and hot from the pan.

After the quiche is cooked and set, the drizzle of syrupy reduced balsamic vinegar wakes up all the flavors with its sweetness and acidity. The quiche needs to rest for a few minutes before you cut it into slices like a pie, but don't let it rest too long—it's still best when it is warm from the oven. Pair it with a glass of dry white wine or an ice-cold yeasty beer and close your eyes: you are in Paris.

SERVES 6 TO 8

DOUGH

- 1½ cups all-purpose flour, plus extra for rolling
- 1 teaspoon kosher salt
- 2 large egg yolks
- 8 tablespoons (1 stick) unsalted butter, cubed and chilled, plus 1 tablespoon at room temperature for greasing the pie plate
- 2 to 3 tablespoons ice water

FILLING

- 8 ounces slab bacon, trimmed and cut into ¼-inch-thick by 1-inch-long lardons
- 4 large eggs
- 8 ounces cream cheese, at room temperature
- 1 cup whole milk
- ½ teaspoon ground nutmeg (preferably freshly grated)
- 2 teaspoons kosher salt
- 1 teaspoon Tabasco

MAKE THE DOUGH: In a food processor fitted with the metal blade, pulse the flour and salt to blend. Pulse in the egg yolks and chilled butter until the mixture resembles coarse crumbs. Do not overmix. Pulse in 2 tablespoons of the ice water through the lid until the dough comes together and forms a rough ball. If it seems dry or loose, pulse in the remaining tablespoon ice water. Transfer the dough to a sheet of plastic wrap and press it into a flattened ball. Wrap in the plastic and refrigerate for 30 minutes.

Preheat the oven to 400°F.

ROLL THE DOUGH AND PREBAKE THE PIE CRUST: Grease the bottom and sides of a 9-inch pie plate with the softened butter and set the plate aside. Turn the dough out onto a lightly floured surface. Sprinkle the top of the dough with flour and use a rolling pin to roll it into a round that is 11 to 12 inches in diameter, adding more flour beneath the dough as needed to prevent it from sticking. Roll the dough up around the pin and transfer it to the prepared pie plate, pressing it gently into the bottom and up the sides. Ideally, there will be about 1 inch of excess dough hanging over the edges. Pinch the excess dough to create a "crimped" top edge. Place a sheet of parchment over the dough and fill with pie weights (dried beans work, too), place it in the oven, and bake for 12 to 15 minutes. Remove the weights and return the pie crust to the oven to bake until the dough turns light brown and firms up, 10 to 12 minutes more. Remove from the oven and let the crust cool completely.

COOK THE BACON: Arrange the bacon lardons in a single layer in a medium skillet, add ¼ cup of water, and cook over low heat until the water cooks out and the bacon is crisp, 10 to 12 minutes. Remove the bacon with a slotted spoon and drain it on a plate lined with paper towels. Reserve the bacon fat.

recipe and ingredients continue

- 2 teaspoons Worcestershire sauce
- 1½ cups coarsely grated Gruyère cheese
- ½ cup finely grated Parmesan cheese
- 6 tablespoons balsamic vinegar

MAKE THE FILLING: In a large bowl, whisk together the eggs, cream cheese, milk, nutmeg, salt, Tabasco, and Worcestershire. Stir in both cheeses and 2 tablespoons of the reserved bacon fat.

BAKE THE QUICHE: Sprinkle half of the crisped bacon lardons over the bottom of the cooled pie crust. Pour the filling into the crust and top with the remaining bacon. Bake the quiche until the filling sets and browns on top, 25 to 30 minutes. Remove it from the oven and set it aside to cool for 10 to 15 minutes.

REDUCE THE VINEGAR AND SERVE: While the quiche is cooling, pour the vinegar into a small saucepan set over low heat. Simmer the vinegar until it has reduced by half, 5 to 8 minutes. It should be slightly syrupy. Transfer the reduced vinegar to a small bowl. Slice the quiche and serve each slice drizzled with a little of the reduced balsamic.

Fried and Steamed Eggs

I don't like an over-easy egg. Once I flip it, the yolk becomes half like a hard-boiled egg and half like a slightly overcooked soft-boiled egg; to me, it's all wrong. Instead, when I'm in the mood for a perfectly fried egg, I cook the eggs in a large pan and add some steam to finish cooking the yolks gently. The yolks will appear to be coated with a thin film of egg white, but they're not overdone—when you break them open, they will be nicely cooked yet still soft and runny in the center.

SERVES 2

- 3 tablespoons unsalted butter
- 4 large eggs
- Maldon salt and freshly ground black pepper

Heat two large skillets over medium heat. When the skillets are hot, add 1½ tablespoons of the butter to each pan. Swirl the butter around in the pans until it is completely melted.

Crack 2 eggs into each pan, leaving room for each egg to spread out and have nice edges. Reduce the heat to medium-low and add 1 scant tablespoon of water to each pan. Cook until the edges of the whites are slightly browned, 2 to 3 minutes. Turn the heat off, cover the pans, and let them sit for 1 minute. Then transfer the fried eggs to individual plates and season them with Maldon salt and pepper.

Béarnaise Sauce

This rich, buttery sauce is such a classic. Made from wine, herbs, shallots, and egg yolks, it goes with everything from steak to fish to roasted vegetables. I learned how to make béarnaise because the great French chef Guy Savoy often had it on his menu. He would dollop it on warm cabbage and top it with caviar—an unusual and divine combination. I encourage you to think about this béarnaise in a new place: since it contains four egg yolks, it could really be the protein that you dollop on vegetables to make them a main course. A perfectly fluffy béarnaise lives between two extremes: raw, undercooked eggs and overcooked scrambled eggs. The clarified butter is simply butter with the milk solids removed—the result is lighter and has a higher smoke point. I love the flavors that the tarragon, chervil, and red wine vinegar provide—the vinegar is like the spark plug of acidity for this whole sauce and is what distinguishes béarnaise from its lemony cousin, hollandaise. Note: If you can't find chervil, add a little more tarragon in its place.

MAKES ABOUT ¾ CUP

½ pound (2 sticks) unsalted butter (to make ⅔ cup clarified butter)

½ cup dry white wine

3 medium shallots, sliced into ¼-inch-thick rounds

6 sprigs fresh tarragon, stems and leaves separated

4 sprigs fresh chervil, stems and leaves separated

4 large egg yolks

1 tablespoon red wine vinegar

Kosher salt and freshly cracked black pepper

CLARIFY THE BUTTER: In a small pot, melt the butter and bring it to a gentle simmer over medium-low heat. This breaks the emulsion and sends the water in the butter to the bottom while the milk proteins rise to the top in a thin layer of foam. Skim the white froth from the surface and then shut off the heat and set the pot aside for 15 minutes. Slowly tilt the pot to pour the clarified butter into a measuring cup or small bowl; leave as much of the white bits in the pot as possible. It doesn't have to be perfect (discard the white bits; you can refrigerate clarified butter, covered, for 2 to 3 weeks).

MAKE THE REDUCTION: In a medium saucepan, combine the white wine, shallots, tarragon stems, and chervil stems. Simmer the mixture over medium heat until it cooks down by about two-thirds (the reduced mixture will be 2 to 3 tablespoons), 10 to 12 minutes. Remove and discard the herb stems and set the reduction aside.

COOK THE EGGS: Fill a medium saucepan with about 3 inches of water and bring it to a simmer. In a metal bowl that will fit over the saucepan without touching the water (like a double boiler), combine the egg yolks with the vinegar. Whisk until the mixture is frothy, 1 to 2 minutes. Place the bowl on top of the pot of simmering water, reduce the heat to low, and cook, whisking constantly, until the eggs have thickened, 5 to 8 minutes. (Imagine if you scrambled eggs but curds never formed. The thickened eggs will look almost like a milkshake—that's the consistency you're aiming for.)

recipe continues

Whisk constantly to avoid uneven cooking and to prevent the egg mixture from forming a crust around the edges of the bowl. Don't rush this step because the sauce needs to be based on fluffy and *cooked* eggs! Keep the heat low, as well, to avoid overheating and scrambling the eggs.

FINISH THE SAUCE: Remove the bowl from the heat and place it on a kitchen towel (to keep it from tipping over as you whisk). Little by little, whisk in the clarified butter. When all the butter is added, whisk in all but 2 tablespoons of the wine reduction, a pinch of salt, and a pinch of cracked black pepper. Chop the tarragon and chervil leaves and stir them into the sauce. Taste for seasoning. Add more of the wine reduction if acidity is still needed.

French Toast Egg-in-a-Hole

The title of this dish makes me dream of two delicious breakfast classics: warm French toast and perfectly runny fried eggs. Visually, it's about seeing that beautiful yolk peeking out from the browned and slightly sweet French toast. The French toast has to be cooked a little longer because the multigrain bread is dense. The two mistakes we often make with French toast are not soaking it enough in the egg mix and, quite simply, not cooking it enough. Take your time with this recipe, because great French toast requires some patience. There is a tasty push/pull between savory (mustard) and sweet (maple syrup) here, so go light on the syrup.

SERVES 4

4 large eggs

1 tablespoon Dijon mustard

1 teaspoon ground ginger

3 to 4 tablespoons maple syrup

¾ cup whole milk

2 teaspoons kosher salt

4 (½- to ¾-inch-thick) slices multigrain bread

6 tablespoons (¾ stick) unsalted butter

4 large eggs

Maldon salt

Preheat the oven to 300°F.

PREPARE THE FRENCH TOAST: In a shallow bowl, whisk together the eggs, mustard, ginger, 1 tablespoon of the maple syrup, the milk, and the kosher salt until smooth. Place the bread slices on a flat surface and use a 2-inch round cookie cutter, or a small glass turned upside down, to punch a hole in the center of each slice. Soak both sides of each slice in the egg mixture so they absorb the liquid but don't become overly soggy, 2 to 3 minutes.

COOK THE FRENCH TOAST: Heat two medium skillets over medium heat and melt 2 tablespoons of the butter in each one. When the butter begins to foam and brown slightly, arrange 2 slices of the bread in each pan. Cook on the first side until the slices brown on the edges, 3 to 5 minutes. Turn the slices over and cook on the other side until they brown on the edges, another 3 to 5 minutes. Place the French toast on a sheet pan, tent it loosely with foil, and keep it warm in the oven.

COOK THE EGGS AND SERVE: Use a paper towel to wipe out the two skillets. Set them over medium heat and melt 1 tablespoon of the remaining butter in each one. Fry 2 eggs sunny-side up in each skillet, until the whites are no longer translucent and the yolks hold their shape but still appear runny, 2 to 3 minutes.

Drizzle the remaining 2 to 3 tablespoons maple syrup over the French toast. Place a fried egg in the center of each plate and set a piece of toast carefully on top of the egg so the yolk peeks out through the hole in the toast. Sprinkle with Maldon salt and serve right away.

RED SAUCE RECIPES

I grew up an Italian American in New York City, so of course my parents and I wandered (and ate our way) through all the Italian neighborhoods, from Little Italy in Lower Manhattan to Arthur Avenue in the Bronx and Hell's Kitchen on Manhattan's West Side. My dad would make these dishes—you know the ones—more than my mom would. He always had a spare can of tomato paste, a can of peeled whole tomatoes, and fresh garlic in the house no matter what. If there were a zombie apocalypse, we would have enough pantry stock on hand to eat these dishes for weeks. The beauty of this kind of highly comforting food is that you can make it in advance and and put it in the fridge overnight so it tastes even better when you sit down to eat it the next day.

Ninth Avenue Childhood Baked Ziti

Except for lasagna, my mom didn't make many baked pasta dishes when I was growing up. The first time I ever had—and fell in love with—baked ziti was in a tiny overly air-conditioned restaurant on Ninth Avenue in New York City. It was a true red-sauce joint, and I remember being cold from the air conditioning and very hungry. The dish arrived at my table boiling hot, bubbling volcanically. I was hooked. It was like an instant fireplace and dinner at the same time. The broiled molten cheesy topping, the unabashed use of garlic, the pasta edges that have crunch like they were fried yet somehow are still al dente inside . . . I always like to eat the edges first, don't you?

SERVES 6 TO 8

½ cup extra-virgin olive oil

2 medium yellow onions, minced

10 large garlic cloves, minced

Kosher salt

1 teaspoon dried red pepper flakes

2 (28-ounce) cans peeled whole tomatoes, with their juices

1 tablespoon sugar

2 teaspoons dried oregano

1 pound ziti pasta

1 cup tightly packed fresh basil leaves

1 pound mozzarella cheese, shredded

2 to 2½ cups finely grated Parmesan cheese (about 8 ounces)

MAKE THE SAUCE: Heat the olive oil in a large skillet set over medium heat. Add the onions and garlic, and season with salt and the red pepper flakes. Cook, stirring from time to time, until the onions become translucent, 3 to 5 minutes. Add the tomatoes and their juices, the sugar, and the oregano, and stir to blend. Cook, stirring occasionally, until the aroma of the tomatoes deepens and the raw garlic mellows, 18 to 20 minutes. Taste for seasoning. Set aside.

COOK THE PASTA: Fill a large pot with 4 quarts of water and bring it to a rolling boil. Add ¼ cup salt and return the water to a boil. Taste the water. It should be salty like seawater. Add the ziti and stir with a large slotted spoon to ensure that the pasta does not clump or stick to the pot as it cooks. Cook until the ziti is still quite firm, 6 to 8 minutes. Drain.

Preheat the oven to 375°F. Set an oven rack in the upper-middle position.

MIX AND REST: Add the ziti to the sauce and stir gently to combine. Allow the mixture to rest on the stove so the pasta can absorb the flavors from the sauce, 5 to 10 minutes. Then stir in the basil. Taste for seasoning.

BAKE AND SERVE: Fill a 10 by 15-inch baking dish with half of the ziti and sauce, and sprinkle half of the mozzarella and half of the Parmesan over the mixture. Top with all of the remaining pasta and sauce and the remaining cheese. Center the dish on a sheet pan and place it on the upper-middle rack of the oven. Bake until the top browns, 15 to 18 minutes. Switch the oven to broil and broil the ziti until the cheese is golden brown and bubbling, 2 to 3 minutes. Serve immediately.

Spaghetti and Meatballs: Goodfellas *vs.* Godfather

There's only one way to know which direction to go with this one: make them both. I vote for half the family cooking meatballs the *Goodfellas* way and the other half cooking them the *Godfather* way. There are some major differences and most of them center around the cooking of the meatballs themselves: In the *Goodfellas* method, the meatballs get browned on all sides and there are onions (not too many!) in the sauce; the *Godfather* version gets wine and tomato paste, and the meatballs aren't browned. The *Godfather* sauce also has sausage in addition to the meatballs. My dad would sometimes add spicy sausages to the mix with the meatballs. I liked it well enough but always felt like the spicy pork takes over the more delicate flavors of the tomato and the beef in the meatballs. It's a choice, but I would likely side with just beef meatballs. Serve these two versions side by side, in contrasting bowls, and let people decide for themselves. You tell me—are you a "goodfella" or a "godfather"?

Goodfellas *Spaghetti and Meatballs*

SERVES 4 TO 6

***GOODFELLAS* SAUCE**

2 tablespoons extra-virgin olive oil

2 medium yellow onions, halved and thinly sliced

5 garlic cloves, thinly sliced

Kosher salt

1 teaspoon sugar

1 teaspoon dried oregano

1 (28-ounce) can peeled whole tomatoes, with their juices

½ cup fresh basil leaves

***GOODFELLAS* MEATBALLS**

1 pound ground beef (80% lean)

½ cup panko bread crumbs, toasted

½ cup finely grated Parmesan cheese

½ cup chopped fresh curly-leaf parsley

Kosher salt

About ¼ teaspoon dried red pepper flakes

1 large egg, lightly beaten

½ cup olive oil

TO FINISH

Kosher salt

12 ounces spaghetti

½ cup finely grated Parmesan cheese

MAKE THE SAUCE: Heat the oil in a medium skillet over medium heat until it warms and spreads to the edges of the skillet, 2 to 3 minutes. Add the onions ("not too many onions!") and garlic, and season with salt. Cook, stirring, until the garlic and onions are translucent, 3 to 5 minutes. Add the sugar, oregano, and tomatoes with their juices. Raise the heat to high and cook, stirring steadily, until the tomatoes break apart and the garlic aroma mellows, 15 to 18 minutes. Add ½ cup of water and cook for a few minutes more, until the sauce tastes cooked and balanced. Taste for seasoning and keep stirring ("Don't forget to stir the sauce!"). Stir in the basil leaves. Keep warm.

MAKE THE MEATBALLS: Put the beef in a large bowl, spreading it across the bottom and up the sides a little. (This will help you to distribute the seasonings evenly throughout the meat.) Sprinkle the toasted bread crumbs, Parmesan, chopped parsley, salt to taste, and the red pepper flakes all over the meat and use your hands to mix the ingredients together. Incorporate the egg. Do not overwork the meat or it will yield tough meatballs.

TASTE TEST: Roll 1 small meatball, about 2 inches in diameter. Heat some of the oil in a small skillet over high heat. When the oil begins to smoke lightly, shut off the heat (to avoid splattering) and add the meatball. Cook for a few minutes, turning the meatball on all sides, until it's browned on the outside but still pink in the middle. Taste for seasoning and texture. If it's too wet, add some more bread crumbs to the mixture. If too dry, add another beaten egg or a splash of cool water. Adjust the seasoning, if needed, as well. Roll the remaining meat mixture into balls. You should get about twenty 2-inch meatballs.

COOK THE MEATBALLS: Heat half of the remaining oil in a large skillet set over medium heat. When the oil begins to smoke lightly, shut off the heat and add half of the meatballs in a single layer, spread somewhat apart so they brown instead of steam. Turn the heat back to high and cook, turning the meatballs so they brown on all sides, 3 to 5 minutes. Press on a few—they should give slightly to light pressure (this is how you know they are still tender in the center). Use a slotted spoon or spatula to transfer them to a tray lined with paper towels to drain any excess fat. Repeat with the remaining oil and meatballs.

recipe continues

COOK THE PASTA: Fill a large pot with 4 quarts of water and bring the water to a rolling boil over high heat. Add a generous handful of salt. Bring the water back up to a boil. Add the pasta and cook, stirring with a slotted spoon to make sure it does not clump or stick to the bottom, until it's al dente, 8 to 9 minutes. Drain the pasta in a large colander.

FINISH THE SAUCE AND MEATBALLS: When you drop the pasta into the water, add the meatballs to the sauce and simmer over very low heat, bubbling slightly, to warm the meatballs through and let them absorb some of the sauce, 3 to 5 minutes. Shut off the heat and allow the sauce and meatballs to rest while your pasta finishes cooking.

SERVE: Transfer the sauce and meatballs to a large bowl and toss in half of the cooked pasta. Add some of the Parmesan cheese. Stir in the remaining pasta. Serve with the remaining cheese in a bowl on the side.

Godfather *Spaghetti and Meatballs*

SERVES 4 TO 6

***GODFATHER* SAUCE**

1 tablespoon extra-virgin olive oil

4 spicy Italian sausages (about 12 ounces total)

5 garlic cloves, thinly sliced

Kosher salt

1 (6-ounce) can tomato paste

2 medium Roma tomatoes, cored and finely chopped

2 teaspoons sugar

1 teaspoon dried oregano

1 (28-ounce) can peeled whole tomatoes, with their juices

2 to 3 tablespoons red wine

½ cup fresh basil leaves

***GODFATHER* MEATBALLS**

1 pound ground beef (85% lean)

½ cup panko bread crumbs, toasted

½ cup finely grated Parmesan cheese, plus extra for serving

1 large egg, lightly beaten

½ cup chopped fresh curly-leaf parsley

Kosher salt

¼ teaspoon dried red pepper flakes

1 tablespoon olive oil

TO FINISH

Kosher salt

12 ounces spaghetti

½ cup finely grated Parmesan cheese

MAKE THE SAUCE: In a medium skillet, heat the olive oil over medium heat. Add the sausages and cook steadily, browning them on all sides, until they are cooked through, 8 to 10 minutes. Remove the sausages (reserve the oil in the skillet) and drain them on a plate lined with paper towels. Add the garlic slices to the skillet and season with salt. Reduce the heat and cook until the garlic browns, about 2 minutes. Then add the tomato paste and sauté it over medium heat, stirring constantly, until it melds with the oil and garlic, 2 to 3 minutes. Add the fresh tomatoes, sugar ("Here's my secret: I add a little bit of sugar"), oregano, and the canned tomatoes and their juices. Cook for a few minutes over high heat, stirring from time to time, until the sauce tastes cooked. Add ½ cup of water and simmer over low heat until the flavors settle and mellow, 5 to 8 minutes. Stir in the wine ("Add a splash of wine") and simmer until the wine blends in with the tomatoes, 3 to 5 minutes. Taste for seasoning. Stir in the basil leaves and sausages.

MAKE THE MEATBALLS: Put the beef in a large bowl and spread it across the bottom of the bowl and up the sides. (This will help to distribute the seasonings evenly throughout the meat.) Add the toasted bread crumbs, Parmesan, egg, chopped parsley, salt to taste, and the red pepper flakes all over the meat and use your hands to mix the ingredients together.

TASTE TEST: Roll 1 small meatball, about 2 inches in diameter. Heat the oil in a small skillet over high heat. When the oil begins to smoke lightly, shut off the heat (to avoid splattering) and add the meatball. Cook until it is browned on all sides and cooked through but still pink in the middle, 2 to 3 minutes. Taste for seasoning and texture. If the meatball is too wet, add some more bread crumbs to the mixture. If it's too dry, add another beaten egg or 2 to 3 tablespoons more of Parmesan. Taste for seasoning. Roll the remaining meat mixture into balls; it should make eighteen to twenty 2-inch meatballs.

COOK THE MEATBALLS: Place the sausages on a flat surface and cut them into 1-inch-thick rounds. Place them, along with the meatballs, in the simmering sauce (you are not going to brown the meatballs, and this is a big difference from how goodfellas cook them). Simmer the sauce over medium to low heat until the meat is cooked through, 10 to 12 minutes. Keep the sauce warm over low heat.

recipe continues

COOK THE PASTA: In a large pot, bring 4 quarts of water to a rolling boil. Add a generous handful of salt. Bring the water back up to a boil. Add the pasta and cook, stirring with a slotted spoon to make sure it does not clump or stick to the bottom, until it is al dente, 8 to 9 minutes. Drain the pasta in a large colander.

SERVE: Shut off the heat and allow the sauce and meat to rest as your pasta finishes cooking. Transfer the sauce, with the meatballs and sausage, to a large bowl and toss with half of the cooked pasta. Add some of the Parmesan cheese. Stir in the remaining pasta. Taste for seasoning. Serve with the remaining cheese in a bowl on the side.

Classic Chicken Parmesan

The perfect chicken Parm is a balancing act between melty cheese, tangy (yet slightly sweet) tomato sauce, and tender breaded chicken. That dream bite? Somewhat crunchy chicken, warm sauce, and melted cheese. Wow. For ingredients, I adore fresh mozzarella, but it belongs on a cheese platter or as part of a classic caprese salad, not in chicken Parm—it's too watery. Here you need the classic supermarket stuff—the kind that comes Cryovac-ed in a firm brick—that gets all melty and bubbly under the broiler, just the way you remember it from your childhood. The combination of fresh garlic in the sauce and garlic powder in the chicken is a must. Make sure your tomato sauce isn't watery—reduce it on the stove longer if you need to, so it doesn't make the dish unnecessarily waterlogged.

SERVES 4 TO 6

CHICKEN

3 cups panko bread crumbs

3 large eggs

2 teaspoons garlic powder

3 boneless, skinless chicken breasts (about 1½ pounds total), pounded into ¼-inch-thick cutlets (any thinner and the meat will start to tear)

Kosher salt

2 tablespoons extra-virgin olive oil

2 tablespoons unsalted butter

TOMATO SAUCE

4 cups Homemade Tomato Sauce (page 146)

½ cup fresh basil leaves

1½ pounds firm whole-milk mozzarella cheese, shredded

1 cup finely grated Parmesan cheese

Preheat the oven to 375°F. Position a rack in the center of the oven.

TOAST THE BREAD CRUMBS: Spread the bread crumbs in a thin, even layer on a sheet pan and place the pan in the oven on the center rack to toast. When the bread crumbs are golden brown, after 5 to 8 minutes, remove the pan from the oven. Transfer the bread crumbs to a medium bowl to cool.

BREAD THE CHICKEN: Crack the eggs into a medium bowl, add a splash of cool water, and beat lightly until smooth. Stir the garlic powder into the bread crumbs. Season the chicken pieces on both sides with salt. Dip each chicken cutlet in the eggs and thoroughly coat both sides in the bread crumbs. Place the breaded chicken in a single layer on a sheet pan. Refrigerate for at least 1 hour or up to 6 hours.

COOK THE CHICKEN: In a large, broiler-safe skillet, heat the olive oil and butter over medium heat, swirling occasionally, until the butter begins to froth. Add the chicken pieces in a single layer and cook until they are golden brown on the first side, 3 to 4 minutes. Gently turn the chicken over and cook on the second side until golden brown, 2 to 3 minutes. Use a slotted spatula to transfer the chicken to a paper-towel-lined plate to drain slightly, reserving the skillet.

BAKE AND SERVE: Preheat the oven to 350°F. Remove the excess fat from the skillet. Add the tomato sauce and cook over medium heat until it is warmed through, 2 to 3 minutes. Remove the skillet from the heat and add the basil. Arrange half of the chicken in a single layer in a broiler-safe 8-inch square baking dish. Top it with half of the tomato sauce and about half of the mozzarella and Parmesan. Add a layer of the remaining chicken, and top that with the remaining sauce and cheese. Place the dish in the oven and bake until it is hot and bubbling, 25 to 30 minutes. Then run the dish under the broiler until the top is golden brown, 2 to 3 minutes.

Homemade Tomato Sauce

This is the tomato sauce that I keep in the fridge for those days when I want something home-cooked but don't feel like preparing a full meal. It's a little different from the recipe I use for baked pasta dishes. It has carrots, which add extra sweetness and texture for a simple pasta dish. It instantly makes meats like chicken, pork, and beef that much more comforting. I also drop it, piping hot, into a bowl of spaghetti along with some fresh basil. I used to make lots of mini pizzas by spooning a bit of tomato sauce on a toasted English muffin and then broiling some slices of mozzarella over the top. I made one for Ava the other day and she said, "Ma, this is the true breakfast pizza." There is something so satisfying about cooking your own sauce. It can almost make you feel like an Iron Chef in your own home!

MAKES ABOUT 5 CUPS

¼ cup extra-virgin olive oil

4 medium yellow onions, halved and thinly sliced

2 medium carrots, peeled and grated

10 large garlic cloves, thinly sliced

½ teaspoon dried red pepper flakes

Kosher salt

2 teaspoons sugar

2 teaspoons dried oregano

2 (28-ounce) cans peeled whole tomatoes, with their juices, lightly crushed

1 cup fresh basil leaves

MAKE THE SAUCE: In a large skillet, heat the olive oil over medium heat. Add the onions, carrots, garlic, and red pepper flakes, season with salt, and cook, stirring occasionally, until the onions are translucent and tender, 5 to 8 minutes.

Add the sugar, oregano, and the tomatoes and their juices. Cook, stirring from time to time, until the tomatoes taste cooked and the raw garlic aroma mellows, 12 to 15 minutes. Taste for seasoning. Add the basil leaves.

Serve immediately or cover and refrigerate for up to 5 days. You can also freeze the tomato sauce in an airtight container or a resealable freezer bag for up to 4 weeks.

Basil Tomato Pasta

I have always enjoyed finding that errant basil leaf in the tomato sauce as I eat a bowl of pasta. Chewing the leaf and having the basil release its floral, grassy notes to the bright tomato and garlic flavors in the sauce? Sublime. Even more sublime? Making a pesto *and* a tomato sauce and adding both to a bowl of pasta, but not fully mixing the sauces together. You keep eating, enjoying the inconsistencies. This creates a great side effect: a varied taste that makes the dish different with every bite so one skews more tomato and the next more basil—it's totally addictive. We are looking for a chunky sauce here, with texture and sweetness from the tomatoes and carrots (they're shredded so they just melt right into the sauce) and from the basil leaves, too. For a chunky sauce like this one, I like a toothy, chewy pasta. My favorites for this recipe are bucatini and perciatelli, tossed al dente in the hot sauce and sprinkled with Parmesan, or with aged provolone for a sharper twist.

SERVES 4 TO 6

TOMATO SAUCE

2 tablespoons extra-virgin olive oil

2 small yellow onions, halved and thinly sliced

2 medium carrots, grated on the large holes of a box grater

5 large garlic cloves, minced

1 teaspoon dried red pepper flakes

Kosher salt

2 teaspoons sugar

1 (28-ounce) can peeled whole tomatoes, with their juices

PESTO

2 cups tightly packed fresh basil leaves, coarsely chopped

1 cup fresh baby spinach leaves, coarsely chopped

1 teaspoon sugar

½ cup extra-virgin olive oil

1 tablespoon kosher salt

PASTA

Kosher salt

1 pound bucatini or perciatelli pasta

2 teaspoons red wine vinegar

½ cup finely grated Parmesan cheese

MAKE THE TOMATO SAUCE: In a large skillet set over medium heat, heat the olive oil until it slides from the center to the edges of the skillet, 2 to 3 minutes. Add the onions, carrots, garlic, red pepper flakes, and a generous pinch of salt. Cook, stirring occasionally, until the onions are translucent, 5 to 8 minutes. Stir in the sugar and the tomatoes and all their liquids. Use a wooden spoon to break up some of the whole tomatoes and cook, stirring from time to time, until the sauce is cooked and the tomatoes meld with the vegetables, 15 to 18 minutes. Add about 1 cup of water and continue cooking until the sauce is chunky and flavorful, another 5 to 8 minutes. Turn off the heat, taste for seasoning, and cover to keep warm.

MAKE THE PESTO: Set aside a few basil leaves for topping the pasta. Into a blender, put the remaining basil, the spinach, the sugar, and the olive oil. Add ¼ cup of cold water and the salt. Pulse until the pesto comes together but is not completely smooth. Taste for seasoning and set aside.

COOK THE PASTA: Fill a large pot with 4 quarts of water and bring it to a rolling boil over high heat. Add ¼ cup of salt and bring the water back to a boil. Taste the water. It should be salty like seawater. Add the pasta and cook, stirring it with a large slotted spoon to ensure that it does not clump or stick to the pot, until it is al dente, 8 to 10 minutes. Drain the pasta, reserving about ½ cup of the cooking water.

FINISH THE DISH: In a large shallow bowl, toss together the pasta, red wine vinegar, and tomato sauce. Add some of the reserved pasta water if the tomato sauce needs some loosening. Dot the pasta with spoonfuls of the pesto and gently, only partially, swirl it in. Sprinkle with the cheese. Top with the reserved basil leaves and serve immediately.

Stuffed Shells

In these stuffed shells, I combine ricotta with pecorino, a salty sheep's-milk grating cheese, because it packs a saltier punch than the classic Parmesan. It also contributes a creamy, milky flavor without being really heavy. For shells that aren't watery, drain your ricotta of any excess liquid—you can drain it in a colander set over a bowl in the fridge for a few hours, or even tie the ricotta in cheesecloth, hang it over a bowl, and put it in the refrigerator to drain overnight. The egg gives a velvety richness to the filling and the soy sauce adds umami—you won't even know that soy sauce was involved when you taste the dish. Best of all, you can put the whole thing together in advance and just bake it when you're ready to eat.

SERVES 4 TO 6

- 2 cups ricotta cheese
- 2 tablespoons extra-virgin olive oil
- 12 sprigs fresh thyme
- Kosher salt
- 1 pound large pasta shells (I like De Cecco #50 size shells)
- 1 cup freshly grated pecorino cheese
- ¼ teaspoon ground nutmeg (preferably freshly grated)
- 1 large egg, lightly beaten
- 1 tablespoon low-sodium soy sauce
- 3 cups tomato sauce, store-bought or homemade (see page 146)

DRAIN THE RICOTTA: Remove the ricotta from its container and place it in a colander set over a bowl. Refrigerate the ricotta for at least 30 minutes or up to 4 hours.

FRY THE THYME: Heat the olive oil in a medium saucepan over medium heat. When the oil begins to smoke lightly, add the thyme sprigs and fry them until they are crispy, 2 to 3 minutes. Transfer the thyme to a paper towel to drain, and season it with salt (reserve the oil in the saucepan).

COOK THE PASTA: Fill a large pot with 4 quarts of water and bring it to a rolling boil over high heat. Add a generous handful of salt and bring the water back to a boil. Taste the water. It should be salty like seawater. Add the pasta shells and cook, stirring them gently with a large slotted spoon to ensure they do not stick, until they are just shy of al dente, 4 to 5 minutes. Drain them and then place them in a large bowl; add the reserved oil from the saucepan and toss. Refrigerate the shells on a sheet pan.

Preheat the oven to 375°F.

PREPARE THE RICOTTA FILLING: In a large bowl, spread the drained ricotta across the bottom and up the sides of the bowl so the seasoning will coat most of the cheese. Season with salt and sprinkle ½ cup of the pecorino in an even layer over the ricotta. Use a small strainer to sift the nutmeg in an even layer over the cheese. Stem the fried thyme over the ricotta, allowing the leaves to fall into the mix; discard the stems. Mix to blend and then stir in the egg and soy sauce.

STUFF AND BAKE: Put the ricotta filling in a resealable plastic bag and cut off the tip of one corner with scissors. Use the bag to squeeze the filling into each shell. Arrange the shells snugly in a single layer in a broiler-safe 13 by 9-inch baking dish. Spoon the tomato sauce over the shells and place the baking dish in the oven. Bake until the shells are browned and crisped, 15 to 18 minutes. Top with the remaining ½ cup pecorino and run under the broiler until bubbling hot and browned, 2 to 3 minutes.

Spinach Manicotti

WITH LEMON

Why did manicotti go out of style? It seems so old-fashioned now, and yet I love the baked pasta tubes. Manicotti are akin to cannelloni. They are both stuffed pastas, often filled with cheese, spinach, and/or tomatoes. You can make them out of flat lasagna sheets, rolled up and baked. For this recipe, I buy manicotti (tube-like) pasta shells, parcook them, and then fill them with fresh spinach, ricotta, and lots of lemon zest. I used to be obsessed with grating only the outer layer of lemon zest to get the floral notes and oils, leaving the bitter white pith behind. Now I love the pith—it adds a pleasantly bitter note that tamps down the natural sweetness of the ricotta. It also heightens the delicate flavor of the spinach, so I encourage you to grate the zest, and then grate even deeper. One large lemon could yield 3 to 4 tablespoons of zest and pith—and trust me, we want all of those flavors in here.

SERVES 6 TO 8

- 1½ cups ricotta cheese
- Kosher salt
- 14 to 16 manicotti pasta shells
- 4 tablespoons extra-virgin olive oil
- 4 cups fresh baby spinach
- 2 cups heavy cream
- 2 large garlic cloves, minced
- Freshly ground black pepper
- 3 cups finely grated pecorino cheese
- 2 teaspoons Worcestershire sauce
- 1 teaspoon Tabasco
- ½ teaspoon ground allspice
- 1 large egg, lightly beaten
- Grated zest (with some pith) and juice of 1 large lemon
- Leaves from 6 sprigs fresh tarragon, coarsely chopped

DRAIN THE RICOTTA: Remove the ricotta from its container and place it in a colander set on a plate. Refrigerate the ricotta for at least 30 minutes or up to 4 hours.

Preheat the oven to 375°F. Position a rack in the center of the oven.

COOK THE PASTA: Fill a medium pot with about 4 quarts of water and bring it to a rolling boil. Add ¼ cup of salt and bring the water back to a boil. Taste the water. It should be salty like seawater. Add the manicotti and cook, stirring them gently with a large slotted spoon to ensure that they do not stick or clump, until they are still quite firm, 3 to 4 minutes. Drain the pasta and transfer it to a large bowl (you'll reuse the empty pot later). Toss the pasta with 2 tablespoons of the olive oil.

WILT THE SPINACH: In a large sauté pan, heat the remaining olive oil over medium heat. When the oil begins to smoke lightly, add the spinach, season it generously with salt, and cook, stirring, just long enough to wilt it, about 1 minute. Quickly remove the pan from the heat and transfer the spinach to a kitchen towel to drain and cool.

MAKE THE SAUCE: Set the pot you used to cook the pasta over medium heat, add the cream and garlic, and bring to a gentle simmer. Season with salt and pepper to taste. Stir in 2 cups of the pecorino, the Worcestershire, and the Tabasco. Taste for seasoning and set aside.

recipe continues

PREPARE THE RICOTTA FILLING: In a large bowl, spread the ricotta out across the bottom and up the sides of the bowl (so the seasoning will coat most of the cheese). Season it with salt and evenly sprinkle ½ cup of the pecorino over the ricotta. Use a small strainer to sift the allspice evenly over the cheese. Mix to blend, adding the egg, lemon zest and pith, and tarragon to the mixture. Coarsely chop about three-fourths of the spinach and stir that into the mix as well.

ROLL THE MANICOTTI: Put the filling in a sealed plastic bag and cut off the tip of one corner with a pair of scissors. Place the hole in the bag at one end of each manicotti and squeeze so the filling goes into the pasta tube. Spoon some of the sauce over the bottom of a 13 by 9-inch baking dish so the pasta won't stick as it bakes. Arrange the filled pasta in tight rows in the baking dish, taking care that the manicotti are snug in the dish. They can even pile up or overlap.

BAKE AND SERVE: Cover the manicotti with about half of the sauce. Place the baking dish on the center rack and bake until the filling is hot in the center when pierced with the tip of a knife, 12 to 15 minutes. Remove the baking dish from the oven. Warm any remaining sauce and spoon it over the manicotti. Sprinkle with the remaining ½ cup pecorino and the remaining spinach. Drizzle with the lemon juice and serve.

Risotto

WITH TOMATOES AND PARMESAN CHEESE

This is a delicious dish that my father would make for me from time to time when we didn't have much food in the house, and now I find myself doing the same. All you need is Arborio rice and a tomato sauce (ideally homemade) that has some texture. Cooking risotto is a process of layering flavors—in this case the shallots, the wine, the tomato sauce—and giving each one its moment alone with the rice before adding another. Be patient. Have you ever tasted uncooked wine in rice? Ruins the mood.

The anchovy oil can come from any glass jar of anchovy fillets; just don't use the oil from a tin—it's too metallic. Risotto can be made using chicken stock (or any stock), but I am partial to water here because I want to savor the starchy, nutty flavors of the rice against the tang of the tomato sauce. (My rule is, if there is no chicken in the dish, why use chicken stock?) I also season the rice with flaky Maldon salt, because I love its crunch and the burst of salt with these flavors.

SERVES 6 TO 8

3 tablespoons extra-virgin olive oil

2½ cups (1 pound) Arborio rice

Maldon salt

2 medium shallots, minced

½ cup dry white wine

3 cups chunky tomato sauce, store-bought or homemade (see page 146)

1 tablespoon anchovy oil (see headnote)

1 cup finely grated Parmesan cheese

½ cup mascarpone cheese

In a medium pot, bring about 2 quarts (8 cups) of water to a simmer over high heat; then reduce the heat to maintain the simmer.

TOAST THE RICE: In a large sauté pan set over medium heat, combine the olive oil and the rice and season with Maldon salt. Stir to coat the rice with the oil and then smooth it out gently so it's in a uniform layer in the pan. Listen for the sound of the rice popping in the heat, and smell the aroma of the rice getting nutty, after 2 to 3 minutes. Stir the rice, moving it around and then smoothing it out so the rice toasts gently, then cook for 1 to 2 minutes more.

COOK THE RICE: Stir in the shallots along with a pinch of Maldon salt and cook, stirring with a wooden spoon, until the shallots are translucent, 2 to 3 minutes. Add the white wine and cook, stirring constantly, until the wine evaporates. Ladle enough of the simmering water into the pan to just cover the rice. Simmer, uncovered, stirring constantly, until the rice has absorbed a fair amount of the liquid.

FINISH THE RICE: From this point, it should take 12 to 15 minutes to finish the risotto. Add the water in small increments, cooking and stirring until it has been absorbed before adding the next ladleful. Cook until the rice is tender but still has a firm bite, like pasta cooked al dente, about 8 minutes. Pour the tomato sauce and anchovy oil into the pan, turn off the heat, and stir the sauce, oil, and half of the Parmesan cheese into the rice. Let the risotto sit on the stove for 5 to 8 minutes so the rice can absorb some of the sauce. Taste for seasoning, then stir in the mascarpone. Serve topped with the remaining Parmesan cheese.

Pork Shoulder Pizzaiola

Pizzaiola is a traditional Neapolitan dish in which a cheaper cut of meat, like pork shoulder, is cooked with wine and tomatoes until tender. My mom used to start cooking the tomato sauce first and then would sear pork chops and spicy pork sausages in another pan. Once the chops and sausages were cooked, she'd drop them right into the sauce. The meat would sit in the sauce on the stove for a good half hour to let all the flavors combine. I always worried that the meat would become cold or overcooked, but it never did. We would fish the meat out and eat it on the spot—so messy, but so tasty. If we could wait, we'd be rewarded, as the meat and sauce were even better the next day, when they had had even more time to comingle. I always loved the flavor of the browned pork chops, but honestly the meat can sometimes be a little dry. So I decided to re-create my mom's sauce with boneless pork shoulder, a cheaper, fattier cut. The anchovies are a classic Italian umami move, and the fish sauce just adds a tasty, salty kick.

SERVES 6 TO 8

- 1 tablespoon extra-virgin olive oil
- 1 pound spicy Italian pork sausages (about 4)
- 2 pounds boneless pork shoulder, cut into 2½- to 3-inch chunks
- Kosher salt
- 2 medium yellow onions, halved and thinly sliced
- 4 large garlic cloves, thinly sliced
- 1 teaspoon dried red pepper flakes
- 3 cups dry white wine
- 1 (28-ounce) can peeled whole tomatoes
- 1 pint cherry tomatoes, stemmed
- 2 anchovy fillets, coarsely chopped
- 1 tablespoon fish sauce
- 1 pound farfalle pasta
- 2 tablespoons unsalted butter, at room temperature

Preheat the oven to 350°F.

COOK THE SAUSAGES: Heat a Dutch oven over high heat and add the olive oil. Use a pair of metal tongs to arrange the sausages in a single layer in the hot oil. Reduce the heat to medium and brown the sausages on all sides until they are cooked through, 8 to 10 minutes. Transfer the sausages to a plate and set aside.

COOK THE PORK SHOULDER: Season the chunks of pork shoulder on all sides with salt. Add the pork to the Dutch oven in a single layer and brown it on all sides, 5 to 8 minutes on each side. Stir in the onions, garlic, and red pepper flakes. Cook, stirring occasionally, until the onions are translucent, 8 to 10 minutes. Add the white wine and cook, stirring often, until all of the liquid cooks out, 12 to 15 minutes. Stir in both the canned and fresh tomatoes, along with the anchovy fillets and fish sauce. Cover the pot and place it in the center of the oven. Cook until the meat is tender when pierced with the tip of a knife, 2 to 2½ hours.

FINISH THE MEAT: Remove the pot from the oven and use a large spoon to skim off any excess fat or impurities from the surface. Let the sauce rest on the stovetop on low heat while you cook the pasta.

recipe and ingredients continue

- 1 cup finely grated Parmesan cheese
- 1 tablespoon red wine vinegar
- ½ cup fresh basil leaves

COOK THE PASTA: Fill a large pot with 4 quarts of water and bring it to a rolling boil over high heat. Add ¼ cup of salt and bring the water back to a boil. Taste the water. It should be salty like seawater. Add the pasta and cook, stirring it with a large slotted spoon to ensure it does not clump or stick to the pot, until it is al dente, 8 to 10 minutes. Drain the pasta, place it in a large bowl, and toss it with the butter and a pinch of salt.

FINISH THE DISH: Stir the sausages into the sauce and then stir in the Parmesan, red wine vinegar, and basil leaves. Taste for seasoning. Divide the pasta among individual bowls and serve the sauce and meat ladled over it, or serve it in a large bowl, family-style.

Note: While I always mix pasta and sauce together, this dish is an exception. The sauce has so much deep, meaty flavor that I like to have the neutral pasta underneath it and everything just spooned on top. One bite of pasta provides relief from all the other flavors, so you keep eating and eating.

VEGETABLE (& FRUIT) SALADS

I used to think a salad meant greens with dressing, but a salad can be so much more. You have the texture of roasted or raw vegetables. You have endless options for vinegars and citrus to brighten the dressings. Temperature is also so important: a chilled plate, a cool head of lettuce, ice-cold cucumbers. Those simple touches can make a meal. I never get tired of trying a new salad, because the varieties and combinations are endless.

Carrot Salad

WITH MISO DRESSING

Go to the supermarket and head for the refrigerated cases in the produce section. Chances are, nestled in the salad dressings or perhaps near the pickled and fermented jars of kimchi and beets, you'll see a few small plastic tubs of shiro miso, a white (or blond) miso paste that is made from fermented soybeans. Its flavor is both salty and sweet and almost like a salted caramel, and it works magic with savory and sweet flavors. You can use a spoonful of shiro miso in just about any dish where you crave an added layer of richness or a slightly salty note. It even tastes good in a caramel sauce for dessert! I have used brown sugar and salt here to bolster the flavors the miso brings to the table. Sweet carrots and tangy green apple make this salad tasty. I love it whisked into a simple red wine vinegar salad dressing, and it's also delicious mixed with honey and spread on sliced cooked chicken. I add a spoonful whenever I find myself thinking, "I need a dash of I don't know what."

This salad is a case study in one ingredient: carrots. They taste varied and more exciting when they're cut into different shapes and combined with accents like miso, scallion, and green apple.

SERVES 4 TO 6

- 2 tablespoons white miso paste (shiro miso)
- ½ cup red wine vinegar
- 1 tablespoon dark brown sugar
- 2 medium shallots, minced
- 1½ tablespoons kosher salt, plus extra as needed
- 1½ tablespoons coarsely ground black pepper
- ½ cup canola oil
- 12 medium carrots, peeled
- 2 medium green apples, cored and halved
- 4 scallions (green and white parts), sliced

MAKE THE DRESSING: In a large serving bowl, whisk the miso and vinegar together until smooth. Add the brown sugar and shallots, and allow the mixture to sit for 5 minutes so the shallots can drink in the vinegar. Then whisk in the salt, pepper, and oil. Taste for seasoning.

PREPARE THE CARROTS: Place the carrots on a flat surface. Cut 4 of the carrots into cubes by slicing them in half lengthwise, then slicing each half again lengthwise, and then cutting the quarters crosswise into ½-inch pieces. Cut 4 of the remaining carrots into thin rounds. Grate the remaining 4 carrots on the large holes of a box grater.

FINISH THE SALAD: Cut the apple halves into thin slices. Add the apple slices, carrots, scallions, and a pinch of salt to the dressing and toss everything together. Serve immediately.

Juicy Chilled Cucumber, Olive, and Feta Salad

There are so many types of feta cheese at the supermarket that it can be confusing: Greek, Danish, French, in brine, not in brine, cow's milk, sheep's milk. Greek feta is the one you know from the classic diner-style Greek salad that feels like three meals in one and takes 45 minutes of chewing to get through. The feta is firm, cubes nicely, and has a pleasantly salty, creamy note with a chalky, chewy undertone. I love it. But when I make a cumber and tomato salad at home, I like French sheep's-milk feta. It's creamier and softer than Greek feta, and, honestly, I just like the flavor more. I also use large, meaty green olives instead of the classic Kalamatas, because I love their texture and mellower flavor. I choose English cucumbers here because I can skip the seeding and they have a great sweet taste. If you have access to farm-stand cucumbers like Kirbys or "burpless," use those!

SERVES 4 TO 6

- ½ small red onion, sliced into very thin rounds on a mandoline
- 2 English cucumbers, peeled and halved lengthwise
- Kosher salt
- 4 tablespoons red wine vinegar
- 1 tablespoon Dijon mustard
- ⅓ cup extra-virgin olive oil
- 2 small inner yellow celery stalks with their leaves, cut crosswise into ¼-inch pieces
- 1 cup green olives (my favorite are Cerignola), pitted and halved
- 2 teaspoons sugar
- 6 ounces feta cheese (preferably French sheep's-milk feta)
- ½ teaspoon ground cumin
- 1 teaspoon dried oregano

SOAK THE ONIONS: Fill a small bowl three-fourths full with cold water and add a few ice cubes. Place the onion rounds in the water and refrigerate for 15 to 20 minutes. This will mellow their raw onion flavor.

DICE THE CUCUMBERS: Place the cucumbers, cut-side down, on a flat surface. Cut each half lengthwise into 3 even slices. Turn the slices on their sides and cut them again into 3 even slices. Now cut the strips into ½-inch cubes. Spoon them into a large serving bowl and toss with a pinch of salt. Refrigerate.

MAKE THE DRESSING: In a medium bowl, whisk 3 tablespoons of the vinegar with the Dijon mustard and olive oil. Taste for seasoning. Stir in the celery (including the leaves) and olives. Remove the onions from the ice water and pat them dry with a kitchen towel. Season the onions with the sugar and add them to the dressing.

ASSEMBLE AND SERVE: Break up the cheese with your fingers and sprinkle it with the cumin, oregano, and the remaining 1 tablespoon vinegar. Remove the bowl of cucumbers from the fridge and pour off and discard any liquid they have released. Add the cheese and all of the dressing to the cucumbers. Toss, taste for seasoning, and serve.

Roasted Sweet Potato Salad

WITH HONEY AND TOASTED PUMPKIN SEEDS

This sweet potato salad can serve many purposes. Sometimes I eat this dish as an afternoon meal to take a break from meat—but not flavor! It is also a wonderful companion to bacon and eggs in the morning, and it works beautifully next to dishes like my Mojo-Marinated Skirt Steak on page 196. What makes this salad really stand out is the miso, honey, and lime juice dressing—it adds umami and a fresh note and just ties into the sweetness of the potato in a great way. Endive is crisp, sturdy, and bitter, which is lovely against the creaminess of the potatoes and the salty, almost butterscotch taste of the miso. This salad is great when the potatoes are warm but is equally delicious when they are cool or even chilled.

SERVES 4 TO 6

4 large sweet potatoes

2 tablespoons low-sodium soy sauce

2 tablespoons white miso paste (shiro miso)

2 tablespoons honey

2 tablespoons rice vinegar

Juice of 1 lime

2 tablespoons extra-virgin olive oil

1 tablespoon Asian sesame oil

Maldon salt

1 head yellow or red Belgian endive, separated into individual leaves

¼ cup pepitas (hulled pumpkin seeds), toasted

Preheat the oven to 400°F. Position a rack in the center of the oven.

COOK THE POTATOES: Arrange the potatoes in a single layer on a sheet pan. Place the pan in the oven on the center rack and bake, undisturbed, until a paring knife slips easily into the center of the largest potato, 1 to 1½ hours. Remove from the oven and set aside to cool.

MAKE THE DRESSING: In a medium bowl, whisk together the soy sauce, miso, honey, rice vinegar, and lime juice. Slowly whisk in the olive oil and sesame oil along with 1 to 2 tablespoons of cool water. Taste for seasoning.

CUT THE POTATOES: Place the potatoes on a flat surface, and with a serrated knife, carefully quarter them lengthwise. Arrange the pieces in a single layer on a serving platter.

ASSEMBLE AND SERVE THE SALAD: Season the potatoes with the Maldon salt. Drizzle some of the dressing liberally over the potatoes. In a medium bowl, toss the endive with some of the remaining dressing. Intersperse the endive leaves between the potatoes and top with the pepitas.

Grilled Zucchini and Charred Pepper Salad

WITH MINT VINAIGRETTE

I love taking a classic salad dressing and inserting just a touch of mayonnaise to offer creaminess unlike any other. The slightly eggy flavor from the mayonnaise is also wonderful with the peppers here. When you clean the charred peppers, leave some of the char on to link up with the grilled notes from the zucchini. Use any type of zucchini available: classic green, yellow, or even the round Eight Ball ones. When you are grilling zucchini, if they are becoming overly charred and are still not tender, place them on a cooler part of the grill so they finish cooking more slowly.

SERVES 4 TO 6

3 tablespoons white wine vinegar

1 tablespoon plus 1 teaspoon Dijon mustard

1 tablespoon mayonnaise

Kosher salt

4 tablespoons extra-virgin olive oil

Leaves from 4 sprigs fresh mint

2 large red bell peppers

2 teaspoons dark brown sugar

3 medium zucchini, ends trimmed, cut lengthwise into ½-inch-thick slices

½ teaspoon cayenne pepper

Maldon salt

Preheat a grill to high (or you can use a gas burner on the stovetop).

MAKE THE DRESSING: In a large bowl, whisk together the white wine vinegar, mustard, mayonnaise, and a pinch of kosher salt. Slowly drizzle in 2 tablespoons of the olive oil, whisking constantly. Taste for seasoning. Add 1 tablespoon of water if the dressing is too strong. Stir in the mint leaves.

CHAR AND PREPARE THE BELL PEPPERS: Place the bell peppers on the hottest side of the grill (alternatively, place them directly on a gas burner on the stovetop). Char the peppers on all sides until the skin burns, 3 to 5 minutes per side, about 15 minutes total. Use tongs to transfer the peppers to a bowl and refrigerate them to cool quickly. (Do not cover the bowl with plastic wrap. This traps the steam and causes the peppers to overcook as they cool.) When they are cool, place the peppers on a flat surface. Remove the top cores and open the peppers up so they lie flat, charred-skin-side up. Use a kitchen towel to wipe a majority of the charred skin away. Turn the peppers over, remove the seeds, and slice the peppers lengthwise into ½-inch-wide pieces. Place them in a medium bowl, sprinkle with the brown sugar, and drizzle with some of the dressing.

COOK THE ZUCCHINI: Place the zucchini slices in a large bowl. Spoon the cayenne into a small sieve or strainer and dust it evenly over the zucchini (or just sprinkle the cayenne over the zucchini as evenly as you can), and then toss the slices with the remaining 2 tablespoons olive oil to coat them. Season the zucchini lightly with kosher salt. Arrange the slices in a single layer on the hottest part of the grill and cook until they are tender to the touch and charred but not falling apart, 4 to 6 minutes. Use a pair of metal tongs to turn the slices over and cook for an additional 4 to 6 minutes. Remove the zucchini from the grill and arrange them in a single layer on a large serving platter.

FINISH THE SALAD: Drizzle some of the dressing over the zucchini and sprinkle with Maldon salt. Arrange the pepper slices like ribbons over the zucchini and serve topped with more dressing.

Grilled Brown Sugar Corn Salad

WITH SCALLIONS

This salad is a summertime greatest hit. There is no way everyone won't devour it! I love it most of all with grilled corn, but roasted corn (or even leftover cooked corn) can be great with these ingredients. I like to serve it and eat it freshly assembled and still warm, but, that said, this salad is also great when it's put together ahead of time and the flavors get a chance to meld together. Serve it warm or chilled, preferably on the patio.

SERVES 3 OR 4

6 large ears fresh corn, shucked

5 scallions

5 tablespoons extra-virgin olive oil

Kosher salt

3 tablespoons apple cider vinegar

1 tablespoon Dijon mustard

Juice of 1 large lime

1 teaspoon freshly ground black pepper

2 teaspoons dark brown sugar

½ cup fresh basil leaves

Preheat a grill to high.

GRILL THE CORN AND SCALLIONS: Rub the ears of corn and the scallions with about 2 tablespoons of the olive oil and sprinkle with salt. Place the corn and scallions on the hottest part of the grill and cook until they are charred on all sides; the scallions will take 3 to 4 minutes and the corn 8 to 10 minutes. Remove them from the grill and let them cool slightly. Cut the kernels off the ears of corn and slice the scallions (green and white parts) into ½-inch lengths.

MAKE THE SALAD: In a large serving bowl, whisk the remaining 3 tablespoons olive oil with the cider vinegar, mustard, lime juice, and pepper. Taste for seasoning. Add the corn and scallions to the bowl, along with the brown sugar and basil, and toss to finish.

Mixed Tomato Carpaccio

WITH PARMESAN CROUTONS

My dad always kept salad plates, and even forks and knives, in the freezer until right before he served a chilled appetizer. He would also keep the wine in there. Sometimes the wine would have shards of ice in it! He didn't care; when he wanted a dish to be cold, everything had to be *cold*. I want this salad to be like jumping into a swimming pool: refreshing, light, stunningly beautiful. This is also great as a super-simple appetizer that can be plated in advance and seasoned just before sitting down to eat. As far as tomatoes go, buy the best ones you see, and don't worry about what type they are. From heirlooms to beefsteaks to cherry tomatoes, any good tomato will do. My favorite heirloom varietiess are the larger Brandywines, Black Cherry, Amana Orange, and Black Krim. For smaller types, I love Sungolds, Black Plum, Coyote, and cherry tomatoes. Temperature is a big ingredient here: I like to plate the juicy tomatoes and keep the plates chilled in the fridge until ready to serve.

SERVES 4

- 6 tablespoons extra-virgin olive oil
- 4 large ripe beefsteak or heirloom tomatoes
- 1 (½-inch-thick) slice sourdough bread, cut into very small cubes
- ½ teaspoon hot paprika
- ¼ cup finely grated Parmesan cheese
- 1 tablespoon Dijon mustard
- 1 tablespoon apple cider vinegar
- Grated zest and juice of 1 lime
- 1 to 2 tablespoons raw sugar (such as Demerara)
- Leaves from 4 sprigs fresh basil
- Maldon salt

SLICE AND PLATE THE TOMATOES: Arrange four appetizer plates on a work surface. Drizzle the center of each plate with about ½ tablespoon of the olive oil, and tilt the plate to spread the oil into a thin layer across the surface. Cut each tomato into thin slices, collecting the tomato juices and seeds in a medium bowl as you slice. Arrange the tomato rounds in a single layer on each plate, filling the plates. I like to arrange some of the slices flat on the plates and fold some in half so there is a little "life" to the layer of tomatoes (the tomatoes have to be very thin in order to fold them delicately and easily). You can refrigerate or freeze the plates at this point and finish when ready to serve.

MAKE THE CROUTONS: In a large skillet set over medium heat, heat 2 tablespoons of the olive oil. Add the bread cubes and sprinkle the paprika over them. Cook, tossing often and reducing the heat to low if needed, until the croutons brown and feel crispy to the touch, 3 to 5 minutes. Use a slotted spoon or spatula to transfer them to a plate lined with paper towels to drain. While they're still hot, sprinkle the croutons with the Parmesan cheese.

MAKE THE DRESSING: To the bowl containing the tomato seeds and juice, add the mustard, cider vinegar, lime zest and juice, and the remaining 2 tablespoons olive oil and whisk to combine.

SERVE: When you're ready to serve the salad, remove the plates from the fridge or freezer and sprinkle the tomatoes with a light, even layer of sugar. Drizzle the dressing over the tomatoes and finish with the basil leaves, Maldon salt, and the croutons.

Chilled Raw Green Bean Salad

WITH HORSERADISH DRESSING

This salad begs to be made an hour or two before serving and then left to marinate and get ice-cold in the fridge. I love to grill a steak or roast some fish and then pull this out at the last second.

I stumbled upon this salad by accident: I made the horseradish dressing to go on top of a steak sandwich. The bowl of horseradish was on the counter, and the green beans were sitting there, too. I blanched the beans, drained them, and dropped them into the dressing. Delicious. A few weeks later I made the salad again with raw beans, and I liked that even better. One note: Use string beans or their smaller cousins, haricots verts, for this salad, as they will be tender when eaten raw. Yellow wax beans can be lovely, too. If the only beans you can find are large and starchy, it's better to hold off on this salad until tender fresh green beans show up in your market. For the horseradish, the best brand of creamed horseradish is Inglehoffer.

SERVES 4

2 tablespoons creamed horseradish (like Inglehoffer Thick-n-Creamy Horseradish)

Juice of 2 large lemons (about ⅓ cup)

1 teaspoon sugar

4 to 5 tablespoons extra-virgin olive oil

1 small bunch fresh dill, chopped (stems and all, about ¼ cup)

Kosher salt

1 pound small to medium green beans, ends trimmed, halved crosswise

MAKE THE DRESSING: In a large bowl, whisk together the creamed horseradish, lemon juice, sugar, 4 tablespoons of the olive oil, the dill, and a pinch of salt. Taste for seasoning. Add more salt or olive oil if needed.

MAKE THE SALAD: Stir the green beans into the dressing and toss to coat. Refrigerate for 30 minutes. Then stir the salad to coat the beans with the dressing again, and marinate for at least another 30 minutes. Serve while the salad is still very cold.

"Peas and Carrots" Salad

WITH CARROT DRESSING

"Peas and carrots" are a classic for a reason, with the comforting, starchy peas made vibrant by the juicy carrots. What originally began as a "mixed veggie" combo on American dinner plates also happens to make an exciting and stunning salad—I combine crunchy-sweet sugar snaps with defrosted frozen peas (don't lie—frozen peas are delicious!), or fresh ones when in season. For the dressing, we take fresh carrot juice and reduce it down to concentrate its sweetness and vibrant color. You can juice your own carrots, but you don't have to; it's fine to just buy the juice at the supermarket. The result is a light dressing with a great texture that is perfect for the sugar snaps. It can be fun to substitute snow peas (the flat ones) for half of the sugar snaps for even more texture and variety. You can make the dressing in advance—just make sure it's nice and cold when you use it. This is a wonderfully refreshing recipe for a hot day. It's also beautiful. To bulk it up as a lunch meal or a light dinner, toss in some cooked shrimp.

SERVES 2 TO 4

1 cup (8 ounces) fresh carrot juice

1 tablespoon mayonnaise

1 tablespoon apple cider vinegar

1 large garlic clove, minced

Kosher salt

2 tablespoons extra-virgin olive oil

Honey or sugar (optional)

12 ounces sugar snap peas, stemmed

1 cup frozen peas, thawed and drained

3 scallions (green parts only), sliced

REDUCE THE CARROT JUICE: In a small saucepan, simmer the carrot juice over medium heat until it's reduced by half, 5 to 8 minutes. Set it aside to cool completely.

MAKE THE DRESSING: In a large bowl, whisk together the mayonnaise, cider vinegar, and garlic. Whisk in the cooled carrot juice, a pinch of salt, and the olive oil. Taste for seasoning. (Note: If your carrot juice lacks sweetness, add a touch of honey or sugar to balance the other flavors.)

MAKE THE SALAD: Toss the sugar snaps and peas in the dressing. Stir in the scallions and serve immediately.

LETTUCE SHOW YOU HOW GOOD SALAD IS!

These are salads I love. Some of the recipes are light and easy. What could be simpler than some arugula, olive oil, and lemon? There are also salads that are more involved and heartier. Bottom line: I keep a few jars of dressing in the fridge at all times so I can make something fast and delicious. A good salad dressing in your back pocket can do that for you, too.

Gem Lettuce and Dill Salad

WITH LEMON DRESSING

There are two things I recommend for any salad: One, dry your greens thoroughly. I wash and spin my greens and then let them sit out, in a single layer on a kitchen towel on the counter, to air-dry for, ideally, a few hours before serving. Watery greens mean a watery (and less tasty) salad. Two, for heartier greens (like Little Gem, romaine, radicchio, and Belgian endive), spread them in a single layer on a sheet pan and season and dress them evenly. Then toss them into a bowl to serve.

What makes the taste of this green salad special is the little bits of bitter pith from the lemon—they accentuate the sweetness of the dill and the lettuce. To get those bits, simply hold the lemon in one hand and take your paring knife in the other. Holding the lemon steady, scrape its skin with the sharp blade until you get small pieces of lemon skin along with some of the pith. The pith adds a little texture and tastes different from the tiny pieces you get when you zest lemon skin.

SERVES 4 TO 6

2 tablespoons lemon peel and pith, scraped off with a paring knife (see headnote)

1 small garlic clove, grated on a Microplane

Juice of 1 large lemon

1 tablespoon honey

1 tablespoon apple cider vinegar

Kosher salt

¼ cup extra-virgin olive oil

4 heads Little Gem lettuce, leaves separated

10 sprigs fresh dill, finely chopped (stems and all)

MAKE THE VINAIGRETTE: In a large bowl, whisk the lemon peel and pith and garlic with the lemon juice, honey, and cider vinegar. Season with salt. Whisking steadily, slowly pour in the olive oil so it blends with the other ingredients. Taste for seasoning.

DRESS THE SALAD: Arrange the lettuce leaves in a single layer on a sheet pan. When you're ready to serve, stir the dill into the dressing and drizzle it over the lettuce leaves. Sprinkle with salt and transfer the dressed lettuce to a bowl. Serve immediately.

Iceberg Giardiniera

I didn't even hear of giardiniera until well into my thirties. Think of all the lost years! It is a versatile Italian condiment that can be used on anything from sausages, sandwiches, and omelets to salads. In Chicago, this topping even finds its way onto pizza! Giardiniera is so refreshing. It's juicy and filled with great textures. The acid from the brine, the crunch of the vegetables—it adds a bona fide pucker note and is a real appetite stimulator. I grab and use it ice-cold, right out of the refrigerator. I enlist both the brine and the vegetables in this super-simple creamy salad dressing, which I love over a chilled iceberg lettuce wedge—it's a nice change from the classic blue cheese–topped wedge. The brine reminds me of pickle juice crashing into an Italian hero sandwich. I often make this salad and serve it alongside hot wings with blue cheese dressing, so I kind of get the best of all worlds.

SERVES 4

1 cup giardiniera vegetables, store-bought or homemade (recipe follows), plus ¼ cup of their brine

1 tablespoon Dijon mustard

2 tablespoons mayonnaise

2 large heads iceberg lettuce, outer leaf layer removed, heads cored and halved, chilled

Freshly ground black pepper

MAKE THE DRESSING: In a medium bowl, whisk together the giardiniera brine, mustard, and mayonnaise. Stir in the giardiniera vegetables. Taste for seasoning.

MAKE THE SALAD: Place each wedge of lettuce on a plate. Top with the dressing and some pepper. Serve immediately.

recipe continues

Iceberg Giardiniera continued

HOMEMADE GIARDINIERA

MAKES ABOUT 4 QUARTS (16 CUPS)

- 12 large garlic cloves, thinly sliced
- 8 celery stalks, cut crosswise into ½-inch pieces
- 5 medium carrots (about 1 pound), peeled and cut into ½-inch-thick rounds
- 2 large red bell peppers, cored, seeded, and chopped
- 1 serrano chile, cut into thin rounds
- 1 medium head cauliflower, cut into smallish florets (a generous 4 cups)
- ¾ cup kosher salt
- 6 cups white wine vinegar
- 1 tablespoon plus 2 teaspoons coriander seeds
- 1 tablespoon plus 2 teaspoons dried oregano
- 1 tablespoon yellow mustard seeds
- 1 tablespoon fennel seeds
- 1 tablespoon whole black peppercorns
- 2 teaspoons dried red pepper flakes
- 1 teaspoon celery seeds
- 1 cup large green olives (I like Castelvetrano or Cerignola), pitted and chopped

SOAK THE VEGETABLES: In a large nonreactive bowl, combine the garlic, celery, carrots, bell peppers, chile, and cauliflower with ½ cup of the salt. Add cold water to cover (about 6 cups) and refrigerate overnight.

MAKE THE BRINE: In a medium pot, combine the vinegar with 4 cups of water and the remaining ¼ cup salt. Bring to a boil, then reduce the heat and simmer, stirring, until the salt dissolves, 2 to 3 minutes. Add the coriander seeds, oregano, mustard seeds, fennel seeds, peppercorns, red pepper flakes, celery seeds, and olives to the brine. Turn off the heat, remove the pot from the stove, and let the brine cool slightly.

FINISH THE GIARDINIERA: Drain and rinse the vegetables, and return them to the same nonreactive bowl. Pour the brine, including all the seasonings, over the vegetables and allow it to cool completely to room temperature, 1 to 2 hours. Cover the bowl with plastic wrap and refrigerate until the giardiniera is completely chilled. Divide the giardiniera between two 2-quart jars and refrigerate for up to 3 weeks.

Note: You can hot-water-process (can) the giardiniera for long-term storage. Sterilize four 1-quart jars and their lids and rings. Instead of adding the seasonings to the hot brine, add a quarter of the spices to each of the four jars. Then pack each jar tightly with the drained vegetables and pour the hot brine over the vegetables. Wipe the jar rims clean with a damp paper towel (the rims must be very clean or the seal won't take). Seal the jars with the lids and rings and prepare a boiling-water bath that's deep enough to completely submerge the jars. Use a pair of sturdy tongs or some thick kitchen towels to submerge the jars in the water, and boil for a full 10 minutes. Carefully remove the jars and let them cool for 1 hour. The unopened jars can be stored at room temperature, but once opened it's important to keep the giardiniera refrigerated. For more canning specifics, consult a book or website on home preserving.

Niçoise Salad

Keeping cans of fancy albacore tuna in the kitchen cabinet, tucked between the instant oatmeal and a few cans of my favorite childhood soup, is almost like an homage to my parents. On days when the fridge was pretty empty and I was hungry, my mom would ask me if I wanted tuna salad or a tuna sandwich so many times that I had no choice but to finally give in. Even now, after a long day standing at the stove, I can always count on a great tuna sandwich or tuna flaked on a salad to bring me to the comfort of home. I ate lots of canned tuna when I came home late from the restaurant in Paris, too.

Niçoise salad originated in Nice, France, home of many great cheeses, fresh herbs, and bountiful olive trees. Traditionally, the olives should be black Niçoise ones, but I love a meaty green olive instead—feel free to use whatever olive variety speaks to you. The devil is always in the details: make sure the lettuce is washed and thoroughly dried to avoid watery flavors or grit; use canned tuna packed in oil for better flavor and richness; make sure the olives are all pitted; and take care to ensure that the potatoes are fully cooked.

SERVES 4 TO 6

- 5 tablespoons extra-virgin olive oil
- 3 tablespoons red wine vinegar
- 2 tablespoons grainy Dijon mustard
- 2 teaspoons capers, plus about 1 tablespoon of the brine
- 1 teaspoon dried oregano
- Kosher salt
- 1 cup (about 5 ounces) haricots verts or small string beans, ends trimmed
- 1 medium shallot, cut into thin rounds and pulled apart into rings
- 10 to 12 baby red potatoes (about 8 ounces)
- 2 small heads Boston lettuce, leaves washed and dried
- 4 medium Roma tomatoes, cored and quartered lengthwise
- 4 large hard-boiled eggs, peeled and quartered
- 2 (5-ounce) cans oil-packed albacore tuna, drained
- ½ cup large green olives, such as Cerignola or Castelvetrano, pitted and halved

MAKE THE DRESSING: In a medium jar with a lid, combine the olive oil, vinegar, mustard, capers and brine, and oregano. Cover, shake well, and set aside.

COOK THE GREEN BEANS AND SHALLOTS: Fill a medium pot three-fourths full with water and bring it to a simmer over medium heat. Add a generous handful of salt. The water should taste like seawater. When the water boils, add the haricots verts and shallots and cook for 2 minutes. Use a slotted spoon to scoop out the beans and shallots (save the water for cooking the potatoes) and transfer them to a large plate, spreading them out in a single layer. Drizzle with a spoonful of the dressing and refrigerate to cool quickly.

COOK THE POTATOES: Add the potatoes to the water and bring it to a simmer over medium heat. Cook the potatoes until they are tender when pierced with the tip of a small knife, 20 to 25 minutes. Transfer the potatoes to a flat surface to cool. Then quarter them, sprinkle with salt, and drizzle with some of the dressing.

ASSEMBLE THE SALAD: On a large serving platter, make a bed of the lettuce leaves. Drizzle with a spoonful of the dressing. Arrange the tomatoes and hard-boiled eggs in an alternating pattern around the edges of the lettuce. Scatter the haricots verts and shallots, as well as the potatoes, in the center area. Use a fork to flake the tuna, then scatter it and the olives on top. Top with any remaining dressing.

Spinach Salad

WITH SOY-GINGER DRESSING

This is a salad that can go two ways. It can be a great zingy companion to any main course, or it can be served topped with roasted chicken (see page 76) or grilled steak for a salad main. I read that we benefit more from spinach when we eat it partially cooked; I also think it tastes best when eaten this way, which is why I wilt most of the spinach for the salad, adding in a bit of raw spinach before serving. You can use larger, leafier spinach here; just tear it into smaller pieces and cook it a few seconds longer. I like to make the dressing in advance and find it is most flavorful when it has a chance to cool to room temperature.

SERVES 2 OR 3

- 2 tablespoons extra-virgin olive oil
- 4 large garlic cloves, thinly sliced
- ½ teaspoon dried red pepper flakes
- Kosher salt
- 1 tablespoon smooth peanut butter
- 3 tablespoons low-sodium soy sauce
- 1 tablespoon honey
- 1 tablespoon grated fresh ginger
- Juice of 1 large lime
- 1¼ pounds baby spinach leaves

SAUTÉ THE GARLIC: Heat 1 tablespoon of the olive oil in a small skillet set over medium heat. Add the garlic, red pepper flakes, and a pinch of salt, and cook, stirring constantly, until the garlic softens, 2 to 3 minutes. Remove the pan from the heat and stir in the peanut butter; then transfer the mixture to a medium bowl.

MAKE THE DRESSING: Whisk the soy sauce, honey, ginger, lime juice, and 2 tablespoons of water into the peanut butter–garlic mixture. Taste for seasoning, and if the dressing seems thick, add 1 more tablespoon of water and taste again.

MAKE THE SALAD: Place a large skillet over low heat and add the remaining tablespoon olive oil. Warm it slightly (about 30 seconds) and then remove the pan from the heat and add about three-fourths of the spinach. Season it lightly with salt and toss with a spoon so the spinach gets coated with the oil and wilts slightly, about 1 minute. The spinach should be only partially wilted and still appear somewhat raw. Pour off any water that might have accumulated in the bottom of the skillet and add the softened spinach and remaining raw spinach to the dressing. Toss to combine and serve in individual bowls.

Thousand Island Tomato and Bacon Salad

Thousand Island is the junk food of the salad dressing category. Yet we love it because it makes us feel fabulously American. I make Thousand Island in a fairly classic way that always tastes so much fresher and zingier than the dressing you get in a bottle. Here I pair it with tomatoes and bacon for a salad that sometimes satisfies my cravings for a Reuben sandwich with potato chips. And to that end, I also use this as a dressed vegetable component on sandwiches and burgers from time to time when I need a special kick. As for the tomatoes, I prefer to buy Sungolds (when in season), grape tomatoes, or Campari tomatoes for this salad. A giant, ripe beefsteak would be great here, too. If you want to keep this dressing vegetarian, sub in 1 tablespoon low-sodium soy sauce for the Worcestershire.

SERVES 4 TO 6

4 thin bacon strips, thinly sliced crosswise

½ cup mayonnaise

⅓ cup ketchup

2 teaspoons capers, chopped, plus 1 tablespoon of the brine

2 teaspoons gherkins, thinly sliced, plus 1 tablespoon of the brine

8 bread-and-butter pickles, chopped, plus 1 tablespoon of the brine

3 tablespoons red wine vinegar

1 tablespoon Worcestershire sauce

Freshly ground black pepper

3 pints cherry tomatoes, halved

Maldon salt

1 tablespoon sugar

COOK THE BACON: Place the bacon pieces in a medium skillet, add ¼ cup of water, and cook over low heat until the water cooks out and the bacon is crisp, 12 to 15 minutes. Drain the bacon on a plate lined with paper towels. (Reserve the bacon fat for another use.)

MAKE THE DRESSING: In a large bowl, whisk together the mayonnaise and ketchup. Stir in the capers and brine, gherkins and brine, pickles and brine, 2 tablespoons of the vinegar, and the Worcestershire. Season with pepper and taste for seasoning.

MAKE THE SALAD: Arrange the tomato halves, cut-side up, on a serving platter. Season them with a light sprinkle of Maldon salt, the sugar, and the remaining tablespoon vinegar. Drizzle with spoonfuls of the dressing and crumble the bacon over the top.

Five-Minute One-Bowl Arugula Salad

Restraint is one of the hardest things to execute when cooking, especially when you're making something simple. For salad, it's very easy to add croutons, cheese, grilled chicken, shrimp, tomatoes . . . the list can go on forever. Here I just want the flavor of tart lemon (the juice and the chopped-up lemon bits) and briny olive oil to counter the peppery arugula. The honey pops in and out of the picture, offering some sweetness. One bowl. Five minutes. Easy, right? Serve this in a simple bowl, for example a wooden one, to give the salad a textured look.

SERVES 3 OR 4

- 1 large lemon
- 3 tablespoons extra-virgin olive oil
- 1 tablespoon honey
- 3 to 4 cups fresh arugula
- Kosher salt

CUT AND JUICE THE LEMON: Slice the lemon into very thin rounds. Remove and discard all the seeds. Pick up the slices, a few at a time, and squeeze them over a large bowl to collect the juice. Then finely chop all of the juiced lemon slices (including the rind) and add them to the bowl.

MAKE THE SALAD: Whisk the olive oil into the lemon juice in the bowl. Drizzle the honey around the sides of the bowl—do not mix it in. Add the arugula and a pinch of salt, and toss to coat it with the lemon-studded dressing, catching some of the honey on the leaves. Serve immediately.

Eggless Caesar Salad

As far as Caesar dressing goes, I'm a fan of the classic made with one small adjustment—I don't add the raw egg yolk because some people are uncomfortable with it and some people don't like it when the eggy taste comes through. Instead, I get a creamy richness from the olive oil and cheese. I do find that the flavor of the anchovy—whether from the mashed anchovy or from the oil in the jar—is imperative because it adds that umami note, salty and rich, which is even more important in a dressing made without the egg yolk. In a pinch, you can use the liquid from a can of oil-packed tuna instead (and crumble the tuna over the salad because why not). Since there's no egg yolk to worry about, you can make the dressing in advance and keep it on the door of the fridge—but please wait to toss it with the romaine (I also like Little Gem lettuce or sturdy non-hydroponically-grown Boston lettuce as backups) until the very last second. Speaking of, I peel away a layer or two of the greener outer leaves from the head of romaine because they overamplify the metallic anchovy notes in the dressing.

SERVES 4

1 tablespoon plus 2 teaspoons Dijon mustard

2 large garlic cloves, grated on a Microplane

1 teaspoon freshly ground black pepper

Kosher salt

⅓ cup fresh lemon juice (from 2 large lemons)

1 tablespoon caper brine

⅔ cup extra-virgin olive oil

½ cup canola oil

4 anchovy fillets, finely chopped, plus 2 teaspoons of the anchovy oil (or 1 tablespoon oil if not using the fillets)

3 medium heads romaine lettuce, outer leaves removed, inner leaves cut crosswise into 1-inch-wide strips

Chunk of Parmesan cheese, for grating

MAKE THE DRESSING: In a blender, combine the mustard, garlic, pepper, and a pinch of salt. Pulse to blend. With the machine running, pour the lemon juice and caper brine into the mix. Then, slowly and with the machine running, drizzle in the olive oil, followed by the canola oil. Transfer the dressing to a bowl. Taste for seasoning. Too lemony? Add more oil. Too oily? Add more lemon. Not coming together? Whisk in a splash of warm water. Stir in the anchovies and anchovy oil. Taste for seasoning, cover the bowl, and refrigerate for at least 30 minutes.

SERVE THE SALAD: Place the sliced romaine in a large bowl and grate a generous amount of Parmesan over it. Add about three-fourths of the dressing and gently toss to coat the romaine. Grate more Parmesan over the salad and serve with the extra dressing on the side.

Chickpea and Celery Salad

WITH TAHINI DRESSING

This salad, made with highly underrated celery and protein-rich chickpeas, is all about contrasts. First, there's the tender chickpeas against the creamy tahini that links up with the juicy, fresh, crunchy celery into a mix that is at once nutty, bright, and refreshing. Then you add some chickpeas that have been fried in olive oil and finished with paprika and flaky salt for a ton of texture and taste. Ideally, make the salad in advance and add the warm fried chickpeas and the parsley at the last minute.

SERVES 4 TO 6

- 1 teaspoon cumin seeds
- 1 teaspoon coriander seeds, toasted and lightly crushed
- ½ cup tahini paste
- 1 large garlic clove, grated
- 2 large lemons: grated zest from 1 lemon and juice from 2 lemons
- Maldon salt
- 8 medium celery stalks, plus the yellow leaves and small inner stalks from the heart
- 1 (15-ounce) can chickpeas, rinsed, drained, and patted dry
- 2 tablespoons extra-virgin olive oil
- 1 teaspoon mild paprika
- 1 cup fresh flat-leaf parsley leaves

TOAST THE CUMIN AND CORIANDER SEEDS: Sprinkle the cumin and coriander seeds in a thin layer in a small sauté pan and warm them gently over medium-low heat until you can smell the spices, 1 to 2 minutes. Remove from the heat and transfer the spices to a small bowl to stop the cooking.

MAKE THE DRESSING: In a large bowl, whisk the tahini with the garlic, lemon juice, toasted cumin and coriander seeds, and a pinch of Maldon salt. The dressing should be fairly thick. Whisk in a little cool water (2 to 3 tablespoons) to thin it out. Taste for seasoning.

PREPARE THE CELERY AND CHICKPEAS: Peel the celery by running the blade of a vegetable peeler down the length of each stalk. This will remove the stringy outer layer that really sticks out like a sore thumb in a salad like this. Cut the stalks crosswise into 1-inch pieces. Pick the yellow leaves from the heart of the celery and add them to the dressing. Finely slice the inner stalks and add them, too, along with the peeled celery pieces and half of the chickpeas. Stir to combine.

COOK THE CHICKPEAS AND FINISH THE SALAD: In a medium sauté pan, heat the olive oil over medium heat until it begins to smoke lightly, 2 to 3 minutes. Add the remaining chickpeas, making sure they are dried of any excess moisture, and cook, stirring, until the chickpeas become crispy, 5 to 8 minutes. Take care as you cook them—they tend to give off water and cause the oil to splatter. Use a slotted spoon to transfer the fried chickpeas to a plate lined with paper towels to drain, and season them with Maldon salt. Use a small strainer or sieve to dust an even layer of the paprika over the chickpeas. Stir the parsley into the salad and top with the fried chickpeas. Serve immediately.

Vegetable Top Salad

WITH WALNUT DRESSING

I love the "nose to tail" vegetable concept behind this salad. You just have to be careful: The flavor of vegetable tops varies from batch to batch. One bunch of carrot tops can have grassy, lovely, tart flavors. One bunch of beets can have super-sweet tops. Then all that can change. You have to taste the tops and make sure they are on point. When you shop for this salad, you want to know about the tops more than the vegetables they are attached to! You are also, hopefully, going to use those tops that are hanging around in your fridge. If you have some droopy tops, refresh them by soaking them in cold water for 20 to 30 minutes. Then dry them and use a scissors to cut them right into the salad. You also need a "classic" green with a tender texture, like peppery arugula, mixed in to act as a home base for all the flavors. The walnuts are best when crushed from whole pieces and left untoasted here. They add to the richness of the dressing and round out the bitter edges from the vegetable tops.

SERVES 2 OR 3

1 cup walnut halves

¼ cup red wine vinegar

2 teaspoons cognac

¼ teaspoon dried red pepper flakes

Kosher salt

¼ cup extra-virgin olive oil

1 cup fresh arugula

3 cups vegetable tops and fresh herbs (such as ½ cup carrot tops, ½ cup parsley leaves, and 2 cups beet tops; you can also mix in other greens like Swiss chard and kale, trimmed of stems and coarsely chopped)

1 tablespoon honey

½ cup finely grated pecorino cheese

MAKE THE DRESSING: Place the walnuts in a plastic bag and use a rolling pin to lightly crush them into smaller pieces. Transfer them to a large bowl and whisk in the vinegar, cognac, red pepper flakes, and a generous pinch of salt. Slowly whisk in the olive oil. Taste for seasoning.

MAKE THE SALAD: In a serving bowl, toss the arugula and the vegetable tops with almost all of the dressing. Drizzle with the honey and sprinkle with the cheese. Serve in the bowl, family-style, or individually plated. Top with the remaining dressing so people can see the nuts right away. Serve immediately.

STEAKS, CUTLETS, RIBS & ROASTS

Let's face it: while everyone loves vegetables, salads, and side dishes, we also love a good steak. I love when I make a tasty marinade that becomes a great sauce for a steak. I love a crispy pork cutlet. I'm even sharing my mom's favorite recipe for a classic steak Diane that gets paired with a steak sauce that might be my favorite on the planet. In short, these recipes are some of the ways I most enjoy cooking and eating meat.

Spicy Pork Loin and Lettuce Wraps

I love pork tenderloin—it is as silky as beef tenderloin, tastes meaty, yet is much lighter than beef—but, being a beef tenderloin, it's expensive! So when I cook it, I want every bite to be worth savoring. These lettuce wraps are the answer because they have contrasting textures, and the natural sweetness of the lettuce enhances the pork. To easily cradle the pork, it's best to use a lettuce with a sturdy (and juicy) "spine" to hold the filling and make it easy to fold and eat—I like soil-grown Boston or Bibb lettuce or large romaine leaves (skip super-tender hydroponic lettuces). Sometimes, I'll even double the lettuce leaves for extra insurance against drips and tears. I also skip peeling the ginger—the skin offers a cool bitter note and a tingly heat.

SERVES 4 TO 6, WITH ABOUT 1¼ CUPS SAUCE

- 1 (2-inch) knob ginger, unpeeled, finely grated on a Microplane
- 3 tablespoons low-sodium soy sauce
- 3 tablespoons fish sauce
- 3 tablespoons honey
- 3 tablespoons distilled white vinegar
- 6 scallions (green and white parts), minced
- 3 medium heads Bibb lettuce (36 to 40 medium to large leaves), washed and dried
- 2 pounds pork tenderloin, trimmed of silverskin
- Kosher salt
- ½ teaspoon sweet paprika
- 2 tablespoons canola oil
- ½ cup fresh cilantro leaves
- 1 small Fresno chile, sliced into very thin rings

MAKE THE SAUCE: In a medium bowl, combine the ginger, soy sauce, fish sauce, honey, vinegar, and scallions. Taste for seasoning and set aside.

GET READY: On a large serving platter, arrange double layers of lettuce leaves, one leaf inside another with the spines of the leaves stacked on top of each other, to create a cup.

SEASON THE PORK: Season the pork tenderloin on all sides with a generous pinch of salt, and then use a small strainer to sift an even layer of the paprika over both sides of the meat.

COOK THE PORK: Heat the oil in a large cast-iron skillet over high heat until it begins to smoke lightly, 2 to 3 minutes. Use tongs to place the pork tenderloin in the hot oil. If you have more than one piece, leave some space between them for maximum browning. Cook until browned, 3 to 5 minutes, and then rotate the pork a quarter turn every 2 to 3 minutes until browned on all sides and an instant-read thermometer inserted into the center reads 145°F (if you prefer your pork more well-done, cook it for a few minutes longer on each side). Transfer the pork to a cutting board and allow it to rest for at least 15 minutes.

ASSEMBLE THE WRAPS: Slice each tenderloin crosswise into thin rounds, 12 to 14 slices per loin, season the slices with salt, and transfer them to a platter. Add any meat drippings to the sauce. Drizzle some of the sauce over the meat and top it with the cilantro leaves and chile slices. Drizzle the lettuce leaves with some of the sauce, too. Fill each lettuce cup with 2 slices of meat, making sure to include some chile slices and cilantro. Top with any remaining sauce and serve.

Black Pepper–Crusted Roast Beef

When I cook roast beef, I want it to taste like its truest self: the classic taste of unadulterated beef. To me, roast beef is the ultimate childhood cut of meat. It was the biggest thing, besides a Thanksgiving ham or turkey, that I remember seeing my mother pull from the oven. Now, you will have some people who like medium-rare and others who like it more cooked. Roast beef is forgiving because it doesn't cook evenly from the center to the ends. I aim for a temperature in the center that registers medium-rare (about 130°F), knowing that the ends will offer some slightly more well-done pieces. For serving, I always top it with a bright, punchy flavor to contrast—here it's a creamy horseradish sauce made with crisp-tart green apples for crunch.

SERVES 8 TO 10

1 (8- to 10-pound) top round beef roast

Kosher salt

½ cup freshly ground black pepper

3 large yellow onions, quartered

¾ cup creamed horseradish (like Inglehoffer Thick-n-Creamy Horseradish)

2 tablespoons extra-virgin olive oil

2 tablespoons red wine vinegar

1 small green apple, peeled, cored, and diced small

1 quart (4 cups) beef stock, store-bought or homemade (page 106)

½ cup grainy Dijon mustard

2 tablespoons inexpensive dry sherry

Preheat the oven to 500°F.

COOK THE ROAST BEEF: Season the beef generously on all sides with salt and then coat it with the pepper. Arrange the onions in the bottom of a roasting pan. Set a roasting rack over the onions and place the roast on top. Place the pan in the oven and roast, undisturbed, for 20 minutes. Then reduce the oven temperature to 350°F and cook until an instant-read thermometer inserted into the center of the roast registers 130°F to 135°F for medium-rare, about 2 hours.

MAKE THE HORSERADISH TOPPING: While the roast is in the oven, in a medium bowl, stir together the creamed horseradish, olive oil, and vinegar. Stir in the diced apple and taste for seasoning. Cover and refrigerate until serving time.

LET THE MEAT REST: Remove the roast beef from the oven and transfer it to a cutting board, placing it upside down on the board; let it rest for 20 minutes. (This allows the juices to flow back through the meat.)

MAKE THE GRAVY: Use a slotted spoon to scoop up the majority of the onions in the roasting pan and place them in a blender. Discard the fat in the pan, put the pan on a stovetop burner, and add the stock to the pan. Bring it to a boil over medium-high heat and cook until it has reduced by half, 8 to 10 minutes. Whisk in the mustard and sherry. Simmer until the gravy thickens slightly, another 8 to 10 minutes. Season to taste. Ladle some of the gravy into the blender and blend it with the onions until smooth. Whisk the smooth onion puree back into the gravy and taste for seasoning.

SERVE: Set the roast, whole, on a platter. Pour the horseradish sauce over the top. Carve the roast into thick slices tableside and serve them with the gravy on the side.

Rib-Eye "Diane"

This is one of the first great steak dishes I remember my mother making. I think the recipe came out of a Julia Child or James Beard cookbook. It's made by searing steaks in a skillet and then building a pan sauce using the drippings plus shallots, green peppercorns, brandy, herbs, and cream for good measure. This all gets poured over the steak. Oh, yes. The connection to "Diane" is that she is the Roman goddess of the hunt, and this sauce was originally paired with venison—although as a kid, I honestly thought Diane was an old friend of my mom's! It always seemed to me that cooking the steak was the easy part, while the sauce required a true show of mastery. You can use this opulent sauce with other steaks, like hanger, filet, or sirloin, but there's just something about the beefy flavor of a rib-eye that makes it an ideal pairing for this peppery, herby sauce. I think the rib-eye has the best flavor of all the cuts of beef.

SERVES 4 TO 6

4 (14-ounce) rib-eye steaks

Kosher salt and freshly ground black pepper

1 tablespoon unsalted butter

5 medium shallots, minced

2 tablespoons green peppercorns packed in brine, drained and lightly crushed

¼ cup brandy

2 tablespoons Dijon mustard

Grated zest and juice of 1 small lemon

2 tablespoons Worcestershire sauce

½ cup beef stock, store-bought or homemade (page 106)

¼ cup heavy cream

Leaves from 6 sprigs fresh flat-leaf parsley, coarsely chopped

1 small bunch fresh chives, coarsely chopped (about ¼ cup)

Maldon salt

COOK THE STEAKS: Season the steaks generously on both sides with salt and pepper. Heat two large cast-iron skillets (large enough to hold two steaks each in a single layer) over high heat until they begin to smoke visibly, 2 to 3 minutes. Turn off the heat and use a pair of tongs to place the steaks in the pans, one by one and in a single layer. Adjust the heat to medium-high and brown the first side, 6 to 8 minutes. Resist the temptation to turn them over or move them as they cook. Once they are browned, turn the steaks over and brown the second side, 5 to 6 minutes. If you are using a meat thermometer, rare registers between 125°F and 130°F; for medium-rare, 130°F to 135°F; and between 135°F and 140°F for medium. Remove the pan from the heat and place the steaks on a wire rack to rest while you make the sauce.

MAKE THE SAUCE AND SERVE: Remove the excess fat from the skillets. Add the butter and shallots to one pan, set the pan over medium heat, and cook until the shallots are translucent, 3 to 5 minutes. To the other pan, add the green peppercorns and brandy and cook until the liquid reduces by half and lifts the tasty steak bits off the bottom of the pan. Transfer the liquid, scraping it from the pan with a heatproof spatula, to the pan with the shallots. Add the mustard, lemon juice, and Worcestershire to the shallots. Swirl the pan so all of the flavors start to meld together. Add the beef stock and cook until the sauce reduces and is thick enough to coat the meat, 3 to 5 minutes. Stir in the cream, parsley, and chives. Simmer for 2 more minutes so the cream integrates. Taste for seasoning. Place the steaks on individual plates, sprinkle with Maldon salt, and spoon the sauce over the top.

Pork Cutlets

This is a big food memory for me. My mom would always gently fry veal or pork cutlets in an even mix of olive oil and butter. She would manage the heat so it was hot enough to slowly brown and form a crust on the meat but slow enough that the meat was super tender. The taste of both the olive oil and the butter adds so much more character to the cutlets than if you deep-fried them in a neutral-flavored oil. It soaks into the bread crumbs and flavors the whole exterior of the meat. Pork top round is surprisingly lean, making the oil and butter necessary to contribute richness. While this is something my mother made consistently, I always considered it a special-occasion dish. The chef in me wants to make so many changes, but this is one dish that I like to keep the same. I don't know that there's any way to improve it!

SERVES 3 OR 4, WITH 2½ TO 3 CUPS SAUCE

3 large eggs

1 cup panko bread crumbs

½ cup fine bread crumbs

½ cup finely grated Parmesan cheese

5 (½-inch-thick) pork cutlets (about 1 pound total) from the top round or loin

Kosher salt and freshly ground black pepper

4 tablespoons extra-virgin olive oil

4 tablespoons (½ stick) unsalted butter

6 Roma tomatoes, cored and cut into bite-size wedges

Pinch of dried red pepper flakes

1 tablespoon maple syrup

Juice of 2 large lemons

¼ cup fresh basil leaves

PREPARE THE PORK: Crack the eggs, dropping the yolks into a small bowl (save the whites for another use, such as the egg white omelet on page 115). Add a touch of cold water to the yolks and whisk to blend. In another bowl, combine both kinds of bread crumbs with the cheese. Season each piece of pork on both sides with salt and pepper. Then dip each slice of pork in the eggs and finally dredge them through the bread crumbs. Place the pork in a single layer on a sheet pan and refrigerate for at least 30 minutes.

COOK THE PORK: In a large skillet, heat 2 tablespoons of the olive oil with 2 tablespoons of the butter over medium heat. When the oil starts to shimmer and thin out in the pan, remove the skillet from the heat and add half of the pork in a single layer. Return the skillet to medium heat and cook until the cutlets are golden brown, 4 to 5 minutes. Gently turn them over and cook until they are browned on the other side and cooked through, 4 to 5 minutes. Use a slotted spatula to transfer them to a paper-towel-lined plate to drain slightly. Season the cooked cutlets with salt and repeat with the remaining oil, butter, and cutlets.

MAKE THE SAUCE: Discard most of the fat from the skillet and add the tomatoes, red pepper flakes, and a few pinches of salt. Cook over medium heat until the tomatoes soften, 2 to 3 minutes. Then add the maple syrup and lemon juice, and simmer until the flavors meld together, 1 to 2 minutes. Turn off the heat.

SERVE: Arrange the cutlets on a large serving platter and top them with the tomato-lemon sauce. Finish with the basil leaves and serve immediately.

Mojo-Marinated Skirt Steak

Skirt steak has great flavor, but it can be tough. The solution is to let it sit in a marinade that can help tenderize the meat before you cook it. This cut in particular shock-absorbs a tangy Cuban-style mojo sauce and ends up being super tasty—just be sure to set aside a few hours to let it soak up the flavor. Here I substitute more readily available tomatillos and fresh lime juice for the traditional sour oranges in the mojo. If you are unable to find tomatillos, substitute two underripe Roma tomatoes. You can eat this steak sliced against the grain into long, thin strips or use it in tacos or to fortify a salad.

SERVES 4

- 2 tablespoons canola oil
- 6 large garlic cloves
- 1 yellow onion, halved and thinly sliced
- Kosher salt
- 2 medium tomatillos (or 1 medium-size green tomato), papery husks removed, rinsed and halved
- ¾ cup fresh lime juice (from 8 to 10 limes)
- Grated zest and juice of 1 large orange
- 16 sprigs fresh cilantro
- 1 teaspoon dried red pepper flakes
- ½ teaspoon ground cumin
- 1 (1½-pound) skirt steak, trimmed of silverskin and sinew and halved crosswise

MAKE THE MARINADE: Set a medium skillet over medium heat and add 1 tablespoon of the oil, the garlic, onion, and a pinch of salt. Add a splash of water and cook until the garlic and onion are tender but not browned, 5 to 8 minutes. In a blender, puree the tomatillos with the lime juice, orange zest and juice, cilantro, red pepper flakes, cumin, and the cooked garlic mixture until smooth.

MARINATE THE MEAT: Put the marinade in a nonreactive baking dish, add the meat, and coat both sides with the marinade. Cover the dish with plastic wrap and refrigerate for 4 to 6 hours.

GET READY: Remove the meat from the marinade and wipe away any excess. Reserve the marinade left in the baking dish. Heat a cast-iron or other heavy-bottomed skillet over medium heat and add the remaining 1 tablespoon oil. When the oil begins to smoke lightly, season the steak on both sides with salt and use a pair of tongs to carefully place it into the hot oil.

COOK THE STEAK: Raise the heat to high and cook the steak until the first side is browned, 3 to 5 minutes. Then turn it over and cook until it is browned on the second side, another 3 to 5 minutes. Flip the steak again and cook for 1 minute to move the juices around inside the meat as it cooks, moving the steak from one side of the pan to the other, and then flip it again and cook for 1 minute, continuing to push the steak around the pan as it sears. Transfer the meat to a flat surface and let it rest for 15 minutes.

SERVE: In the same skillet, bring the reserved marinade to a simmer over medium heat. Cook for 3 to 4 minutes to reduce it. Taste for seasoning. Use a sharp knife to slice the meat against the natural grain (this will tenderize it further). Top with the cooked marinade and serve.

I find that moving the meat from one side of the pan to the other helps to internally baste the meat—like shaking a snow globe to keep the snow active inside. While searing does *not* lock juices inside meat, moving the meat (and blood) back and forth makes the meat juicier. This is a great technique for thin steaks like skirt steak or hanger steak, as well as for filet mignon or strip steak.

I get so many questions about knowing when a steak is done. It's a tough call because every cut and piece of meat is different. The simplest way to check for doneness is to make a small incision in the thickest part of the steak and take a peek. It should be a little less cooked than you would like, to allow for carry-over cooking—this is the resting time before you carve it. So if you want a medium-rare steak, for example, pull it when it's still deeply pink in the center. Here are the temperature ranges for doneness if you're using a meat thermometer:

Rare: 125°F to 130°F (warm in the center but very red)

Medium-rare: 130°F to 135°F (pink/red mixed in center, juicy)

Medium: 135°F to 140°F (pale pink center)

Medium-well: 140°F to 155°F (some slight juiciness and a hint of remaining pale pink in the center)

Well-done: 155°F to 165°F (no traces of red or pink)

St. Louis Ribs

WITH BROWN SUGAR RUB AND BARBECUE SAUCE

When I was a kid, we always had the kind of ribs you get from Chinese restaurants—never from American barbecue places. My dad didn't like sweet and tangy American ribs, and if my dad didn't like something, we didn't eat it! So here is my rewrite of my childhood pork ribs made in the decidedly American barbecue style that I always wanted: with a mix of sweet and spicy dry rub on the meat and a juicy, sloppy sauce to finish. Some might see it as a barbecue sin, but I'm telling you, when you make this, people will eat everything down to the bone—and they might even try to gnaw on the platter, too. (And if you're wondering, St. Louis–style ribs have had the cartilage and rib tips removed, so they are more uniform, for easier cooking and a nice presentation.)

SERVES 6 TO 8, WITH 2 CUPS BARBECUE SAUCE

- ⅔ cup packed dark brown sugar
- ¼ cup hot paprika
- ¼ cup chili powder
- ¼ cup kosher salt, plus more for finishing
- 1 teaspoon ground mace (or nutmeg)
- 2 racks St. Louis–style pork ribs (5 to 5½ pounds total)
- 1½ cups ketchup
- ½ cup Dijon mustard
- ¼ cup Worcestershire sauce
- 1 tablespoon blackstrap molasses
- 1 cup red wine vinegar
- 1 large lime, halved

MAKE THE RUB: In a medium bowl, thoroughly combine ⅓ cup of the brown sugar with the paprika, chili powder, salt, and mace. Rub the mixture all over the racks of ribs. Wrap the ribs in plastic wrap and refrigerate for at least 8 hours or up to 24 hours.

MAKE THE SAUCE: In a large pot, combine the ketchup, mustard, Worcestershire, the remaining ⅓ cup brown sugar, the molasses, and the vinegar. Bring the mixture to a simmer over medium-low heat and cook, stirring from time to time, until the sauce thickens and smells cooked, about 30 minutes. Turn off the heat and cover the pot to keep the sauce warm.

Preheat a charcoal or gas grill to high. Preheat the oven to 350°F.

GRILL-MARK THE RIBS: Place the ribs directly on the hot grill and grill them just long enough to flavor and leave a nice dark grill mark without cooking them fully, 8 to 10 minutes per side.

FINISH COOKING THE RIBS: Set a wire rack on a rimmed sheet pan and place the rib racks, bone-side up, on the rack. Divide the warm sauce between two bowls and set one bowl aside for serving. Brush the sauce from the first bowl onto both sides of each rack of ribs. Cover the whole pan with a layer of foil, crimping it around the edges, and bake the ribs for 1½ hours. Remove the foil and turn the racks over. Wrap the foil back tightly over the ribs (or use a new piece) so they are covered. Place the pan in the oven and bake until the ribs are nicely browned and tender, 1 to 1½ hours more. The meat should come off the bone easily. If it does not, cover and bake longer. Remove the pan from the oven, take off the foil, and set the meat aside to rest for 15 minutes.

SERVE: Transfer the racks to a flat surface and cut between the bones to separate each rack into individual ribs. Season the meat with salt. Spoon the reserved sauce over the ribs. Squeeze the lime over them and serve.

FISH DISHES YOU REALLY WANT TO MAKE

This is a tough topic to tackle at home. People always tell me they prefer to order fish when they are eating out. It's expensive, it's hard to know what to buy, and it's not always clear which is the best way to cook it. I look a lot at the Monterey Bay Aquarium Seafood Watch website (seafoodwatch.org) for which fish are okay to eat (caught sustainably) and when to buy them (yes, fish have seasons, just like produce!). I encourage you to check out their website. The recipes here are simple ones that you can use as jumping-off points. For example, the recipe for sea bass can be applied to other types of fish fillets according to what's available in your area.

Salmon Carpaccio

WITH FRESH LIME

Since the salmon is served raw and the dish is so spare, this is an instance where most of the success lies with good ingredients. If you can get your hands on some wild salmon that doesn't break the bank, that is the best choice for flavor and color; if you can't find it, tuna or fluke—the freshest you can find—is a good second choice. Ideally, for this dish you would use fish that has never been frozen. Freshness and great ingredients are paramount in raw fish dishes. You can slice and plate the salmon in advance and then season it with the citrus, salt, and spices at the last minute. I see this as a refreshing appetizer, but it can also be ramped up to main-course size.

SERVES 4 TO 6

- 1 tablespoon coriander seeds
- 1 tablespoon white sesame seeds
- 4 tablespoons extra-virgin olive oil
- Maldon salt
- 2 large limes
- 1 (1-pound) salmon fillet (preferably wild salmon), skin on, pin bones removed

TOAST THE SPICES: In a small sauté pan, combine the coriander seeds and sesame seeds with 1 tablespoon of the olive oil. Toast for a minute over low heat to wake up the flavors. Remove from the heat, season with Maldon salt, and transfer the mixture to a bowl to cool for 1 minute. Lightly zest the limes into the spice mix and stir to blend (reserve the zested limes).

CUT THE SALMON: Place the fish, skin-side up, on a cutting board. Starting at one end of the fillet and using a sharp knife, cut thin slices at a slight angle, arranging them on individual plates (or a platter) as you slice. Make a single layer of fish slices, as thin as you can. Once the plates are covered with fish (you should get 25 to 30 slices from a 1-pound fillet), cover the plates with plastic wrap and refrigerate.

MAKE THE DRESSING AND SERVE: In a medium bowl, juice the 2 limes and combine with the remaining 3 tablespoons olive oil. Remove the plates from the refrigerator and uncover them. Sprinkle the fish with Maldon salt and the toasted seeds, sprinkling all around so that every bite is seasoned. Drizzle the dressing over the top, sprinkle with Maldon salt, and serve immediately.

Lobster Newburg

If you're going to serve lobster, go big or go home. In the summertime, my favorite way to eat lobster is either on a lobster roll or steamed with a pot of melted butter and some corn alongside. But when it gets cold out, I like to make lobster Newburg because it's such a cozy, belly-warming winter dish. Full disclosure: I have also made this dish a few times after feeling chilled from a long day of summer sun on a windy beach. In this recipe, the lobster gets cooked two ways: first, in salted hot water, and second, rewarmed in the sauce made with leeks, Marsala, cognac, and cream. It's a fine line between cooking the whole lobster long enough to make it tender and overcooking it—you don't want the meat to become rubbery when it hits this velvety fortified sauce. I love that affordable ingredients, like celery and leeks, are combined with the some of the most expensive, like cognac and lobster, in this dish.

SERVES 6

Kosher salt

2 teaspoons Tabasco

20 whole black peppercorns

4 dried bay leaves

3 (1½-pound) live lobsters

8 tablespoons (1 stick) unsalted butter

4 medium shallots, thinly sliced into rings

3 celery stalks, thinly sliced, plus 2 inner yellow stalks with the leaves

1 cup dry vermouth

4 sprigs fresh tarragon: 2 finely chopped (stems and all), 2 left whole

3 large leeks (white and pale green parts only), halved lengthwise, thoroughly washed, and cut into medium dice

2 tablespoons all-purpose flour

COOK THE LOBSTERS: Fill a large, deep pot (one that will hold all the lobsters) with 5 to 6 quarts of water and bring it to a rolling boil over high heat. Add a generous handful of salt, the Tabasco, the black peppercorns, and the bay leaves. Turn off the heat and stir the water to combine the flavors. Allow the water to sit for 2 minutes so it becomes more like a hot bath than a boiling cauldron (the lobster meat will be tenderer as a result). Plunge the lobsters into the water, taking care that they are completely submerged, and turn the heat back on to medium so the water simmers. Cook until the shells and heads turn red, about 9 minutes. There is no way to tell if a lobster is cooked without separating the head from the tail and looking at the doneness of the tail meat. The meat should be white, fairly firm to the touch, and no longer translucent. Use a frying spider or slotted spoon to remove the lobsters from the water and transfer them to a colander to drain and cool.

SHELL THE LOBSTERS: When the lobsters are cool enough to handle, carefully extract the meat from the tails, claws, and legs. Take care that the claw meat does not contain any cartilage. Slice the tail meat into 1-inch-thick rounds, leave the claws and knuckles whole, and refrigerate everything until you're ready to serve.

Set the tail shells aside for serving. Reserve the heads and all of the other shells for making the stock. (I like to remove the lungs, which can impart a bitter flavor; you can find them running along both sides of the inner layer of the lobster heads.) Use a sharp knife or cleaver to chop the bodies into smaller pieces.

MAKE THE STOCK: Add 2 tablespoons of the butter to a large skillet and melt it over medium heat. Stir in the shallots and sliced celery, and season with salt to taste. Add all of the lobster heads (except the tail shells). Cook

recipe and ingredients continue

½ cup dry Marsala wine, plus extra if needed

½ cup cognac

½ cup heavy cream

Juice of 1 small lemon, plus extra if needed

¼ cup finely grated Gruyère cheese

6 cups fresh baby spinach

over high heat, tossing to make sure any excess moisture cooks out but the mixture does not burn. Remove the pan from the heat and carefully add the vermouth—step back in case the liquor flames. Then carefully return the pan to the heat. Add the 2 whole sprigs of tarragon and cook over medium heat until all of the vermouth has evaporated, 3 to 5 minutes. Add about 3 cups of water and a pinch of salt and simmer gently until the stock is flavorful, 15 to 20 minutes.

Strain the stock into a medium bowl, pressing down on the shells to extract the maximum flavor. Discard the shells and allow the stock to cool at room temperature (it should yield about 1½ cups; you do not need a lot of stock, but you do need as much flavor as possible).

MAKE THE SAUCE: In a medium skillet, melt 5 tablespoons of the butter over medium heat and add the leeks. Season them with salt and cook until they are tender, 3 to 5 minutes. Stir in the flour and cook over low heat, stirring constantly, until the flour is integrated, 2 to 3 minutes. Add the Marsala and cook until it has all but cooked out, 3 to 5 minutes. Remove the pan from the heat, then add the cognac and step back (it might flame up). Gently return the pan to the heat and cook until the cognac has all but cooked out, another 3 to 5 minutes. Add the stock and stir to blend. Cook for a minute or two and then add the cream and season with salt; cook until the sauce is reduced by a third, 2 to 3 minutes. Taste for seasoning and stir in the chopped tarragon, lemon juice, and cheese. Turn off the heat and allow the sauce to cool slightly (sauces, like meat, need a few minutes to rest before serving).

Preheat the oven to 350°F.

Place the tail shells on a sheet pan and let them warm up in the oven for 3 to 5 minutes.

FINISH THE DISH: Warm the sauce over low heat. Melt the remaining 1 tablespoon butter in a large skillet over medium-high heat. Add the spinach and toss just to lightly wilt it, about 1 minute, and then season it with salt. Drain the spinach of any excess liquid and arrange some on each of six plates (or on a large platter, if serving family-style). Remove the tail shells from the oven and set each one, upside down, on top of the spinach. Add the lobster meat to the warm sauce and gently heat the meat, stirring to coat it in the sauce. Taste the sauce for seasoning, adding salt and a splash of Marsala or lemon juice if needed. Divide the lobster meat and the sauce into individual portions, filling the lobster shells with the meat and sauce. Extract the claws from the sauce and place one on top. Coat with all the remaining sauce.

Mini Maine Crab Cakes

This is such a tried-and-true recipe. If you can get fresh jumbo-lump crabmeat, that's the best crab for crab cakes because it has such a smooth texture and great flavor. It's also very expensive. Lump crab, which is different from jumbo-lump in that the pieces of crab are not as big and there are usually a lot more bits of shell in the meat, also works well. Backfin crab is good, too, but really take care to make sure there are no shell fragments in the meat. Crunching down on one tiny shell can ruin an entire crab cake. For this recipe, we are making about thirty-six bite-size crab cakes. You can certainly double or triple the size of each crab cake and serve them as an appetizer or main course. No matter how much crab mix I make, there is never any left over.

MAKES ABOUT 36 BITE-SIZE CRAB CAKES

- 2 cups panko bread crumbs
- 2 tablespoons unsalted butter
- 1 small yellow onion, minced
- 1 small red bell pepper, cored, seeded, and minced
- 2 large garlic cloves, minced
- Kosher salt
- 6 sprigs fresh flat-leaf parsley, coarsely chopped (stems and all)
- 5 large eggs
- ½ cup mayonnaise
- 1 tablespoon red wine vinegar
- 1 tablespoon Dijon mustard
- 1 tablespoon capers, drained
- 2 teaspoons Tabasco
- 2 teaspoons Worcestershire sauce
- 1 pound lump crabmeat, drained of excess moisture and picked through to remove any shells
- 1 quart (4 cups) canola oil, for frying
- Lemon wedges, for serving
- Tartar sauce (see page 208), for serving (optional)

Preheat the oven to 375°F. Position a rack in the center of the oven.

TOAST THE BREAD CRUMBS: Spread the panko bread crumbs in a thin, even layer on a rimmed sheet pan and place it in the oven on the center rack. When the bread crumbs are golden brown, after 5 to 8 minutes, remove the pan from the oven. Transfer the bread crumbs to a medium bowl to cool.

COOK THE ONION MIXTURE: In a medium sauté pan, melt the butter over medium heat. Add the onion, red bell pepper, garlic, and a pinch of salt and cook until the onions are translucent, 3 to 5 minutes. Stir in the parsley and remove from the heat. Set aside to cool.

MAKE THE CRAB MIXTURE: In a large bowl, lightly beat 2 of the eggs. Add the mayonnaise, vinegar, mustard, capers, Tabasco, and Worcestershire and whisk. Add the crabmeat and the cooled onion mixture and stir to combine. Taste for seasoning. Form the mixture into about 36 bite-size crab cakes, place them on a sheet pan, cover with plastic wrap, and refrigerate.

BREAD THE CRAB CAKES: Crack the remaining 3 eggs into a medium bowl, add a splash of cold water, and whisk to blend. Dip each crab cake thoroughly in the egg and then dredge it through the toasted bread crumbs, making sure the entire surface, including the sides, is evenly coated. Place the crab cakes in a single layer on a sheet pan. Refrigerate for at least 30 minutes.

COOK THE CRAB CAKES: Line a sheet pan with paper towels, and set it aside. In a medium pot, heat the oil to 350°F on an instant-read thermometer. Drop a couple of the crab cakes into the oil and cook until they are golden brown, 2 to 3 minutes on each side. Transfer the crab cakes to the prepared sheet pan and season them with salt. Fry the rest in batches—don't crowd the pan or the crumbs won't brown.

SERVE: Arrange the crab cakes on a serving platter. Serve the lemon wedges and tartar sauce, if using, on the side.

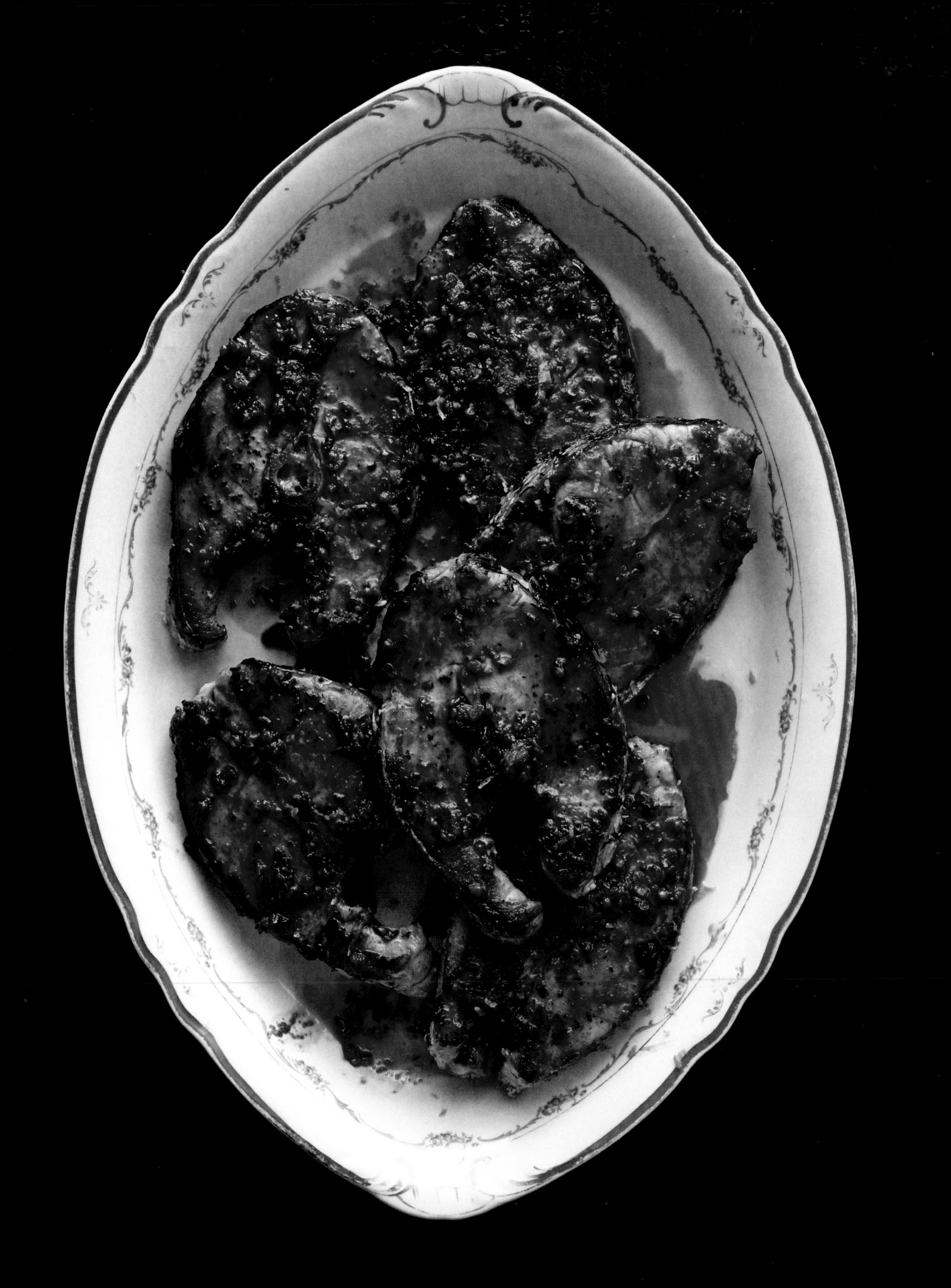

Cod Steaks

WITH HARISSA

Any large, sturdy, and steaky fish will do here. I like cod, but you can choose tilefish, bass, Spanish mackerel, or sea trout—they're all great options. For the best flavor and most moistness, I like to use steaks instead of fillets because the steaks are "on the bone," and bones contribute flavor. If steaks are unavailable, use skin-on fillets and cook them the same way. The most important thing is to choose a fish that can stand up texturally to the spices in the harissa. Why harissa? This flavorful North African condiment packs a spicy heat, but it is surprisingly warm and doesn't blow out your palate. It's a heat that unfolds more gradually and elevates the delicate flavor and steaky texture of the cod. While the harissa is super tasty when made fresh, I also like to make a batch of harissa and let it sit in the fridge for a few weeks.

SERVES 6

- 2 tablespoons extra-virgin olive oil
- 2 teaspoons caraway seeds
- 2 teaspoons coriander seeds
- ½ teaspoon cumin seeds
- 2 tablespoons sweet paprika
- 1 teaspoon dried red pepper flakes
- 4 large garlic cloves, sliced
- 1 large red bell pepper
- 1 small Fresno chile
- 1 tablespoon red wine vinegar
- Leaves from 4 sprigs fresh mint, coarsely chopped
- 2 tablespoons canola oil
- 6 (6- to 8-ounce) cod steaks, on the bone
- Kosher salt and freshly ground black pepper
- Grated zest and juice of 1 large lemon

TOAST THE SPICES: In a large sauté pan, warm the olive oil over medium heat. Add the caraway, coriander, and cumin seeds, the paprika, and the red pepper flakes. Reduce the heat to medium-low, add the garlic, and gently fry until fragrant, 1 to 2 minutes.

CHAR THE PEPPERS: Place the bell and Fresno peppers directly on a gas flame. Char on all sides until the skin burns. Refrigerate to cool them quickly. When cool, peel and discard the skin. I use a clean kitchen towel to wipe the skin away. Try to avoid rinsing, as it washes away flavor. Place the peppers on a flat surface, and open, stem, seed, and slice them.

MAKE THE HARISSA: Transfer the oil, spices, and roasted peppers to a food processor. Turn the processor on and, while it's running, gradually add the vinegar and mint. Taste for seasoning and set aside.

COOK THE COD: Wipe out the sauté pan, set it over high heat, and add the canola oil. When the oil smokes lightly, after 2 to 3 minutes, season the cod steaks with salt and pepper and place them in a single layer in the pan, leaving space between them. Reduce the heat and cook the fish, undisturbed, until it is browned on the bottom, 5 to 8 minutes. Use a spatula to turn the steaks over and cook until the flesh becomes opaque, another 5 to 8 minutes, depending on the thickness.

SERVE: Transfer the cod steaks to a serving platter, sprinkle with the lemon zest, and squeeze the lemon juice directly over the fish. Brush the fish liberally on both sides with the harissa.

Fritto Misto

Fritto misto is a fancy term for mixed fried items that are served as an appetizer, usually with a tart, acidic sauce for dunking. This is the simplest and best batter recipe because you can use it to fry just about any kind of fish or vegetable with great results. The alcohol tells the flour to relax, and the result is a crispy, delicate coating with a flavorful hint of beer that is especially delicious with fish. The batter is great with shrimp or squid as well as parcooked squash or onions. The key here is frying the fish and then immediately serving it so the seafood is piping hot. Frying the basil and lemon pieces as additional ingredients makes the dish really fun to cook and eat. A bit of bitter lemon peel, a bite of sweet, grassy basil, a briny, crisped shrimp . . . these little extras make you want to eat a giant platter of this dish—and people will do just that.

The tartar sauce can be made a couple of days ahead and stored in the fridge. The flavor will only improve as the ingredients have more time to sit.

SERVES 4 TO 6

TARTAR SAUCE

- ¾ cup mayonnaise
- 2 tablespoons finely chopped dill pickle, plus 1 tablespoon of the brine
- 1 tablespoon Dijon mustard
- 2 teaspoons chopped capers, plus 1 tablespoon of the brine
- 2 teaspoons Worcestershire sauce
- 1 teaspoon Tabasco
- 4 sprigs fresh tarragon, finely chopped (stems and all)
- Grated zest and juice of 1 large lemon

MAKE THE TARTAR SAUCE: In a medium bowl, whisk together the mayonnaise, dill pickle and brine, mustard, capers and brine, Worcestershire, Tabasco, tarragon, and lemon zest and juice. Taste for seasoning, transfer to a serving bowl, cover with plastic wrap, and set aside.

PREPARE THE BATTER: Pour the beer and vodka into a medium bowl and slowly whisk in the flour, paprika, sugar, baking soda, and sparkling water. The batter should be fairly thick (thick enough to coat the shrimp before frying) but also easy to stir. If it is too thick, add more sparkling water. If it's too thin, add more flour. Set the batter aside in a warm place.

SEASON THE SHRIMP: In another bowl, toss the shrimp with the garlic. Season lightly with salt and set aside.

GET READY: Pour the oil into a large heavy-bottomed pot (or a deep fryer) and heat it slowly over medium heat to 350°F. (Use an instant-read or deep-frying thermometer to monitor the temperature.) Line two sheet pans with paper towels. Fill a small bowl with the tartar sauce and place it in the center of a platter.

FRITTO MISTO

1 (8-ounce) bottle of beer, such as Heineken

¼ cup vodka (the cheaper, the better)

1 cup all-purpose flour, plus extra if needed

1 teaspoon hot paprika

½ teaspoon sugar

½ teaspoon baking soda

½ cup sparkling water

1 large garlic clove, grated on a Microplane

2 pounds large (16/20-count) shrimp (about 36 shrimp), peeled and deveined

Kosher salt

1 quart (4 cups) canola oil, for frying

Leaves from 6 sprigs fresh basil

1 large lemon, sliced into *very* thin rounds, preferably using a mandoline

4 (5-ounce) flaky medium-thick fish fillets (such as bass, bream, or porgy), each cut crosswise into 5 equal pieces

FRY: Drop a basil leaf in the oil to test the heat level. It should rise to the surface and fry quickly, taking no more than 1 minute to crisp. Once the oil is hot enough, fry all of the basil leaves and then use a slotted spoon or frying spider to transfer them to one of the prepared sheet pans; while hot, sprinkle with salt. Now fry the lemon slices in the same oil until they're crispy, 1 to 2 minutes. Transfer them to the pan containing the basil. Dip the shrimp in the batter and drop them, in small batches, into the oil. Fry until they are crispy on both sides, turning them with a slotted metal spoon, 2 to 3 minutes. Transfer the shrimp to the second sheet pan and season them immediately with salt. Lastly, batter the fish pieces and fry them until they are crisp and golden brown, 2 to 3 minutes. Transfer them to the pan holding the shrimp and turn off the heat under the oil.

SERVE: Arrange the shrimp and fish around the bowl of tartar sauce on the serving platter and intersperse the basil leaves and lemon slices around and on top. Serve immediately.

Mussels

Mussels are relatively inexpensive at the seafood counter, and when you steam their shells open, the liquid is so delicious. To me, it tastes more like the sweet ocean than like cooked shellfish. Here I keep the flavors simple, with fresh basil and white wine highlighting the natural sweetness of the mussels and their liquid. I love mixing peppery arugula with basil in pestos, but if you lean more classic, use all basil. You might be wondering why I bother chopping the arugula and basil just before blending. Well, the heat from a blender can actually turn the herbs and change their flavor, so if you add them to the blender already chopped, it will take less time to get to pesto, and the less blending, the better!

SERVES 4

- 1 cup tightly packed fresh arugula leaves, chopped
- 1 cup tightly packed fresh basil leaves, chopped
- 1 teaspoon sugar
- 5 tablespoons extra-virgin olive oil
- Kosher salt
- 4 pounds fresh medium-size to small mussels, thoroughly rinsed and debearded
- ¾ cup dry white wine
- 2 large garlic cloves, thinly sliced
- 2 tablespoons unsalted butter

MAKE THE PESTO: In a blender, combine the arugula, basil, sugar, 3 tablespoons of the olive oil, and a pinch of salt. Add ¼ cup of water and pulse until the pesto is well combined but not completely smooth. Taste for seasoning.

COOK THE MUSSELS: Rinse the mussels one final time to make sure they are free of any sand or grit (even a little grit can ruin an entire dish). Heat a large, deep skillet over high heat. Add the remaining 2 tablespoons olive oil and the mussels in as much of a single layer as you can. Add the white wine and garlic, and cook, uncovered, shaking the pan slightly, until all of the mussels open, 3 to 5 minutes (if any don't open after 5 minutes, discard them).

FINISH: Once the mussels open, shut off the heat and stir in the pesto and the butter. Simmer over medium heat to allow the flavors of the sauce to come together, 1 to 2 minutes. Taste for seasoning. To serve, transfer to a large bowl and toss to combine the mussels with the cooking liquid. You can also serve the mussels directly from the pot along with a loaf of bread and some bowls for collecting the shells as you eat.

Seared Striped Bass

My father always cooked smaller whole fish in the oven. It was only when I started cooking professionally that I explored pan-searing fish. The high heat creates a crispy, delicious skin and cooks the fish quickly, letting you spend less time in the kitchen and more time with friends and family. This basic recipe for pan-searing sea bass is elegant enough for a dinner party but quick enough for a weeknight meal. You can apply the technique to many types of fish, like mahi-mahi, swordfish (with some fresh lime), salmon, or flounder. I often think a simple fish dish gives the cook more confidence to cook it properly and leaves room for some dramatic accompaniments, like Grilled Zucchini and Charred Pepper Salad (page 163) or Roasted Broccoli with Garlic and Tamari (page 52).

SERVES 4

4 (6-ounce) skin-on striped bass or sea bass fillets

Kosher salt

¼ cup canola oil

Grated zest and juice of 1 large lemon

Preheat the oven to 350°F.

COOK THE FISH: Season the fish on both sides with salt. Heat the oil in a large ovenproof skillet over medium heat. When the oil begins to smoke lightly, after 2 to 3 minutes, remove the pan from the heat and add the fillets, skin-side down, in a single layer, leaving space between the pieces. Return the pan to the heat and cook over high heat until the skin becomes crispy, 5 to 8 minutes.

FINISH IN THE OVEN: Place the skillet in the oven and bake until the fish is is cooked through, 5 to 8 minutes. Sprinkle the lemon zest and then some lemon juice over the fish. Arrange the fillets on a platter and serve.

Poached Salmon

WITH RICE WINE–BUTTER SAUCE AND BASMATI RICE PILAF

It would be wonderful if we could master a set of rules for poaching fish and apply them successfully every time. Truth is, fish differs so much that you have to go case by case with the seasoning and the cooking time. The thickness of the fish, the variety, the weight, the size, the temperature of the poaching liquid: there are so many variables. The best rule is to watch the fish closely as it cooks. Poaching is deceptive because the fish looks cooked on the outside when it could still be raw on the inside, so it's best to check the interior. Whether you like your fish medium-rare or well-done, be sure to avoid poaching it in boiling liquid—that will not only overcook the fish but also make it tough. A slow, gentle simmer is best. I love how the flavors of the poached salmon and dill sink into the floral rice here. It's pure comfort food.

SERVES 6, WITH 6 TO 8 SERVINGS OF RICE

BASMATI RICE PILAF

2 cups basmati rice

2 dried bay leaves

2 tablespoons unsalted butter

1 medium yellow onion, finely diced

Kosher salt

POACHED SALMON

1 large lemon, sliced into 5 or 6 rounds

1 small bunch fresh flat-leaf parsley

16 whole black peppercorns

4 dried bay leaves

Kosher salt

5 (5- to 6-ounce) salmon fillets, skin removed

SOAK THE RICE: In a medium bowl, combine the rice with 4 cups of cold water. Set it aside for 30 minutes. Drain the rice, reserving the soaking water.

COOK THE RICE: Heat a medium sauté pan over medium heat and add the bay leaves, butter, and onion. Season with salt and cook until the onion becomes translucent but not brown, 3 to 5 minutes. Stir the rice into the onion mixture and cook for 2 minutes, until you hear it crackling. Add the reserved soaking water and stir gently. Season again with a generous amount of salt and bring the liquid to a simmer over medium heat.

Cook the rice over medium-low heat, uncovered and undisturbed, for about 8 minutes. Take a fork (so as not to damage the rice), flake a few grains off the top, and taste for doneness. It may need another 2 to 4 minutes to cook through. When the rice is tender, remove the pan from the heat and allow it to rest (as you would a roast beef) for 10 minutes before forking it gently into a bowl.

MAKE THE POACHING LIQUID: In a large, deep skillet, combine 4 cups of water with the lemon, parsley, peppercorns, bay leaves, and a generous pinch of salt. Stir to combine and bring to a simmer over medium heat. Taste for seasoning. The liquid should be acidic and salty. Remove the pan from the heat and allow the liquid to cool for a few minutes.

COOK THE SALMON: Carefully add the salmon pieces to the poaching liquid, leaving space between them. Allow the salmon to sit in the liquid,

recipe and ingredients continue

1Tbsp
1tsp
K
SABATIER

RICE WINE–BUTTER SAUCE

4 tablespoons (½ stick) unsalted butter

2 medium shallots, minced

Kosher salt

1 tablespoon rice vinegar

1 teaspoon sambal oelek chile paste

2 sprigs fresh dill, finely chopped (stems and all)

off the heat, for a minute or two, and then return the pan to very low heat. The poaching liquid should not boil or even simmer. Let the fillets poach until they are cooked in the center, 6 to 10 minutes (depending on the thickness of the fillets). To check the doneness, use a slotted spatula to transfer a fillet to a kitchen towel and use the tip of a paring knife to check the center. If you like a medium-rare fillet, it should be light pink and tender in the middle; for a more well-done fillet, it should be firm and opaque all the way through. When the fillets are cooked to your liking, transfer them to the towel to drain before placing them on a serving platter. Reserve ¼ cup of the poaching liquid.

MAKE THE SAUCE: In a small sauté pan set over medium heat, melt 1 tablespoon of the butter and add the shallots with a pinch of salt. Cook until the shallots are tender, 2 to 3 minutes. Add the reserved poaching liquid and simmer over high heat until the liquid is reduced by half, 1 to 2 minutes. Whisk in the remaining 3 tablespoons butter, the rice vinegar, sambal oelek, and dill. Taste for seasoning and pour the sauce over the fish. Serve with the rice on the side.

Classic Shrimp Scampi

This is one of those iconic dishes that doesn't need any updating or improving because it's so good as it is. A great scampi should always be about allowing the subtle sweetness and brininess of the shrimp to coexist peacefully with the garlic and oil. You need some butter to balance the taste of the sauce, and you need olive oil for cooking the shrimp. (Olive oil burns and turns very bitter at high heat.) Once these ingredients come together, you will understand. Serve this dish with buttered pasta or loaves of seriously crusty bread. I have also been known to go overboard and offer buttery garlic bread on the side.

SERVES 3 OR 4

2 tablespoons extra-virgin olive oil

1½ pounds "colossal" (8/10-count) shrimp (15 or 16 shrimp), peeled and deveined

Kosher salt

2 tablespoons unsalted butter

2 large garlic cloves, grated on a Microplane

¾ cup dry white wine

½ teaspoon dried red pepper flakes

2 dashes Tabasco

2 dashes Worcestershire sauce

½ cup fresh flat-leaf parsley leaves, chopped

Grated zest and juice of 1 large lemon

QUICK-SEAR THE SHRIMP: Heat the oil in a large skillet over medium heat. Season the shrimp with salt, and once the oil begins to smoke lightly, remove the pan from the heat and quickly arrange the shrimp in it in a single layer with a little space between them. Return the pan to the heat, raise the heat to high, and brown the shrimp on the first side, adding 1 tablespoon of the butter in small pieces around the shrimp to add flavor as they brown, 1 to 2 minutes. Turn the shrimp over and cook until the other side is browned, 1 to 2 minutes. The goal here is not to fully cook the shrimp but to brown the exterior and develop flavor. Transfer the shrimp to a sheet pan.

MAKE THE SAUCE: In the same skillet, add the remaining 1 tablespoon butter and the garlic, a pinch of salt, and the white wine. Simmer over medium heat, stirring, until the wine all but evaporates and the garlic is tender, 3 to 5 minutes.

COOK THE SHRIMP AND SERVE: Arrange the shrimp in the sauce and warm them through over low heat, basting them with the sauce. Sprinkle with the red pepper flakes. Cook until the shrimp turn pink but are still tender, 2 to 3 minutes more. Stir in the Tabasco, Worcestershire, parsley, lemon zest, and lemon juice. Taste for seasoning and serve.

Whole Roasted Fish, Ava-Style

Ava loves this dish because it reminds her of her grandfather. I told her the story of how my dad would cook fish in this simple, special way by literally tossing it, somewhat like a football, onto a roaring-hot sheet pan in a preheated oven. He would cook it until the eyes of the fish turned white, and we would devour it as is. Ava likes opening the oven and putting the fish on the hot sheet pan—it's almost like searing something, except instead of it being on the stovetop, it's in the oven. She loves the dramatic moment when the fish arrives at the table on a platter, and she enjoys the act of flaking the fish off the bone and squeezing the baked lemon slices from the fish cavity over it. We do this with bass, mackerel, bluefish . . . any fish that is tasty cooked whole.

SERVES 2 TO 4

- 2 whole Boston or Spanish mackerel (1½ to 2 pounds each), scaled and gutted
- 2 large lemons, cut into 5 rounds each
- 8 sprigs fresh thyme
- ¼ cup extra-virgin olive oil
- Maldon salt and freshly ground black pepper

Preheat the oven to 450°F. Place a foil-lined sheet pan in the oven to preheat.

COOK THE FISH: Stuff the fish cavities with the lemon slices and thyme sprigs. Rub the oil over the outside of each fish and season them on both sides with Maldon salt and black pepper. Open the oven and, without removing the hot sheet pan, place the fish on it, spacing them apart from each other. Cook the fish until the flesh is tender and flakes at the meatiest part closest to the head, 12 to 15 minutes.

SERVE: Use a large metal spatula (or two smaller ones) to transfer the fish to a large serving platter. Top with Maldon salt and pepper and serve right away.

MY FAVORITE SOUPS

Chef Guy Savoy once told me that the mark of a great chef is a great bowl of soup. No matter what kind of day it is, I always feel ready to have some soup. I find it cooling in the summer and belly-warming in the winter. I also think soup can be a great expression of a culture. An Italian wedding soup, a great egg drop soup, a tasty avgolemono soup—they all use similar ingredients but yield great, varied results. Some of these recipes involve only a few ingredients and a little cooking; others are more involved. Either way, there is a soup here for you.

Shrimp Bisque in a Bread Bowl

The only thing required to truly call a soup a bisque is that it be thickened with rice. Rice is a wonderful ingredient to give body to soup without the heaviness of flour or the distinctive flavors of potato or corn. You can make this soup and serve it as is or go the extra mile and make these delicious bread bowls to hold the soup. There's something about making a bread bowl with fine ingredients that I find so homey and satisfying. If you don't have the time to make the bowls yourself, you can buy either individual round sourdough rolls or a large, sturdy round loaf for serving the soup family-style.

SERVES 6 TO 8

- 6 tablespoons (¾ stick) unsalted butter
- 1½ pounds medium (28/30-count) shrimp, peeled (reserve the shells) and deveined
- ¼ cup Pernod or pastis (see Note)
- Kosher salt
- 1 dried bay leaf
- Leaves from 4 sprigs fresh basil
- 2 small yellow onions, minced
- ½ teaspoon cayenne pepper
- 2 tablespoons long-grain white rice
- 2 celery stalks, peeled and thinly sliced crosswise
- 2 small carrots, peeled and thinly sliced crosswise
- 1 (28-ounce) can peeled whole tomatoes, drained
- 1 tablespoon Worcestershire sauce
- 1 teaspoon Tabasco
- 2 cups heavy cream
- Juice of 1 large lemon
- 6 sprigs fresh tarragon, chopped (stems and all)
- 8 Bread Bowls (recipe follows)

MAKE THE SHRIMP STOCK: In a large heavy-bottomed pot, melt 2 tablespoons of the butter over medium heat and then add the reserved shrimp shells. Cook, stirring, until the shells brown slightly, 5 to 8 minutes. Add the Pernod and cook until it has evaporated, 5 to 8 minutes. (Do not rush this step.) Add 8 cups of water, a pinch of salt, and the bay leaf, and simmer over medium heat for 20 minutes. Taste the stock. If it seems watery, cook it for another 5 to 8 minutes; otherwise, strain the stock through a fine-mesh sieve into a large bowl. Press down on the shells as you strain the stock to maximize the flavor. Discard the shells (don't clean the pot—you'll use it again). Set the stock aside.

COOK THE SHRIMP: In a large sauté pan, warm 1 tablespoon of the butter over low heat and stir in the shrimp along with a generous pinch of salt. Cook, stirring, just until the shrimp turn pink, 2 to 3 minutes. Transfer the shrimp to a medium bowl and stir in the basil. Refrigerate.

MAKE THE SOUP: In the same heavy-bottomed pot you used for the stock, combine the remaining 3 tablespoons butter with the onions, cayenne, rice, celery, carrots, and a pinch of salt. Cook over medium heat until the vegetables are tender, 10 to 12 minutes. Add the tomatoes and the shrimp stock. Simmer until the vegetables are soft, 15 to 20 minutes. Stir in the Worcestershire, Tabasco, and cream, and simmer until all the ingredients meld together, 2 to 3 minutes. Taste and adjust the seasoning.

FINISH THE SOUP: Add about one-fourth of the soup to a blender and puree it. Pour the puree back into the soup pot and then puree another one-fourth of the soup. Return it to the pot (this way, the soup has body but also some texture left from the vegetables). Bring the soup to a simmer. Taste for seasoning. Stir in the shrimp, lemon juice, and tarragon. Gently ladle the soup into the finished bread bowls and cover with the reserved tops. Serve immediately.

recipe continues

BREAD BOWLS

Use these bread bowls for the shrimp bisque (or another thick soup), for sandwiches (especially egg sandwiches), cheese platters, or as bread for a smoked salmon tartine. More simply, bake them to serve as a great loaf alongside stew or soup. The cottage cheese and touch of caraway give this bread a hearty texture and a great layered flavor. Reserve the interior of the bread to dry for bread crumbs.

MAKES 8 BREAD BOWLS

2¼ teaspoons active dry yeast

2 tablespoons extra-virgin olive oil

3 cups bread flour

2 teaspoons caraway seeds

3 tablespoons honey

1 tablespoon blackstrap molasses

1 tablespoon kosher salt

1 cup whole-milk cottage cheese

1 large egg

PERNOD OR PASTIS

These are anise-flavored liqueurs from France. They add a fennel-like flavor to this bisque that is uniquely tasty. Sip a glass of it while cooking the bisque to get into the mood! It's transporting.

PREPARE THE YEAST: In a medium bowl, dissolve the yeast in ½ cup of warm water (between 110°F and 120°F). Set the bowl aside until the yeast bubbles and froths a little, 5 to 10 minutes.

MAKE THE DOUGH: Oil a medium bowl with 1 tablespoon of the olive oil and set it aside (the oil prevents the dough from sticking to the sides of the bowl as it rises). In the bowl of a stand mixer fitted with the paddle attachment, combine the flour, caraway seeds, honey, molasses, and salt and mix on low speed until blended. Blend in the cottage cheese and the egg, then add the yeast mixture and mix until the dough starts to form a ball, 5 to 8 minutes. Transfer the dough to the oiled bowl, cover with a kitchen towel, and set it in a warm place until doubled in volume, 1½ to 2 hours. Gently push the air out of the dough, cover, and let it rise again, 1 more hour.

Preheat the oven to 400°F. Arrange oven racks in the upper-middle and lower-middle positions.

SHAPE THE DOUGH: Grease two sheet pans with the remaining tablespoon of olive oil. Divide the dough into 8 equal pieces, shape them into balls, and place 4 balls on each sheet pan. Flatten the balls gently with your hand.

BAKE THE BREAD: Place the sheet pans on the oven racks, immediately reduce the oven temperature to 350°F, and bake, undisturbed, until the tops are light to medium brown, 20 to 25 minutes. The interior of the bread should register 185°F to 190°F on an instant-read thermometer. Remove the pans from the oven; keep the oven on. Allow the rolls to rest for at least 30 minutes before turning them into bread bowls.

FINISH THE BREAD BOWLS: Slice off the tops of the rolls and set them aside. Carefully hollow out the center of each roll to make a bread bowl. Place the hollowed-out bowls and the sliced-off tops on the sheet pans and bake for 5 to 10 minutes to firm the texture. Remove them from the oven and fill each bowl with about 1 cup of soup. Top each bowl with the roll's top and serve.

Corn Chowder

All chowder needs in order to be called a chowder are potatoes, onions, and, usually, some form of pork. In this corn chowder, corn kernels add texture and sweetness, while the cobs help build in even more flavor. I always feel like I am throwing away an ingredient when I put the corncobs in the trash; here the cobs show their worth by infusing more corn flavor in the soup. As far as the bacon goes, your choice can affect the chowder greatly. A more peppery, smoky bacon can be tasty, but it will obscure the sweetness of the corn. I like a good-quality but mellow bacon for this soup so it becomes a key player but leaves room for the other ingredients to shine as well.

SERVES 4 TO 6

1 tablespoon extra-virgin olive oil

6 thin bacon strips, thinly sliced crosswise

2 medium red onions, minced

Kosher salt and freshly ground black pepper

12 large ears fresh corn, husked, kernels sliced off the cobs, kernels and cobs reserved separately

2 tablespoons dark brown sugar

3 medium Idaho potatoes (I like to leave them unpeeled), diced small

1 large garlic clove, minced

1 quart (4 cups) half-and-half

1 small bunch fresh chives, cut into 1-inch lengths

MAKE THE SOUP BASE: In a soup pot, combine the oil and bacon and cook over medium heat, stirring with a wooden spoon, until the bacon becomes crisp, 5 to 8 minutes. Use a slotted spoon to remove the bacon and set it aside on a plate lined with a paper towel. Add the onions to the pot, season with salt and pepper, and cook until they are translucent, 5 to 8 minutes. Add the corn kernels and 1 tablespoon of the brown sugar and cook over medium heat, stirring occasionally, until the corn becomes translucent and tender, 8 to 10 minutes. Turn off the heat and leave the pot on the stove.

MAKE THE CORN STOCK: Meanwhile, put the corncobs in a medium pot and add enough water to cover them (about 8 cups). Bring the water to a simmer over medium heat. Add a pinch of salt and the remaining 1 tablespoon brown sugar, and simmer gently over medium-high heat until the liquid reduces by half, 12 to 15 minutes. Strain the stock through a fine-mesh sieve set over a large bowl and discard the cobs.

COOK THE POTATOES: Put the potatoes in the medium pot where you cooked the corn and add enough corn stock to cover them. Simmer over medium heat until the potatoes are tender, 8 to 10 minutes. Add the potatoes and any remaining cooking liquid, as well as any remaining unused corn stock, to the pot of cooked corn kernels. Add the garlic and the half-and-half and simmer for 2 to 3 minutes. Taste for seasoning. Stir in the bacon and chives, and serve right away.

Tom Yum Soup

Many of the dishes that you make at home can just be a variation of what you eat every day at work or when you are out and about. I profess to be no expert on Thai cooking, but I do love this soup, and there's no reason why I shouldn't make it at home. I find the flavors of lemongrass, chiles, and cilantro beyond delicious and really comforting. It's so bright and invigorating that I use this soup as a refreshing reset for my palate after a long day of tasting various foods on the set of *Chopped*.

SERVES 4 TO 6

- 2 tablespoons coconut oil
- 2 lemongrass stalks, tough outer layers removed and discarded, cut into 3-inch-long pieces and tied together with string
- Kosher salt
- 3 large garlic cloves, minced
- 16 cremini mushrooms, thinly sliced
- 5 cups vegetable stock
- 1 (15.5-ounce) can unsweetened coconut milk
- 2 tablespoons low-sodium soy sauce
- 1 (3-inch) knob fresh ginger, peeled and grated
- 1 tablespoon rice vinegar
- 1 small Fresno chile, thinly sliced into rings
- 8 sprigs fresh cilantro, chopped (stems and all)
- 3 ounces firm tofu, cut into small cubes
- 4 scallions (green and white parts), thinly sliced

MAKE THE SOUP BASE: In a large heavy-bottomed pot, melt the coconut oil over medium heat and add the lemongrass. Season with salt and cook, stirring, for 2 to 3 minutes to wake up the flavors. You will smell the fragrant aroma as it heats. Add the garlic and mushrooms, and cook, stirring often, until the mushrooms are tender, 2 to 3 minutes. Add the vegetable stock and simmer until the liquid reduces by about half, 15 to 20 minutes.

FINISH AND SERVE: Add the coconut milk to the soup base and simmer over medium-low heat until the soup is fully combined and slightly thickened, 5 to 8 minutes. Taste for seasoning. Remove and discard the bundle of lemongrass. Stir in the soy sauce, ginger, rice vinegar, chile, cilantro, tofu, and scallions. Taste for seasoning and serve hot.

Beef and Barley Soup

The key to a hearty, full-flavored beef and barley soup is to cook the meat, stock, and aromatics together for a long time (to tenderize the meat), but not to take all of the vegetables along for the whole ride. Instead, you cook the vegetables separately and to their own desired doneness so they retain some texture when the soup is finished. Basically this is a braise that then becomes a soup. Pearl barley is wonderfully chewy against the deep beefy notes from the stock and oxtails. We are, in essence, taking a stock and, by cooking meat in it, converting it into a meaty broth.

SERVES 6

- 2½ pounds (1½- to 2-inch) beef oxtail pieces
- Kosher salt and freshly ground black pepper
- 3 tablespoons canola oil
- 2 cups dry red wine
- 10 cups beef stock, store-bought or homemade (page 106)
- 2 dried bay leaves
- 1 cup pearl barley
- 3 medium yellow onions, minced
- 4 large garlic cloves, minced
- 4 large carrots, peeled and diced
- 1 medium leek (light green and white parts), washed well and minced
- 2 tablespoons Dijon mustard
- 1 tablespoon red wine vinegar

Preheat the oven to 375°F. Position a rack in the center of the oven.

COOK THE OXTAILS: Season the oxtails with salt and pepper on all sides. In a large, ovenproof heavy-bottomed pot with a lid, heat 2 tablespoons of the oil over medium heat. When the oil begins to smoke lightly, after 2 to 3 minutes, add the oxtails in a single layer. Brown them on the first side, 5 to 8 minutes, and then carefully turn them over and brown the second side, another 5 to 8 minutes. Add the red wine and cook until all of the liquid evaporates, 5 to 8 minutes. Then add the stock and bay leaves and bring to a boil over medium heat. Skim off any impurities that rise to the surface, then cover the pot and place it in the oven on the center rack. Cook until the oxtails are tender when pierced with the tip of a knife, 2½ to 3 hours. Use a slotted spoon to transfer the oxtails to a large bowl and set aside to cool. Cover the pot to keep the cooking liquid warm.

COOK THE BARLEY: In a medium pot, bring 4 cups of water to a boil over medium heat. Stir in the barley and cook until it is tender and the water has all but evaporated, 25 to 30 minutes. Drain and season with salt.

COOK THE VEGETABLES: In a large sauté pan, heat the remaining 1 tablespoon oil over medium heat. Add the onions, garlic, carrots, leek, and a pinch of salt, and cook, stirring occasionally, until the vegetables are tender, 8 to 10 minutes. Stir in the mustard.

FINISH: Over medium heat, bring the cooking liquid to a simmer. Pull the meat from the oxtail bones, discard the bones, and add the meat and vegetables to the pot. Remove the bay leaves. Stir in the barley and vinegar. Taste for seasoning and serve.

Broccoli Cheddar Soup

Broccoli cheddar soup is the macaroni and cheese of the soup world. It's an excuse to eat cheese, and broccoli is a brilliant, healthy cover for it. Adult home cooking is often loaded with memories and an obsession to re-create Mom's exact recipes. Let me disclose this: my mother *never* made this cold-weather American classic when I was growing up. She also skipped dips, baked pasta casseroles, green bean casseroles, and sweet potato casseroles with marshmallows, too. Maybe that's why I enjoy delving into these important American icons with my daughter, Ava. I finally feel like I have permission to explore dishes that were overlooked in my own childhood and to share them with her instead. We are building our own memories with classics like this soup.

SERVES 6 TO 8

4 medium heads broccoli

5 tablespoons extra-virgin olive oil

Kosher salt

1 medium yellow onion, minced

¼ teaspoon ground nutmeg (preferably freshly grated)

¼ cup all-purpose flour

½ cup dry white wine

1 quart (4 cups) whole milk

2 cups heavy cream

1 cup grated Gruyère cheese

2 cups grated extra-sharp cheddar cheese, plus extra for serving

1 tablespoon Worcestershire sauce

1 tablespoon apple cider vinegar

Preheat the oven to 400°F. Position a rack in the center of the oven.

PREPARE THE BROCCOLI: While the oven is preheating, trim the tough stems from the heads of broccoli. Cut 1 head into bite-size florets to make 2 cups. Chop the rest into ½-inch pieces.

ROAST THE BROCCOLI: Arrange the 2 cups broccoli florets (not the chopped pieces) in a single layer on a parchment-lined sheet pan and drizzle them with 1 tablespoon of the olive oil and a generous pinch of salt. Place the pan in the oven on the center rack and roast until the broccoli is tender and browned on top, 18 to 20 minutes. Remove it from the oven and set aside.

MAKE THE SOUP: In a large heavy-bottomed pot, combine the onion with the remaining 4 tablespoons olive oil, the nutmeg, and a pinch of salt. Cook over medium heat until the onions become translucent, 3 to 4 minutes. Whisk in the flour and the white wine. Cook, stirring constantly, until the wine evaporates and the flour is fully blended in, 3 to 5 minutes. Stir in the chopped broccoli and a pinch of salt, cover, and cook until the broccoli is tender, 10 to 12 minutes. Add the milk and cream, and bring to a simmer over medium heat; then cook for 5 to 8 minutes. Taste for seasoning.

FINISH AND SERVE: Puree about three-fourths of the soup in small batches in a blender, pouring it back into the pot after each batch (since you're not pureeing all of the soup, it will retain a slightly chunky texture). Stir in the Gruyère and cheddar. Shut off the heat and allow the cheese to melt gently into the hot liquid, stirring it occasionally. Then stir in the Worcestershire. Taste for seasoning. Stir in the roasted broccoli and the vinegar. Taste again for seasoning. Divide the soup among individual bowls and sprinkle each one with some more cheddar before serving.

Chilled Beet Soup

WITH HOMEMADE CRÈME FRAÎCHE

One thing about vegetables: sometimes it takes one vegetable (carrots) to make another vegetable (beets) taste more like itself. This soup is really about tasting and combining flavors. It's not about standing at the stove and cooking a hot soup. You have to feel around the flavors a little, taking care that the carrot and beet meld together as the base. Making homemade crème fraîche is sort of next-level: it's less sour than store-bought and gives a deep, creamy note to dishes. We need that cream here because this is a really lean recipe. Homemade crème fraîche takes eight hours to thicken at room temperature; so if you don't have time, simply buy crème fraîche or sour cream and skip right to the soup.

SERVES 4, WITH 1¾ CUPS CRÈME FRAÎCHE

CRÈME FRAÎCHE

1 pint (2 cups) heavy cream

2 tablespoons buttermilk

Kosher salt

SOUP

2 tablespoons extra-virgin olive oil

1 medium red onion, minced

Kosher salt

1 tablespoon red wine vinegar

1 tablespoon honey

1 quart (4 cups) fresh beet juice

2 cups fresh carrot juice

4 to 6 sprigs fresh dill, coarsely chopped (stems and all)

MAKE THE CRÈME FRAÎCHE: In a glass bowl, stir together the cream and buttermilk. Cover the bowl with plastic wrap and let it sit on the counter for 8 to 10 hours. We are asking the buttermilk and cream to become thick and sour. It's not romantic, but it's definitely delicious. Once the mixture is thick, stir in a pinch of salt and refrigerate the crème fraîche. This can be made in advance and keeps for at least a few days, covered, in the refrigerator.

COOK THE ONION: In a medium skillet set over medium heat, combine the olive oil and onion along with a pinch of salt. Cook until the onion becomes translucent, 2 to 3 minutes. Add ½ cup of water and cook until all of the water evaporates, 3 to 5 minutes. Stir in the vinegar and honey. Turn off the heat and set aside to cool.

MAKE THE SOUP: In a medium bowl, whisk together the beet juice, carrot juice, and cooked onion mixture. Taste for seasoning. Place the bowl in the refrigerator and chill the soup, stirring it occasionally to ensure proper cooling.

SERVE: Serve in a large bowl, family-style, or ladle into individual bowls. Top each serving with a dollop of the crème fraîche and a sprinkling of dill.

Juicy Carrot Soup

Here raw ingredients are combined to create a tasty "clean" soup for warm weather. I like orange carrots best for this because they always taste the sweetest and offer the best texture. (Sometimes the fancy heirloom stuff is not the best ingredient to use.) Ginger juice tastes better (and is less work) when you leave the skin on; simply rinse off any dirt before juicing. Note: You can most easily make this soup by purchasing the carrot and ginger juices ready-made. When I have some friends over, I love a first course that's sitting on ice (quite literally) and is ready to go. It takes the pressure off cooking!

SERVES 6

- 1½ quarts (6 cups) fresh carrot juice
- ¼ cup fresh ginger juice (store-bought or from 8 to 10 ounces fresh ginger; see Note)
- Juice of 2 large oranges (about ½ cup)
- Juice of 1 large lemon (about ¼ cup)
- 2 tablespoons honey
- Kosher salt and freshly ground black pepper
- ⅓ cup extra-virgin olive oil
- 1 small jicama, peeled and cut into 1-inch cubes
- 1 teaspoon ground ginger
- ½ small jalapeño, cut into thin rounds (see Note)

MAKE THE SOUP: In a blender, combine the carrot juice, ginger juice, orange juice, lemon juice, honey, and salt and pepper to taste, and blend on medium-low speed until smooth. With the blender running on medium speed, slowly pour in the olive oil. Taste for seasoning and then refrigerate for at least 1 hour or up to 8 hours. Chill six soup bowls in the refrigerator, too.

GARNISH AND SERVE THE SOUP: Toss the jicama, ground ginger, and jalapeño together in a medium bowl and season with salt. Divide the jicama mixture among the chilled soup bowls. Pour the soup over the jicama (it becomes a hidden crunchy, spicy treat) and serve.

Ginger Juice: On a flat surface and using a large chef's knife, cut the ginger into ½-inch slices and run them through a juicer according to the manufacturer's instructions.

Note: For less heat, simply remove the seeds and ribs from the jalapeño.

Italian Chicken Soup

This is loosely based on a childhood favorite of mine, *stracciatella* ("little rags") soup. The "little rags" refers to the eggs that are swirled into the soup and cooked in the broth, looking like little rags. It's hearty, flavorful, and easy to put together. What makes the flavor of this soup so special is the use of a whole chicken cooked in the pot to yield a rich, clean broth. The secret is not to overcook the chicken, so you can put all the meat back into the broth. The salt comes more from the Parmesan cheese than from salt itself. I even tried this recipe subbing in my Thanksgiving turkey after almost all of the meat had been carved from it. *Acini di pepe* ("seeds of pepper") is a very small pasta that almost looks like pearl couscous. If you can't find it, use any tiny pasta, any shape.

SERVES 4 TO 6

- 2 tablespoons extra-virgin olive oil
- 3 medium carrots, peeled and cut into 1-inch-thick rounds
- 3 medium celery stalks, peeled and cut into 1-inch pieces
- 24 pearl or other small onions, peeled if fresh, thawed if frozen, halved
- Kosher salt and freshly ground black pepper
- 1 (3½- to 4-pound) whole chicken
- 1 small bunch fresh thyme, stems tied together with string
- 6 cups chicken stock, store-bought or homemade (page 107)
- 8 ounces acini di pepe pasta
- ½ cup finely grated Parmesan cheese
- 2 cups fresh baby spinach

START COOKING THE SOUP: In a pot that's large enough to hold the chicken, add the olive oil along with the carrots, celery, and onions. Season the vegetables generously with salt and pepper, and cook over medium heat, stirring occasionally, until the onions become translucent, 5 to 8 minutes. Add the chicken, thyme, stock, and water to cover (2 to 3 cups). Bring to a gentle simmer, skimming the surface with a ladle or shallow spoon as impurities rise up, and then reduce the heat to low and cook slowly until the thickest part of the chicken thigh reaches an internal temperature of 165°F and the juices at the thigh joint run clear, 50 to 55 minutes.

COOK THE PASTA: Bring a medium pot of water to a boil and season it with a generous handful of salt. The water should taste like seawater. Drop the pasta into the water and cook until tender, 5 minutes. Drain the pasta in a fine-mesh strainer.

FINISH THE CHICKEN: Taste the chicken stock and adjust the seasoning as needed. Use a slotted spoon to transfer the chicken to a large bowl. Let it cool for a few minutes and then remove and discard the skin. Remove the breast and thigh meat, taking care that there are no bones, and break the meat into bite-size pieces. Flake the meat off the wings as well.

FINISH THE SOUP: Remove and discard the thyme sprigs. Stir in the pasta. Season the chicken meat with salt and then stir it into the soup. Add the cheese and spinach, taste for seasoning, and serve hot.

BAKING FOR BREAKFAST

Breakfast and brunch are meals where we can go for broke. Baking a tasty treat, from muffins to scones to focaccia, can be so satisfying. These baked goods fill your kitchen with the smells of a bakery. There is something very relaxing about baking, and over the years, it has become my hobby. Why would a chef make baking her hobby? It's a question I have asked myself more than once. Usually a hobby serves as a respite from one's profession. If you can believe it, pastry chefs are very different creatures from savory chefs. They measure. They are precise. They sometimes put most of their trust (and work) into a pan in the oven and have to hope for the best. I love how different making fresh doughnuts or a coffee cake can be from braising chicken thighs and making some rice pilaf. I love the pockets of free time I find myself with when I bake. The waiting in front of the oven can give me time to think, drink coffee, and daydream. It also gives me time to scramble eggs, cook bacon or sausages, make toast or waffles or whatever other dishes I want to serve with my baked goods. I always joke that for my next career, I will be a pastry chef. In the meantime, let's have some scones . . .

Waffles

WITH CRISPY QUINOA

Obviously, various sizes of waffle irons will change the yield on this recipe. I make it in my parents' ancient (tiny) waffle iron that gets volcanically hot and produces about 12 of these waffles. This recipe always seems to make the perfect amount for 4 to 6 people. The quinoa adds a sneaky and gloriously nutty boost of protein to your waffles. I add some to the batter for texture and density and then crisp the rest to serve over the top. It's almost like that lovely bit of cornmeal on the underside of a slice of pizza. The vanilla and apple cider vinegar are the flavor boosts here. I recommend dousing these waffles with maple syrup and serving them with butter. I even put marmalade and raspberry jam on the side for people who want a fruity flavor. This is a great way to use leftover cooked quinoa—you'll need about ¾ cup.

MAKES ABOUT 12 WAFFLES, SERVING 4 TO 6

- ¼ cup red quinoa
- 3½ cups buttermilk
- 3 large eggs, lightly beaten
- 1 teaspoon vanilla extract
- 2 teaspoons apple cider vinegar
- ⅓ cup sugar
- 3 cups all-purpose flour
- 1 tablespoon baking powder
- 2 teaspoons kosher salt
- 1 teaspoon ground cinnamon
- ¾ teaspoon baking soda
- ¾ cup (1½ sticks) unsalted butter, melted, plus 1 tablespoon for toasting the quinoa; plus extra for greasing the waffle iron and for serving
- Maple syrup, unsalted butter, and jam (optional), for serving

Preheat the oven to 350°F. Position a rack in the center of the oven.

COOK THE QUINOA: In a medium-size ovenproof sauté pan, combine the quinoa and 1½ cups of water, and bring to a simmer over medium heat. Place the pan in the oven on the center rack and bake, without stirring, until the grains fluff slightly and uncoil, 12 to 15 minutes. Fluff the quinoa with a fork and taste for doneness (it should have a pleasant pop in the center). Set it aside to cool.

MAKE THE BATTER: In a large bowl, whisk together the buttermilk, eggs, vanilla, vinegar, and sugar. Stir in the flour, baking powder, salt, cinnamon, baking soda, the ¾ cup melted butter, and all but 1/2 cup of the cooked quinoa, stirring just until the batter is somewhat smooth, without any pockets of unmixed flour. Do not overmix. This will yield about 6½ cups of batter. Set the batter aside to rest for a few minutes while you crisp the remaining quinoa.

CRISP THE QUINOA: Melt the 1 tablespoon butter in a medium sauté pan over medium heat. Add the remaining ½ cup cooked quinoa and cook, stirring, until it crisps and crackles, 3 to 5 minutes. Transfer the quinoa to a paper-towel-lined plate to absorb the extra butter, and set aside.

MAKE THE WAFFLES: Brush the surface of a waffle iron with some melted butter. For each 4-inch waffle square, use about ½ cup of the batter. Cook the waffles according to the waffle iron's instructions (you want the waffles to be golden brown, not too thick, and cooked through). Brush the waffle iron with melted butter before you make each waffle. Transfer cooked waffles to a sheet pan and keep them warm in the oven until all are cooked.

SERVE: Drizzle a little maple syrup over the waffles and top them with the crisped quinoa. Arrange the waffles on a serving platter. Serve with more maple syrup, extra butter, and jam (optional) on the side.

Gluten-Free Vanilla-Raspberry Muffins

Thanks to almond flour, these gluten-free muffins have a wonderful flavor, with the brightness from the raspberries providing a great counter to the richness from the nut flour. I sprinkle sugar and lemon zest over the muffins right when they come out of the oven. The sugar immediately adheres and semi-melts, offering sweetness and great texture as well. Other muffins that include lemon in the batter—but not grated on top—can't match the brightness of grating the zest right over the top.

MAKES 12 MUFFINS

Nonstick cooking spray
1¾ cups almond flour
1 cup granulated sugar
1 teaspoon baking powder
1 teaspoon baking soda
1 teaspoon kosher salt
1 cup (2 sticks) plus 2 tablespoons unsalted butter, cut into small cubes, at room temperature
2 large eggs
3 large egg yolks
3 tablespoons buttermilk
1 tablespoon vanilla extract
1½ cups fresh raspberries
¼ cup coarse sugar
Grated zest of 1 large lemon

Preheat the oven to 350°F. Position a rack in the center of the oven. Spray a 12-cup muffin tin with cooking spray and then add a muffin liner to each cup. Coat the liners with cooking spray as well.

MAKE THE BATTER: In the bowl of a stand mixer fitted with the whisk attachment (or using a handheld mixer), mix the almond flour, granulated sugar, baking powder, baking soda, salt, and butter on low speed until the mixture resembles coarse crumbs, 3 to 5 minutes. With the mixer on low speed, slowly add the whole eggs, egg yolks, buttermilk, and vanilla.

FINISH AND BAKE: Remove the bowl from the mixer and use a rubber spatula to gently fold in the berries. Divide the batter among the prepared muffin cups, filling them to the top. Place the muffin tin in the oven on the center rack and bake until the muffins are golden brown on top and a knife inserted into the center of one emerges clean (aside from perhaps a streak of raspberry), 18 to 20 minutes. Remove the tin from the oven and immediately sprinkle the coarse sugar and lemon zest over the muffins. Let the muffins cool in the tin for 15 to 20 minutes, then carefully remove them from the tin and arrange on a serving platter. Store the muffins covered loosely in plastic. If storing overnight, refrigerate.

Blueberry–Brown Sugar Muffins

This is a perfect morning muffin recipe because everything is made with a whisk in a bowl—no power tools required. Cream cheese gives these muffins a luxurious texture, and the olive oil and brown sugar give them great flavor. The jam surprise in the center adds extra moisture and an even deeper fruit flavor, while the fresh blueberries add water to the muffin equation—and the combination of jam and berries is sublime. I have eaten three or four of these by myself before anyone else got to them, pretending that the batter only made eight muffins instead of a dozen. Now my secret is out! These are also great fork-split and toasted in a hot skillet or by carefully running them under the broiler.

MAKES 10 TO 12 MUFFINS

- Nonstick cooking spray
- ½ cup cream cheese, at room temperature
- ¾ cup extra-virgin olive oil
- 2 tablespoons whole milk
- ½ cup packed dark brown sugar
- ¼ cup granulated sugar, plus ¼ cup extra for sprinkling
- 2 teaspoons kosher salt
- 4 tablespoons (½ stick) unsalted butter, melted
- 1 tablespoon vanilla extract
- 1 large egg
- 1 cup whole-wheat flour
- 2 tablespoons all-purpose flour
- 1 teaspoon baking powder
- 1 teaspoon baking soda
- 2 cups fresh blueberries
- 1 cup blueberry jam
- Grated zest of 1 large lemon

Preheat the oven to 350°F. Position a rack in the center of the oven. Spray a 12-cup muffin tin with cooking spray and then add a muffin liner to each cup. Coat the liners with cooking spray as well.

MAKE THE BATTER: In large bowl, whisk together the cream cheese, olive oil, and milk until smooth. Whisk in the brown sugar, the ¼ cup granulated sugar, the salt, butter, vanilla, and egg. Use a wooden spoon to gently stir in both flours, the baking powder, and the baking soda. Carefully stir in the blueberries. Do not overmix (or you risk your muffins turning blue!).

ASSEMBLE: Fill each prepared muffin cup halfway with the batter, put a spoonful of jam in the center of the batter, and top with another layer of batter to cover, filling each muffin cup a little over three-fourths full.

BAKE: Place the muffin tin in the oven on the center rack and bake until the muffins are golden brown on top and a knife inserted into the center of one emerges clean, 20 to 25 minutes. Sprinkle the tops with the extra ¼ cup granulated sugar and sprinkle the lemon zest over the sugar. Remove the muffins from the tin and let them cool for a few minutes before eating. You can smell the zest as they cool, and get a hint of the blueberry as well. Store the muffins covered loosely in plastic. If storing overnight, refrigerate.

Cacao Nib Muffins

WITH DARK CHOCOLATE GLAZE

These muffins are for those mornings when you want dessert dressed up in a breakfast-appropriate costume—they're all about the chocolate, without any relief or apologies! These are really fun because they are easy enough and have that one unusual ingredient to make them stand out: cacao nibs. Nibs are actually dried, roasted, and crushed cacao beans. They are wonderfully bitter, like a coffee bean, and have an amazing crunchy texture. If nibs are not available, simply omit. You won't actually taste the white wine in the batter but it lifts the flavors up a little (like vinegar in a salad), and alcohol always keeps flour in line and therefore gives you a better chance at making a truly tender muffin.

MAKES 12 MUFFINS

MUFFINS

Nonstick cooking spray

2 large eggs

2 large egg yolks

½ cup plus 2 tablespoons sugar

7 tablespoons extra-virgin olive oil

5 tablespoons unsalted butter, melted

2 tablespoons dry white wine

1½ tablespoons maple syrup

1 tablespoon vanilla extract

¾ teaspoon kosher salt

¾ cup all-purpose flour

¼ cup fine cornmeal

1 teaspoon baking powder

1½ cups semisweet chocolate chips

2 tablespoons cacao nibs

GLAZE

⅔ cup heavy cream

⅔ cup (about 5 ounces) chopped dark chocolate (60% to 70% cacao)

Preheat the oven to 350°F. Position a rack in the center of the oven. Spray a 12-cup muffin tin with cooking spray and then add a muffin liner to each cup. Coat the liners with cooking spray as well.

START THE BATTER: In the bowl of a stand mixer fitted with the whisk attachment, whip the eggs, egg yolks, and sugar on medium-high speed until the mixture is pale yellow and thick, 5 to 8 minutes. In separate medium bowl, whisk together the olive oil, melted butter, wine, maple syrup, vanilla, and salt.

FINISH THE BATTER: With the mixer on low speed, slowly pour the olive oil mixture into the egg mixture. Stop the mixer and add the flour, cornmeal, baking powder, chocolate chips, and cacao nibs. Turn the mixer back on to low speed and mix only until the batter is combined. (Once you start to add the dry ingredients, don't overmix or it will toughen the texture of the muffins.) Use a rubber spatula to scrape down the bottom and sides of the bowl to ensure that no dry spots remain in the batter.

BAKE THE MUFFINS: Spoon the batter into the prepared muffin cups, filling them to the top. Place the muffin tin in the oven on the center rack and bake until the muffins are golden brown on top and a knife inserted into the center of one emerges clean, 18 to 20 minutes. Remove the tin from the oven and gently remove the muffins from the tin. Set aside to cool.

MAKE THE GLAZE: While the muffins are cooling, bring the cream to a boil in a small saucepan set over medium-low heat. Put the chopped dark chocolate in a small heatproof bowl and immediately pour the hot cream over the chocolate. Let it sit for a few minutes to melt, and then whisk to combine.

FINISH THE MUFFINS: Stir the glaze and spoon it generously over each muffin. Store the muffins covered loosely in plastic. If storing overnight, refrigerate.

Cheese Focaccia

This is a super-simple focaccia recipe where the pecorino cheese both acts as a salty seasoning and adds great richness. The cheese is added twice—once in the dough before baking (which gives it a tangy note) and once right after (for saltiness and texture on top). The flavor of the olive oil in the bread comes out, too, and plays so nicely with the cheese. I love dunking the focaccia in good grassy olive oil or good balsamic vinegar.

MAKES 16 TO 20 SQUARES

- 3½ cups (about 1 pound) bread flour
- 2¾ cups (about 1 pound) semolina flour
- 2 teaspoons kosher salt
- 2 teaspoons sugar
- 4 teaspoons (about 15 grams) active dry yeast
- 2½ cups warm water, between 110°F and 120°F
- ¼ cup extra-virgin olive oil, plus extra as needed
- 2 cups finely grated pecorino cheese
- Balsamic vinegar, for dunking (optional)

MAKE THE DOUGH: In the bowl of a stand mixer fitted with the dough hook, mix the two flours with the salt, sugar, and yeast. Add the warm water and the olive oil, and knead on medium speed until the dough comes together, forms a ball on the hook, and develops a sheen, 12 to 15 minutes. Lightly coat a large bowl with olive oil and place the dough in the center. Cover the bowl with plastic wrap and set it aside at room temperature to rise until it has tripled in volume, 2 to 3 hours.

SECOND PROOFING: Grease a half sheet pan with a little olive oil and press the dough into it as best you can. It will shrink back and only fill about half of the pan. Let it rest for 20 minutes, and then sprinkle 1 cup of the pecorino over the dough and press it in, stretching the dough to cover the whole pan. Cover the pan with plastic wrap and set it aside at room temperature until the dough rises nearly to the plastic wrap, 1½ to 2 hours.

Preheat the oven to 450°F. Position a rack in the center of the oven.

BAKE: Remove the plastic wrap from the pan and use your index finger to press rows of dimples into the dough, spacing them a few inches apart. Place the pan in the oven on the center rack and bake for 15 minutes. Reduce the oven temperature to 350°F and bake until the focaccia is golden brown, about another 25 minutes. Remove the pan from the oven and sprinkle the remaining 1 cup pecorino over the focaccia. Let it rest for at least 10 minutes in the pan before cutting it into squares. Serve the focaccia with more olive oil or balsamic for dunking if you like. Store leftover focaccia in an airtight container for up to 3 days.

Marble Coffee Cake

My mother often made the classic coffee cake with the super-crunchy top, but I love the novelty and flavors of a marble coffee cake; it also makes for a stunning presentation. It almost feels like a flashy cousin of coffee cake. The chocolate chips are critical because they collaborate brilliantly with the cinnamon and allspice in the topping and offer tartness as well. The flavor ends up being dominated by spiced cocoa and pecans. The crunch factor is also high. There is almost too much topping here (if that is even possible), so the crumbs fall on the plate as you eat. They are so great to gather up and taste all the nuances in flavor as you sip searing-hot coffee or tea.

SERVES 10 TO 12

BATTER

- 4 tablespoons (½ stick) unsalted butter, plus 1 to 2 tablespoons for greasing the pan, at room temperature
- 1 cup granulated sugar
- 2 large eggs
- 1½ cups sour cream
- 2 teaspoons vanilla extract
- 2 cups all-purpose flour
- 2 teaspoons kosher salt
- 1 teaspoon baking soda
- 1 teaspoon baking powder
- 1 teaspoon ground cinnamon

FILLING AND FINISHING

- ¾ cup pecan halves, coarsely chopped
- ¾ cup packed dark brown sugar
- ¾ cup semisweet chocolate chips
- 4 tablespoons unsweetened Dutch-process cocoa powder
- 1½ teaspoons ground cinnamon
- ½ teaspoon ground allspice
- 2 to 3 tablespoons confectioners' sugar

Preheat the oven to 350°F. Position a rack in the center of the oven. Grease a 10½ by 3½-inch Bundt pan with 1 to 2 tablespoons room-temperature butter and set it aside.

START THE BATTER: In the bowl of a stand mixer fitted with the paddle attachment, beat the 4 tablespoons butter on high speed until it becomes fluffy, about 2 minutes; then add the sugar. Beat the butter and sugar together until light and fluffy, 5 to 8 minutes. Scrape down the sides of the bowl with a rubber spatula and then beat in the eggs, one by one, mixing well after each addition. Beat in the sour cream and vanilla.

FINISH THE BATTER: In a medium bowl, whisk together the flour, salt, baking soda, baking powder, and cinnamon. Remove the bowl from the mixer and fold the dry ingredients into the batter. Do not overmix.

MAKE THE FILLING: In a medium bowl, combine the pecans, brown sugar, chocolate chips, 3 tablespoons of the cocoa powder, the cinnamon, and the allspice.

MAKE THE MARBLE: Add about one-third of the batter to the prepared Bundt pan, using a large spoon to gently even it out and taking care to get it into the grooves. Sprinkle one-third of the filling over the batter. Add half of the remaining batter and half of the remaining filling. Finish with the remaining batter and sprinkle the remaining filling on top. Stick a tablespoon into the batter and pull it back out. Rotate the pan a quarter turn and repeat until you have dunked the spoon in and pulled it out four times. This is what creates the marble effect.

BAKE: Place the Bundt pan on the center rack of the oven and bake until a small knife or a toothpick inserted into the center of the cake emerges clean, 50 to 55 minutes. Let the cake cool in the pan for about 10 minutes before unmolding it onto a cake plate. The topping will now be on the bottom and will spread around the cake on the plate. Set the cake aside to cool for at least 30 minutes more.

SERVE: Combine the confectioners' sugar and the remaining 1 tablespoon cocoa powder in a small strainer or sieve and dust the top of the cake before slicing and serving. Cover any remaining cake with plastic and refrigerate it.

Very Large Cherry-Strawberry Scones

These are oversized and obscene *on purpose.* They are meant to be broken into small pieces, hot out of the oven, and shared communally. I have made them to serve alone with a pot of tea or to put out as the opener for a fun brunch. Serve bowls of honey and jam on the side for drizzling or dunking. Note: The raw scones freeze beautifully—freeze them on a baking sheet until they are no longer tacky to the touch, then wrap them tightly in plastic wrap and store them in a resealable freezer bag for up to three weeks.

For the batter, frozen butter is ideal, but really cold butter works, too.

MAKES 6 LARGE SCONES

- Nonstick cooking spray
- 14 medium strawberries, hulled and quartered
- ⅓ cup plus 4 tablespoons sugar
- 2 cups all-purpose flour, plus extra for shaping
- 1 teaspoon baking powder
- ¼ teaspoon baking soda
- 1 teaspoon kosher salt
- 8 tablespoons (1 stick) unsalted butter, frozen
- ½ cup sour cream
- 1 large egg
- ½ cup dried cherries

Preheat the oven to 400°F. Position a rack in the center of the oven. Line a sheet pan with parchment paper.

COOK THE STRAWBERRIES: Heat a medium sauté pan over medium heat and coat it with cooking spray. (We are using cooking spray because we don't want to add any more butter or oil to the scones.) Add the strawberries and 1 tablespoon of the sugar, and cook over medium heat until the liquid is released from the fruit, 2 to 3 minutes. Quickly transfer the berries to the prepared sheet pan to cool.

MAKE THE DOUGH: In a medium bowl, mix together the flour, ⅓ cup of the sugar, the baking powder, baking soda, and salt. Using the large holes of a box grater, grate the frozen butter over the dry ingredients (alternatively, cut the butter into small cubes and add them to the bowl). Work the butter into the flour with your fingers until it looks like finely grated cheese. In a small bowl, whisk together the sour cream and egg, and then use your fingers to work the mixture into the flour mixture. Gently mix in the cherries and strawberries. Mix only to combine the ingredients. Nothing more. Do not overmix.

FORM THE SCONES: Line the sheet pan with a clean piece of parchment. Lightly flour your work surface and turn the dough out onto it. Gently press the dough into a rough 1-inch-thick round, about 5 inches in diameter. Use a knife to cut the round into 6 equal wedges (like a pie). Place the wedges on the prepared sheet pan, leaving some space between them, and sprinkle the tops with the remaining 3 tablespoons sugar.

BAKE: Place the pan in the oven on the center rack and bake until the scones are golden brown, 15 to 18 minutes. Set them aside to cool for a few minutes before serving. The scones are best when eaten as soon as they are baked, but you can also keep them in an airtight container. Refrigerate if keeping them overnight.

DOUGHNUTS & CAKES

These are some of my favorite cake recipes. The red velvet with the fresh and freeze-dried strawberries is tasty and dramatic when you put it on the table. It might be the cake I am most proud of in this section because I omitted the classic red food coloring and opted to bring about the red color through natural ingredients. Cake has to be worth it. We don't eat cake out of hunger. We enjoy it recreationally. Growing up in Midtown Manhattan, there was a doughnut shop in the lobby of my building. The aroma of freshly fried dough filled the lobby every day. It's pure nostalgia when I enter a doughnut shop now.

I wanted a quick doughnut recipe and developed the one on page 257. I suggest frying and eating them fairly quickly, while they're still warm. They're the perfect treat to make for those of us who struggle with having enough patience to actually wait for a cake to cool completely before frosting and eating it. You also need patience to properly cream butter and sugar. I take my time with this step because it yields a fluffier texture in cakes and muffins. There are some classic cake recipes to build on—a good vanilla cake, for example—that you can take in your own direction by switching up the frostings or toppings. Have fun with it.

Red Velvety Strawberry Cake

I've always loved the acidity of red velvet cake but I wanted to find a way to skip the red food coloring. I find that reduced red wine in the cake, plus a mix of fresh and dried strawberries with a hint of red wine vinegar in the frosting, does the trick to create a more "natural" red color and a good strawberry flavor.

Freeze-dried strawberries are a great ingredient for desserts. I love to mix them with confectioners' sugar to coat doughnuts and butter cookies. They are tart, which is always a needed flavor in desserts to counter the sweet, and they are also a vibrant red and naturally add drama.

SERVES 10 TO 12

CAKE

1 (750mL) bottle inexpensive fruity red wine, such as a Merlot or Pinot Noir

1¾ cups (3½ sticks) unsalted butter, at room temperature, plus 2 tablespoons at room temperature for greasing the pans

2 cups packed dark brown sugar

2 teaspoons baking soda

1½ teaspoons kosher salt

2 tablespoons vanilla extract

6 large eggs, at room temperature

2⅔ cups all-purpose flour

¾ cup unsweetened Dutch-process cocoa powder

1 cup buttermilk

FROSTING

18 ounces cream cheese, at room temperature

2 teaspoons red wine vinegar

3½ cups confectioners' sugar, sifted

1 pint fresh strawberries, hulled and finely chopped

3 (1.2-ounce) packages freeze-dried strawberries (2½ to 3 cups)

REDUCE THE RED WINE: In a medium saucepan, simmer the red wine over medium heat until it has reduced by about two-thirds to about 1½ cups), 10 to 12 minutes. Set it aside to cool.

Preheat the oven to 350°F. Position a rack in the center of the oven. Thoroughly grease the bottoms and sides of two 9-inch cake pans with the 2 tablespoons butter.

START THE BATTER: In the bowl of a stand mixer fitted with the paddle attachment, cream the 1¾ cups (3½ sticks) butter with the brown sugar, baking soda, salt, and vanilla on medium speed to combine, 3 to 4 minutes. Raise the speed to medium-high and beat until the mixture is fluffy, another 5 to 8 minutes. With the mixer on medium speed, add the eggs, one by one, beating until each one is fully incorporated before adding the next.

FINISH THE BATTER: In a separate bowl, sift together the flour and cocoa powder. With the mixer on low speed, alternate adding the flour mixture, the buttermilk, and the reduced red wine, starting and ending with the flour mixture and using a rubber spatula to scrape the bottom and sides of the bowl as needed. Do not overmix.

BAKE THE CAKE: Divide the batter evenly between the buttered cake pans, smoothing out the tops with a spatula. Place the pans in the oven on the center rack and bake until the tip of a small knife inserted into the center of each cake emerges clean, 45 to 50 minutes. Let the cakes cool for 10 minutes in the pans and then unmold them onto a wire rack set over a rimmed baking sheet. Let them cool for at least 30 additional minutes.

MAKE THE FROSTING: In a large bowl, whisk together the cream cheese, vinegar, and confectioners' sugar until smooth. Gently fold in the fresh strawberries and all but one-fourth cup of the freeze-dried strawberries.

ASSEMBLE THE CAKE: Place one cake layer on a flat surface. Frost the top and sides with a scant half of the frosting. Top the first layer squarely with the second one, and gently press the two layers together. Frost the top and sides of the cake with the remaining frosting. Sprinkle the cake with the remaining freeze-dried strawberries. Serve immediately or refrigerate, covered, for up to 3 days. (If refrigerating, let the cake stand at room temperature for 2 hours and up to 6 hours before slicing and serving, and wait until just before slicing to sprinkle it with the remaining freeze-dried strawberries.)

Vanilla Cake

WITH MARSHMALLOWY FROSTING

As long as your butter is soft and your milk is close to room temperature, this cake is literally a piece of cake to make. I am partial to the classic Swans Down brand of cake flour because I grew up watching my mom bake with nothing but. (You can always find a few boxes in the "suburbs" of the baking aisle, a.k.a. the lower shelves.) A few small details make all the difference with this recipe: Make sure the mixer bowl is very clean and cool to the touch when you whip your egg whites. And sift your dry ingredients—it really does help with the "fluff" factor. You can also frost this cake with whipped cream to save time.

SERVES 12 TO 14

CAKE

- 1¼ cups (2½ sticks) unsalted butter, at room temperature, plus 2 tablespoons for greasing the pans
- 2¼ cups sugar
- ⅛ teaspoon ground nutmeg (preferably freshly grated)
- 1½ cups whole milk, at room temperature
- 1 tablespoon plus 2 teaspoons vanilla extract
- 4½ cups cake flour
- 2 tablespoons baking powder
- 1 teaspoon kosher salt
- 7 large egg whites

FROSTING

- ¼ teaspoon cream of tartar
- 1⅓ cups sugar
- 2 large egg whites
- 1 tablespoon light corn syrup

Preheat the oven to 350°F. Position a rack in the center of the oven. Thoroughly grease two 9-inch cake pans with the 2 tablespoons butter.

START THE BATTER: In the bowl of a stand mixer fitted with the paddle attachment, cream the 1¼ cups butter with the sugar and nutmeg on medium speed until the mixture is smooth and fluffy, 8 to 10 minutes. (Do not rush this step; the sugar is softening and fluffing the butter and this is part of what gives a great cake its great texture.) Reduce the mixer speed to low and add the milk in a slow, steady stream. Add the vanilla.

COMBINE THE INGREDIENTS: In a medium bowl, sift together the flour, baking powder, and salt. Remove the bowl from the mixer and use a rubber spatula to fold the dry ingredients into the batter until combined—the batter shouldn't have any pockets of dry flour. Do not overmix; overmixing makes for a tough, chewy cake. Transfer the batter to a large bowl, and wash and dry the stand mixer bowl, leaving no trace of fat behind (which would prevent the egg whites from whipping up nicely).

ADD THE EGG WHITES: In the clean bowl of the mixer fitted with the whisk attachment, whip the egg whites on medium speed until soft peaks form, 2 to 3 minutes. Using a rubber spatula, gently fold the egg whites into the batter. Divide the batter between the buttered cake pans, smoothing out the tops and taking care to treat the batter gently so it doesn't deflate.

BAKE: Place the cake pans side by side in the oven on the center rack and bake until a small knife or toothpick inserted into the center of each cake emerges clean, 30 to 35 minutes. Let the cakes cool in the pans for about 15 minutes. Then run a paring knife around the edges to release each cake from the pan and unmold them onto a wire rack to cool completely.

MAKE THE FROSTING: Pour about 2 inches of water into a medium roasting pan. Set the roasting pan over a burner and bring the water to a gentle simmer over medium heat. Dip an instant-read thermometer into the simmering water to clean any impurities off the end and to test that the thermometer works. In a clean stainless-steel bowl, combine 5 tablespoons of water with the cream of tartar, sugar, egg whites, and corn syrup. Gently lower the bowl into the simmering water. Turn off the heat under the water. Use a whisk or a handheld mixer to whip the mixture until the egg whites are fluffy, about 3 solid minutes. Do not leave the mixture unattended or stop beating at any time in this process or the egg whites may cook and get lumpy.

Remove the bowl from the hot water bath and quickly take the temperature of the frosting. You want it to reach 140°F. If it's not there yet, immediately put the bowl back in the water and resume beating for 2 to 3 minutes more , until the temperature of the frosting reaches 140°F.

ASSEMBLE: Place one of the cooled cake layers upside down on a cake plate and spread a thin layer of the frosting on top. Add the second cake layer, right-side up, squarely on top of the first, and frost the top and sides of the cake with all of the remaining frosting. The cake is best eaten freshly baked, but cover any leftovers with plastic wrap and store at room temperature overnight. If there are still leftovers the next day, refrigerate.

Orange Pound Cake

The classic version from my childhood memory bank is a lemon pound cake that my mother made for my dad all the time. In fact, she would often make a lemon dessert if they had an argument and were just making up! It had a tart flavor I grew to love over time. I also loved when my parents were getting along! Dad would honestly eat almost the whole dessert in a day or two. Lemon, or any citrus, mixed into a dessert provides that addictive contrast between sweetness and acidity. This led to my adult interpretation: Why not use oranges? I char them for this cake so they are *almost* candied but are also pleasingly bitter, hyper-floral, and a little smoky, too. They get finely chopped so you encounter fun, chewy bits all throughout the cake. If you have access to varied types of oranges, feel free to experiment. I love classic supermarket juice oranges, which are, to me, the "OG" childhood oranges.

This cake is excellent served warm with a nutty ice cream like butter pecan or pistachio. I also like to serve it with the frosting on the side—sort of like the cake version of putting bread and a dish of butter on the table.

SERVES 8 TO 10

CAKE

- 1 cup (2 sticks) unsalted butter, at room temperature, plus 2 tablespoons for greasing the pan
- 2 medium juice oranges: one sliced into ¼-inch-thick rounds yielding, ideally, about 12 slices (remove any seeds from the slices); the other one juiced
- 1½ cups sugar
- 5 large eggs
- 1½ cups plus 2 tablespoons cake flour
- 1 teaspoon kosher salt

Preheat the oven to 350°F. Position a rack in the center of the oven. Grease a 9 by 5-inch loaf pan with the 2 tablespoons butter.

CHAR THE ORANGES: Line a sheet pan with parchment paper and arrange the orange slices on it in a single layer. Place the pan in the oven on the center rack and bake until the oranges are golden brown, 20 to 25 minutes. (Check from time to time and remove the orange slices as they turn brown and get crispy and charred around the edges.) Set aside to cool. Place the cooled orange slices on a cutting board and coarsely chop them. Set aside.

MAKE THE BATTER: In the bowl of a stand mixer fitted with the whisk attachment, beat the 1 cup butter and the sugar on medium speed until the mixture is fluffy and pale, 6 to 8 minutes. Add the eggs, one by one, beating after each addition before adding the next. In a separate medium bowl, sift together the flour and salt. With the mixer on medium-low speed, add the flour mixture, the orange juice, and the chopped charred orange and mix until just combined, using a spatula to scrape the bottom and sides of the bowl to ensure no dry patches remain. Do not overmix or you'll have a tough cake.

recipe and ingredients continue

FROSTING

- 8 tablespoons (1 stick) unsalted butter, at room temperature
- 1 (1-pound) box confectioners' sugar
- 1 teaspoon kosher salt
- 1 tablespoon vanilla extract

BAKE: Pour the batter into the buttered loaf pan and tap the pan gently against the counter so the batter settles into an even layer. Place the pan in the oven on the center rack and bake until golden brown and a small knife inserted into the center of the cake emerges clean, 40 to 45 minutes. Remove the pan from the oven and let the cake cool in the pan for 20 minutes. Then unmold the cake onto a wire rack set over a sheet pan.

MAKE THE FROSTING AND SERVE: In the bowl of a stand mixer fitted with the paddle attachment, beat the butter and confectioners' sugar until fluffy, 5 to 8 minutes. Then beat in the salt and vanilla. Serve the cake on a plate, in slices, with the frosting on the side for spreading as people see fit.

Powdered Cake Doughnuts

I always thought doughnuts were a treat that I would buy at the bakery and never make at home, but placing a platter of warm just-fried doughnuts in front of family and friends is really rewarding! I grew up with a doughnut shop in the lobby of my building. I forever hold to that standard of tasty, fresh childhood doughnuts. I wanted to re-create that feeling. The cakey-ness gets a lift from the yeast, and the sour cream and buttermilk add a bit of tanginess. If you like, you can add spices to the confectioners' sugar—my absolute favorite way to serve these doughnuts is rolled in confectioners' (powdered) sugar that's accented with an excessive amount of cinnamon. A little cocoa powder can be really nice, too.

MAKES 10 TO 12 DOUGHNUTS

- 2 cups all-purpose flour, plus 1 cup for dusting
- 1½ cups cake flour
- 1 cup granulated sugar
- 2 teaspoons baking powder
- ½ teaspoon baking soda
- 2 teaspoons kosher salt
- ¼ teaspoon ground nutmeg (preferably freshly grated)
- 1 (¼-ounce) envelope active dry yeast
- ¾ cup buttermilk, at room temperature
- 2 teaspoons vanilla extract
- 1 large egg
- 3 large egg yolks
- ⅓ cup full-fat sour cream
- 2 quarts (8 cups) canola oil, for frying
- 1 to 1½ cups confectioners' sugar

MIX THE DRY INGREDIENTS: In a large bowl, sift together the all-purpose flour, cake flour, granulated sugar, baking powder, baking soda, salt, and nutmeg. With your hand, make a well in the center of the dry ingredients and add the yeast to the well.

MAKE THE DOUGH: In a medium bowl, whisk together the buttermilk, vanilla, whole egg, and egg yolks, and set the mixture aside. Place the sour cream in a heatproof bowl and warm it gently over a pot of simmering water (like a makeshift double boiler) for 2 to 3 minutes. Once the sour cream is warm, remove the bowl from the saucepan, pour the sour cream directly over the yeast, and allow the sour cream and yeast to sit for 2 to 3 minutes. Then use a wooden spoon to stir the sour cream mixture into the dry ingredients. Stir the buttermilk mixture and mix it into the flour mixture until it is integrated, without any pockets of unmixed flour.

CUT THE DOUGHNUTS: Sift a generous layer of all-purpose flour onto two rimmed sheet pans and set them aside. Turn the dough out onto a clean, lightly floured surface. The dough will be sticky. Sift more flour on top of the dough, flour your hands, and pat the dough into a ¾-inch-thick sheet. Dip a 2¾-inch round cutter in flour so the dough won't stick to it, stamp out a round of dough, and gently transfer the round to one of the floured pans. Continue to cut out rounds as close together as possible to avoid making too many scraps, flouring the cutter every time to prevent sticking. Gather the scraps and roll them into a ball. Flatten the ball and cut out a few additional doughnuts; discard any scraps that remain.

FINISH: Dip a 1-inch cutter in flour and cut a round out of the center of each doughnut to make the hole. Save the small dough holes and set them on one of the floured pans. Let the doughnuts and the holes rest for 8 to 10 minutes.

recipe continues

HEAT THE OIL: In a large heavy-bottomed pot, heat the canola oil over medium heat until it reaches 350°F. Use a deep-frying thermometer to monitor the temperature. Line a sheet pan with a double layer of paper towels.

FRY: Sift the confectioners' sugar onto a sheet pan and set it aside. Use a slotted spoon to submerge 5 doughnuts in a single layer in the hot oil. Fry until the bottoms are browned, 3 to 4 minutes. Using the slotted spoon, carefully turn each doughnut over and fry until golden brown on the second side, 3 to 4 minutes. Again using the slotted spoon, transfer the doughnuts to the paper-towel-lined sheet pan to drain. Repeat with the remaining doughnuts, taking care to allow the oil to come back up to temperature between batches. Fry the doughnut holes as well—they will take 2 to 3 minutes to become golden brown. Let all of the doughnuts cool for at least 10 minutes; then coat them on each side by rolling them in the confectioners' sugar.

EAT: The doughnuts are best eaten immediately. I like to put the full pan of confectioners' sugar and just-fried doughnuts right on the counter and watch them disappear. The doughnuts can be stored, wrapped in plastic wrap, for up to 2 days.

Chocolate Cake

WITH WHITE CHOCOLATE-KAHLÚA GLAZE

I am an avid baker, mostly because I have spent so much of my adult life cooking chicken breasts and making salads. Desserts have always been like a change of scenery to me. Icing a cake is a refreshing, satisfying break for this savory chef. This two-layer chocolate cake is a winner. You can serve it with this white chocolate glaze (that gets an extra kick from Kahlúa) or make the same glaze with dark chocolate instead. I love to load the top of the glazed cake with brandied cherries, too. (I secretly want every cake to be a Black Forest cake.)

SERVES 10 TO 12

CAKE

- 1 cup (2 sticks) unsalted butter, at room temperature, plus 2 tablespoons for greasing the pans
- 1½ cups sugar
- 2 large eggs
- 3 large egg yolks
- 1 tablespoon vanilla extract
- 2 cups all-purpose flour
- ½ cup unsweetened Dutch-process cocoa powder
- 1 teaspoon kosher salt
- ½ teaspoon baking powder
- ½ teaspoon baking soda
- 1 cup buttermilk, at room temperature

GLAZE

- 1½ cups heavy cream
- 2 tablespoons Kahlúa liqueur
- 12½ ounces chopped white chocolate (about 2 cups; see Note)

Preheat the oven to 350°F. Position a rack in the center of the oven. Thoroughly grease the bottoms and sides of two 9-inch cake pans with the 2 tablespoons butter.

START THE BATTER: In the bowl of a stand mixer fitted with the paddle attachment, cream the 1 cup butter with the sugar on medium speed until the mixture is smooth and fluffy, 8 to 10 minutes. (Do not rush this step; the sugar is softening and fluffing the butter and this is part of what gives a great cake its great texture.) Scrape down the sides of the bowl with a rubber spatula and then, with the mixer on medium speed, beat in the eggs and egg yolks, one at a time, combining well after each addition before adding the next. Then beat in the vanilla.

FINISH THE BATTER: In a medium bowl, sift together the flour, cocoa powder, salt, baking powder, and baking soda. With the mixer on medium-low speed, add half of the buttermilk to the batter and blend until smooth. Add half of the dry ingredients, mix on low speed until mostly combined, and then repeat with the remaining buttermilk and dry ingredients, scraping down the sides and bottom of the bowl as needed. Once the batter is well combined, with no pockets of unmixed flour (scrape the bottom and sides of the bowl to be sure), stop mixing.

BAKE THE CAKE: Divide the batter between the buttered cake pans. Tap the pans on the counter to level the batter, and place the pans on the center rack in the oven. Bake until a cake tester or a small knife inserted into the center of each cake comes out clean, 50 to 55 minutes. Let the cakes cool in the pans for 10 minutes. Then unmold the cakes onto a wire rack set over a rimmed sheet pan. Set aside to cool for about 20 minutes.

MAKE THE GLAZE: In a medium saucepan, bring the heavy cream and Kahlúa to a simmer over medium heat. Place the white chocolate in a heatproof bowl, set the bowl on top of the saucepan (the bottom of the bowl should not touch the cream), reduce the heat to low, and heat the chocolate gently, stirring it occasionally with a rubber spatula, until it is melted, 2 to 3 minutes. Remove the bowl from the saucepan, pour the warmed cream mixture into the melted chocolate, and stir gently to combine until the ganache is smooth. Keep warm.

ASSEMBLE: Place one of the cooled cake layers upside down on a cake plate and spread a thin layer of the glaze in the center. Add the second cake layer, right-side up, squarely on top of the first, and frost the top and sides of the cake with the remaining glaze. The cake is best eaten freshly baked, but cover any leftovers with plastic and leave at room temperature overnight. If there are still leftovers the next day, refrigerate.

Note: Don't use white chocolate chips. Buy white chocolate bars instead and finely chop as much as you need. White chocolate bars melt more fluidly than chips, which often become pasty when melted. You may think they'll act the same as other chips, but they won't!

Tiramisu Swiss Roll

I am all about the flavor combo of tiramisu—cocoa, coffee, Marsala, creamy sweetened mascarpone—more than I actually like eating the dessert itself (whenever I eat it, I always feel as if I am wading through a heavy mousse). I imagined this fantastic flavor combo—bitter cocoa, coffee, and Marsala—in a different form. Why not a cake? In this Swiss roll, you get all of that deliciousness in one simple-to-make-and-serve package. Serving a slice, with its spiraled swirl, always makes me nostalgic for one of those snack cake–style packaged treats. Only this homemade version is ten times better than any store-bought indulgence. This is the kind of cake that tastes best of all as leftovers, when the flavors have had time to soak into one another, eaten out of hand and standing in front of the fridge!

SERVES 10 TO 12

CAKE

1 cup (2 sticks) unsalted butter, plus 2 tablespoons at room temperature for greasing the sheet pan

2 cups sugar

2 cups all-purpose flour

1 teaspoon baking soda

1 teaspoon kosher salt

¼ cup unsweetened Dutch-process cocoa powder, plus ¼ cup for sifting

1 tablespoon instant coffee or espresso

2 large eggs, lightly beaten

½ cup buttermilk, at room temperature

3 teaspoons vanilla extract

12 ounces (about 1½ cups) mascarpone cheese

3 tablespoons sweet Marsala wine

1 cup heavy cream

GLAZE

⅔ cup heavy cream

2 tablespoons dark rum

2 tablespoons honey

1 cup chopped dark chocolate (about 6 ounces; preferably 66% cacao)

Preheat the oven to 350°F. Position a rack in the center of the oven. Grease the bottom and sides of an 18 by 13-inch rimmed sheet pan with some of the room-temperature butter, line the pan with parchment paper, and then grease the parchment with butter as well. Spread a large, clean kitchen towel on a flat surface and cover it with a sheet of parchment paper.

MIX THE DRY INGREDIENTS: In a medium bowl, sift together the sugar, flour, baking soda, and salt.

MIX THE WET INGREDIENTS: In a medium saucepan, melt the 1 cup butter with 1 cup of water over medium heat, and then whisk in the cocoa powder and instant coffee until smooth, 2 to 3 minutes.

MAKE THE BATTER: Pour the wet ingredients over the dry ingredients and stir to combine. Stir in the eggs, buttermilk, and 2 teaspoons of the vanilla. The batter should be smooth, without any pockets of unmixed flour. Take care not to overmix.

BAKE THE CAKE: Pour the batter onto the prepared sheet pan, using an offset spatula to spread it out evenly. Place the pan in the oven on the center rack and bake until a small knife inserted into the cake comes out clean, 18 to 20 minutes. Remove the pan from the oven and turn the cake out onto the parchment-covered towel. Gently peel off and discard the layer of parchment sticking to the cake. Cover the cake with a clean kitchen towel to keep it moist while you make the filling.

MAKE THE FILLING: In the bowl of a stand mixer fitted with the whisk attachment, beat the mascarpone cheese and Marsala together until smooth and slightly fluffy, 3 to 5 minutes. Transfer the mixture to a large bowl. Combine the cream and the remaining

recipe continues

1 teaspoon vanilla in the (now empty) mixer bowl, and beat until soft peaks form, 2 to 3 minutes. Use a rubber spatula to fold the whipped cream into the mascarpone mixture. Set the filling aside.

MAKE THE GLAZE: In a medium saucepan, combine the cream with the rum and honey, and heat over medium heat until it thickens slightly, 3 to 5 minutes. While the cream is heating, place a heatproof bowl over the saucepan (the bottom of the bowl should not touch the cream) and add all but 1 piece of the chocolate to it. Stir occasionally until the chocolate is melted, 2 to 3 minutes. Remove the bowl from the saucepan and add the warmed cream mixture to the melted chocolate. Whisk to blend, and cover the bowl with plastic wrap to keep the glaze warm.

GET READY: Position the cake on the parchment-covered towel so a longer side is facing you; you will be rolling up the cake lengthwise like a jelly roll. Spread the mascarpone filling over the cake, leaving a 1-inch border around all four sides. Sift a layer of cocoa powder over the filling.

ROLL THE CAKE UP: Starting at the long edge nearest you and with one hand holding each end, pick up the edges of parchment under the cake and roll the cake, tightly, away from you, so it starts to form a roll. Move your hands to the center of the cake, ensuring that the cake is being rolled tightly into a log. Tuck the first edge underneath itself and just keep going; roll the rest of the cake up, gently but firmly. Take care not to roll the parchment up inside the cake! (I've done it.) You want the cake to roll up around the cream filling as tightly as possible. (Don't worry if the cake cracks slightly or is uneven when you roll it up: people won't care because it's so delicious.)

WRAP IN PLASTIC: Wrap the rolled cake in a double layer of plastic wrap and gently twist the ends to tighten it up slightly. Refrigerate the cake for at least 30 minutes or up to 12 hours.

GLAZE AND SERVE: Remove the plastic wrap and place the cake on a wire rack set over a sheet pan. Pour the glaze evenly over the cake. If the glaze has cooled too much and thickened to where it won't pour easily, simply rewarm it gently over low heat on the stove just long enough to loosen the texture, 1 to 2 minutes. Grate the reserved chunk of chocolate over the top and then sift cocoa powder over everything. Let the glaze set for 20 to 30 minutes, then transfer the cake to a platter and serve.

COOKIES & SUCH

I think I could write a new chapter of cookie recipes every year. I have my favorite classics—a buttery shortbread, a chocolate chip, or a chocolate chunk. (Yes, there is a difference!) I have some that are outside the box, like gluten-free flourless coconut macaroons and lentil-based cookies loaded with spices. I always like a good nut brittle for crunch, too. This is a fun chapter to bake your way through for the holidays or to pull out one recipe that speaks to you and make it your project on a rainy Sunday.

Coconut Pecan Macaroons

The richness of the coconut and the toasty pecans keep me coming back for more with this simple recipe. Not only do they do the work that ingredients like butter, cream, and egg yolks normally do in so many other cookie recipes (tenderizing, leavening), they are also the driving flavors and textures and they offset the fluffy, airy quality of the egg whites. I like turning the macaroons into a gluten-free dessert by sandwiching sorbet between two of them; the macaroons also pair well with fresh fruits or even a jar of jam for dunking. Lemon curd would be great as well.

MAKES 18 TO 24 COOKIES

Nonstick cooking spray

¾ cup pecan halves

4 large egg whites

1⅓ cups sugar

1 cup sweetened shredded coconut

Preheat the oven to 350°F. Position a rack in the center of the oven. Line two rimmed sheet pans with parchment paper and lightly coat the parchment with cooking spray.

TOAST THE PECANS: Place the pecans on a rimmed sheet pan and bake them until they become toasty and golden brown, 5 to 8 minutes. Remove from the oven (keep the oven on) and transfer the nuts to a plate to cool completely, then finely chop them.

MAKE THE BATTER: In the clean bowl of a stand mixer fitted with the whisk attachment, whip the egg whites on medium-high speed until they form soft peaks, 3 to 5 minutes (you will see the trail of the whisk in the whites). Reduce the mixer speed to medium and gradually add the sugar, whisking until all of it is mixed in and the whites are glossy and stiff, 2 to 3 additional minutes.

FINISH: Remove the bowl from the mixer and use a rubber spatula to gently fold the toasted pecans and the coconut into the egg whites. Drop generous tablespoons of the batter onto the prepared sheet pans. Try to keep the cookies aerated and fluffy—don't press down on the batter. Make sure you leave at least 1 inch of space between the cookies so they can brown slightly.

BAKE: Place the pans in the oven on the center rack and bake for 5 minutes. Rotate the pans and bake until the cookies are light brown, 8 to 10 more minutes. Do not allow them to get too dark. Remove the pans from the oven and let the cookies cool and set on the pans for 3 to 5 minutes. Use a flat metal spatula to transfer them to a wire rack to cool completely. The cookies will keep in a container with a fitted lid at room temperature for up to 2 days.

WHIPPING EGG WHITES

When whipping whites, make sure the bowl and whisk are clean and free of any traces of fat or impurities—the egg whites will never stiffen if there is even a drip of oil or hint of egg yolk in the bowl. There are various stages of egg whites, and recipes will often call for "soft" peaks or "stiff" peaks depending on how they'll be used. My question always is: How do we know what to look for? As the whites are whipping in the mixer, look for the distinct trace and trail of the whisk in the egg whites as the beater spins around in the bowl. For the first couple of minutes, the whites are frothy and gain some volume but don't take shape. In the next couple of minutes, you can start to see the traces the whisk leaves in the whites as the mixer spins. The color also whitens. These are signs of the "soft peak" (think mountain peaks) stage. Soft-peak whites are often used for softer meringues and to lighten batters for waffles or pancakes. With 2 to 3 minutes more whisking, the traces of the whisk become more pronounced in the whites. If you lift the whisk out of the bowl, the whites will cling stiffly to the whisk. Stiff-peak whites are often used for other types of meringues, Pavlova, and more elaborate dishes like soufflés. This is the final stage. If you continue to mix, the whites become a duller color and break into chunks. This is when they are officially overbeaten. Best course of action? Start again!

Gluten-Free Butter Cookies

These fragile cookies taste wonderfully of almonds and honey. I am partial to a fairly delicate honey here and to good-quality almonds. They make the cookies flavorful yet light. You can experiment with various flavors of honey: chestnut honey is tasty and orange blossom honey has a more deeply floral note. These cookies are wonderful made with hazelnut or pecan flour, too. You can make your own nut flour by finely grinding nuts in the food processor before making the cookie dough (which comes together in minutes)—just make sure not to grind them for too long or you'll have nut butter instead of nut flour. For times when there's a holiday or office party, it's invaluable to have a great cookie recipe that doesn't include wheat flour, so no one feels excluded.

MAKES ABOUT 3 DOZEN COOKIES

2½ cups almond flour (made from blanched almonds), plus extra for rolling

1 teaspoon ground cinnamon

1 teaspoon kosher salt

1 cup (2 sticks) unsalted butter, chilled and cubed

¼ cup honey

1 tablespoon vanilla extract

MAKE THE DOUGH: In a food processor fitted with the metal blade, pulse together the almond flour, cinnamon, and salt. Then pulse in the butter, honey, vanilla, and 1 tablespoon of water until the dough forms a loose ball. Turn the dough out onto a piece of parchment paper and cover it with another sheet of parchment. Press down to flatten the dough until it is about ¾ inch thick. Wrap the parchment loosely around the dough to protect it and refrigerate for at least 30 minutes or up to 6 hours.

GET READY: Preheat the oven to 350°F. Set oven racks in the upper-middle and lower-middle positions. Line two sheet pans with parchment paper.

ROLL THE DOUGH: Spread some almond flour on a flat surface (to prevent the dough from sticking). Use a rolling pin to roll the dough until it's about ½ inch thick. Use cookie cutters to cut out rounds or different shapes. You can use this dough for holiday cookie shapes, or whatever other occasion you are celebrating. With a metal spatula, carefully transfer the cookies to the prepared sheet pans, leaving at least 1 inch of space between them.

BAKE: Place the pans in the oven, one on each rack, and bake until the cookies are golden brown, 5 to 7 minutes. Allow them to cool on the pans for 2 to 3 minutes, and then use a metal spatula to transfer them to a wire rack. Store the cookies in a plastic container with a fitted lid at room temperature for up to 2 days.

Molasses Cookies

Molasses cookies and warm spice cookies are two favorites of mine. I use blackstrap molasses for these, which is the darkest and least sweet kind of molasses because it is made from the third round of boiling concentrated sugarcane juice. It doesn't have any heavy sulfur notes and it tastes almost like lightly burned sugar. I also use shortening to give the cookie a distinctive crunchy texture. Like when you eat a crispy piece of bacon. The absence of butter flavor here leaves more room for the spices, molasses, and vanilla to take center stage. I eat these cookies warm and sprinkled with sugar right after baking. I sometimes stick two together with some caramel sauce in between or sandwich them around bold-flavored ice creams like rum raisin, cinnamon, or butter pecan.

MAKES 24 TO 30 COOKIES

- ½ cup packed dark brown sugar
- ⅓ cup blackstrap molasses
- ¼ cup solid vegetable shortening
- 1 large egg yolk
- 1 teaspoon vanilla extract
- 2 teaspoons ground cinnamon
- 1½ teaspoons ground ginger
- 1 teaspoon baking soda
- 1 teaspoon kosher salt
- ½ teaspoon ground cloves
- 1 cup all-purpose flour, plus extra for rolling

MAKE THE DOUGH: In the bowl of a stand mixer fitted with the paddle attachment, beat together the brown sugar, molasses, shortening, egg yolk, vanilla, cinnamon, ginger, baking soda, salt, and cloves. Remove the bowl from the mixer. Sift the flour over the batter and gently stir it in—just until mixed. Gather the dough into a ball and place it on a piece of plastic wrap, flattening it into a thick 6-inch round. Enclose the dough in the plastic wrap and refrigerate it for at least 1 hour and up to 12 hours.

GET READY: Preheat the oven to 350°F. Place oven racks in the upper-middle and lower-middle positions. Line two sheet pans with parchment paper.

CUT OUT THE COOKIES: Divide the dough in half and place one piece on a lightly floured surface. Use a rolling pin to roll the dough into a sheet about ½ inch thick, adding more flour on top or under the dough if needed to prevent sticking. Use a 2-inch round cookie cutter (or a decorative one) to stamp out cookies as close together as possible. Place the cookies on one of the prepared sheet pans, leaving at least 1 inch of space between them. Repeat with the remaining dough.

BAKE: Bake the cookies until they are golden brown, 6 to 8 minutes. Remove the pans from the oven and let the cookies cool on the pans for 2 to 3 minutes. Then use a metal spatula to transfer them to a wire rack. These cookies taste best when freshly baked, but can be stored in a plastic container with a fitted lid at room temperature for up to 3 days. If you won't be able to eat or serve them all within 3 days, it's better to bake half the dough and refrigerate (or freeze) the rest to bake later. If you freeze the dough, simply leave it in the fridge overnight to thaw before rolling, cutting, and baking.

Brown Butter–Chocolate Chunk Cookies

This is all about that first bite: the butter gets browned, so it offers a nutty caramel taste, and then there's also the brown sugar note and the chunks of chocolate. When these are hot from the oven, they literally melt in your mouth. I like the heft of chocolate chunks, but you can easily sub in the same amount of chips here. I love to fold in untoasted walnut pieces for added texture and a nutty taste. Walnuts are also generally the cheapest nut at the grocery store. Store them, and all your nuts, in the freezer for a longer shelf life. Nuts get rancid quickly, especially if they are sitting in your cupboard at room temperature.

MAKES ABOUT 3 DOZEN COOKIES

- ¾ cup (1½ sticks) unsalted butter, at room temperature
- ½ cup granulated sugar
- ½ cup packed dark brown sugar
- 1 large egg
- 1½ teaspoons kosher salt
- 2 teaspoons vanilla extract
- 1 cup plus 2 tablespoons all-purpose flour
- ½ teaspoon baking soda
- 1 (11.5-ounce) bag semi-sweet chocolate chunks
- 1 cup chopped walnuts (optional)

BROWN THE BUTTER: In a small sauté pan set over medium heat, melt 4 tablespoons (½ stick) of the butter, swirling the pan often, until the white bits in the bottom of the pan turn light brown and the butter smells nutty, 2 to 3 minutes. Immediately pour the brown butter into a small bowl and let it cool for at least 10 minutes or up to 30 minutes.

MAKE THE DOUGH: In the bowl of a stand mixer fitted with the paddle attachment, cream the remaining 8 tablespoons (1 stick) butter with the granulated and brown sugars on medium-high speed until smooth, light, and fluffy, 8 to 10 minutes. Add the egg, salt, and vanilla and beat on medium speed until blended. Remove the bowl from the mixer. Sift the flour and baking soda into the bowl, and then stir in the cooled brown butter, stirring only until the mixture is combined and no pockets of unmixed flour remain. Stir in the chocolate chunks and walnuts (if using).

GET READY: Preheat the oven to 350°F. Set oven racks in the upper-middle and lower-middle positions. Line two sheet pans with parchment paper.

BAKE THE COOKIES: Using your hands, roll generous tablespoons of the dough into balls and arrange them on the lined sheet pans, leaving at least 1 inch of space between them (they will spread as they cook). Place the pans in the oven, one on each rack. Bake until the cookies are light brown on the top and edges, 8 to 10 minutes (they'll look a little underdone). Remove the pans from the oven and allow the cookies to cool on the pans for 5 minutes. Then use a metal spatula to transfer them to a wire rack. Let them cool for another 5 to 10 minutes before serving. Store the cookies in a plastic container with a fitted lid at room temperature for up to 2 days.

Dark Chocolate Peanut Butter Bars

These are like the best possible version of a chocolate–peanut butter candy bar. Take a bite and you get a distinct layer of chocolate (not too sweet) and then a distinct layer of peanut butter (creamy, toasty, nutty). It's sublime. I cut these into bars or wedges and keep them in the fridge because I like them best when they're just a little cooler than room temperature. You could also freeze them for a few hours and serve them extra-cold.

For the cookie crumbs, use a chocolatey and not too buttery cookie—I like chocolate wafer cookies. You want a cookie that has a cocoa note but not much else. It's the pleasantly bitter, almost tart, flavor note that serves to break up the sweetness. You can break the cookies up by putting them in a sealed plastic bag and crushing them with a rolling pin or by pulsing them a couple of times in a food processor.

MAKES 16 SLICES

- 11 tablespoons (1 stick plus 3 tablespoons) unsalted butter, melted
- 2 cups (8 to 9 ounces) finely ground chocolate cookie crumbs
- ½ teaspoon ground cinnamon
- 16 ounces full-fat cream cheese, at room temperature
- ½ cup sugar
- 2 large eggs
- ¾ cup (8 ounces) smooth peanut butter
- ½ cup heavy cream
- 3½ ounces semisweet chocolate, finely chopped (a generous ½ cup)

Preheat the oven to 350°F. Position a rack in the center of the oven.

MAKE THE CRUST: Brush the bottom and sides of a 9-inch springform pan with about 1 tablespoon of the melted butter. In a medium bowl, combine the remaining melted butter with the cookie crumbs and cinnamon, and stir to combine. Transfer the crumbs to the buttered pan and press them into an even layer over the bottom of the pan (not up the sides). Use a cup measure or a glass to press the crumbs down firmly. Place the pan in the oven on the center rack and bake until the crust is firm, 15 to 18 minutes. Set the pan aside to let the crust cool for at least 20 minutes. Keep the oven on.

MAKE THE PEANUT BUTTER FILLING: In the bowl of a stand mixer fitted with the paddle attachment, beat the cream cheese and sugar on medium-high speed until completely smooth, 3 to 5 minutes. Add the eggs and peanut butter, and beat on medium-high speed until smooth. Pour the filling over the cooled crust, using a spatula to spread it out evenly, and place the pan back in the oven. Bake until the filling is firm and doesn't jiggle when you gently shake the pan, 12 to 15 minutes. Remove the pan from the oven and set it aside to cool for at least 30 minutes or up to 1 hour.

MAKE THE CHOCOLATE TOP: In a small saucepan, bring the cream to a gentle simmer over medium heat. Place the chopped chocolate in a heatproof bowl, set it over the saucepan like a makeshift double boiler (the bottom of the bowl shouldn't touch the cream), and shut the heat off completely. Stir the chocolate from time to time as it melts. When the cream is warm and the chocolate is somewhat melted, take the bowl off the saucepan, pour the cream over the chocolate, and stir until blended. If the cream and chocolate are at similar temperatures, the result is a glossier ganache! Gently spread the chocolate over the peanut butter layer in the springform pan and refrigerate until the chocolate is firm, at least 2 hours.

SERVE: Unlatch and remove the sides of the springform pan. Warm a knife in hot water, wipe it dry, and cut a narrow wedge of the bar, as you would cut a slice of cake. Repeat, warming the knife and wiping it dry before each cut so the bars look neat and the layers show up distinctly; you should get 16 wedges. The bars can be stored in a sealed plastic container in the refrigerator for up to 2 days.

Bleecker Street Cannoli

This is an iconic dessert for me, so you can imagine the standards I held myself to when creating a homemade version. Of course, the cannoli not only had to compare to those from my favorite Italian bakeries in Little Italy but had to *surpass* them. My two favorite cannoli go-tos in NYC are Ferrara Bakery on Grand Street and Rocco's on Bleecker Street.

I tasted my very first cannoli when my dad brought some home from Rocco's in the classic cardboard bakery box tied a hundred times with red-and-white bakery string. It took him what seemed like five minutes to open the box! He rustled the paper and pulled out the first cannoli. I took a bite—I'll never forget how the crunchy shell collapsed as I bit into it and then tasted the burst of creamy-sweet ricotta studded with chocolate and touched with hints of lemon and cinnamon. I still go down to Rocco's and stand at that same counter and eat that same cannoli. It's a memory I can re-create at that bakery and one that I love to re-create at home for Ava.

A great cannoli really comes together in two parts: there's the shell, which must be thin and crispy, and then the filling, which has to have that flavor of ricotta and light lemon with the crunch of the little chocolate chips. The key to shells that stay crisp is ricotta that isn't too wet—if your ricotta has an excess of liquid, you must drain it in a cheesecloth-lined strainer for at least half an hour before making the filling. To make the shells, you'll need 6 to 8 cannoli molds—metal tubes that you wrap the dough around before frying. You can find them online at baking supply sites or at brick-and-mortar kitchenware stores.

MAKES 20 TO 24 CANNOLI

DOUGH

- 2 cups all-purpose flour, plus extra for rolling the dough
- 1 tablespoon granulated sugar
- 1 teaspoon kosher salt
- 1 tablespoon plus 2 teaspoons unsalted butter, cut into small pieces and chilled
- 1 large egg yolk, lightly beaten
- ⅓ cup dry white wine

MAKE THE DOUGH: In a medium bowl, sift together the flour and granulated sugar. Add the salt. Work the butter pieces in with your fingers until the dough resembles coarse crumbs. Using your hands, work in the egg yolk and white wine until the dough is smooth. Wrap the dough in plastic wrap and let it rest in the refrigerator for a few minutes while you make the filling.

MAKE THE FILLING: Sift together the confectioners' sugar, cinnamon, and allspice in a medium bowl. In another medium bowl, whisk the ricotta until it's smooth. Stir the sugar mixture into the ricotta, mixing until blended. In a third bowl, use a whisk to whip the cream until it is fairly stiff (it's a small amount—I find it easier to whisk by hand than to use a mixer). With a rubber spatula, gently fold the whipped cream into the ricotta mixture. Stir in the chocolate chips and a few light gratings of lemon zest. Cover the bowl with plastic wrap and refrigerate.

GET READY TO FRY: In a medium heavy-bottomed pot, heat the oil over medium heat to 350°F. Make an egg wash by whisking the egg with a splash of cool water in a small bowl; set it aside.

FILLING

- ¾ cup confectioners' sugar, plus more for dusting
- 1 teaspoon ground cinnamon
- ¼ teaspoon ground allspice
- 2 cups ricotta cheese, preferably whole-milk
- ¼ cup heavy cream
- ¼ cup mini semisweet chocolate chips
- 1 lemon

- 1 quart (4 cups) canola oil, for frying, plus extra for greasing the molds
- 1 large egg

FORM THE DOUGH: While the oil is heating, sift an even layer of flour over your work surface and flour a rolling pin. Unwrap the dough and set it on the floured surface. Roll the dough out until it is about ⅛ inch thick. Use a 3- or 4-inch round cookie cutter, the rim of a glass, or small bowl to cut out rounds, as close together as possible, from the dough. You should end up with 20 to 24 rounds. Put a little oil on a paper towel and wipe the outsides of the cannoli molds to lightly grease them. Wrap each round of dough around a mold, then use your finger to dot a little egg wash on the bottom edge before pressing the round over to seal it in place. Use your hands to gently and slightly flare the edges away from the mold.

FRY THE SHELLS: Line a sheet pan with a double layer of paper towels and set it aside. Once the oil hits 350°F, start frying the shells: Using a pair of tongs, hold the end of one pastry-wrapped mold as you submerge it in the oil. Fry the shell until it's crispy and golden brown, 2 to 3 minutes (fry just one at a time until you get the hang of the process). Use tongs to fish out the shell. Cover your hands with a folded kitchen towel to protect them from the heat and immediately, but gently, slide the shell off the mold (the shell has to be removed from the mold immediately after coming out of the oil). Set the shell aside on the paper-towel-lined sheet pan to drain and cool. Repeat with the rest of the dough.

FILL THE SHELLS AND SERVE: Just before serving, transfer the ricotta filling to a pastry bag fitted with a smooth tip and pipe the filling into the cannoli shells. (Alternatively, use a plastic bag with one corner cut off.) Fill the cannoli shells from both sides so that the cream runs the entire length of the shell. Dust the cannoli with confectioners' sugar and serve immediately. You can store the unfilled cannoli shells in a sealed plastic container at room temperature for up to 2 days; the filling can be stored in an airtight container in the refrigerator for up to 2 days as well.

Lentil cookies
for a prince.

Lentil Cookies

These cookies are really unusual. Somehow they remind me of a very special icon I happened to cook for many times at my restaurant, Butter: Prince. Yes, I serve these cookies on my very special Prince plate to remember him. He was a consummate vegetarian and he loved when things had lots of hidden flavor. These cookies are like that. Under the disguise of healthy lentils, the raisins, apricots, cognac, cinnamon, and allspice all work underground to offer many warm flavors. You can glaze them with some melted white chocolate or even a simple caramel.

MAKES 36 TO 40 SMALL COOKIES

- ¾ cup (1½ sticks), plus 1 tablespoon unsalted butter, at room temperature
- ⅔ cup dried brown lentils, rinsed
- 1 cinnamon stick, about 3 inches long
- 1 cup golden raisins
- 2 tablespoons cognac
- 1 cup granulated sugar
- 1 large egg, lightly beaten
- 2 teaspoons ground cinnamon
- ½ teaspoon ground allspice
- 2 teaspoons kosher salt
- 1¼ cups whole-wheat flour
- ¾ cup all-purpose flour
- 1 teaspoon baking powder
- ¼ cup dried apricots, chopped into small pieces
- Confectioners' sugar, for dusting

COOK THE LENTILS: In a medium skillet, melt 1 tablespoon of the butter over medium heat. Add the lentils and cook, stirring with a wooden spoon, until they toast lightly and become coated with the butter, 2 to 3 minutes. Add 3 cups of water and the cinnamon stick, and cook until the lentils are completely tender and all the water has evaporated, 30 to 45 minutes. Discard the cinnamon stick and set ½ cup of the lentils aside in a small bowl. Transfer the remaining lentils to a food processor and process until smooth. Set the pureed lentils aside to cool.

Preheat the oven to 350°F. Arrange oven racks in the upper-middle and lower-middle positions. Line two sheet pans with parchment paper.

MAKE THE BATTER: In a medium bowl, combine the raisins and cognac; set aside. In the bowl of a stand mixer fitted with the paddle attachment, combine the ¾ cup (1½ sticks) butter and the granulated sugar and blend on medium speed until combined. Raise the speed to medium-high and cream the mixture until it is smooth and aerated, 5 to 8 minutes. Add the egg and beat on medium speed until combined. Add the lentil puree, cinnamon, allspice, and salt and beat until incorporated. Remove the bowl from the mixer.

FINISH THE BATTER: Set a sieve over the bowl of batter and sift the whole-wheat flour, all-purpose flour, and baking powder directly into the bowl. Use a rubber spatula to gently combine, and then stir in the reserved whole lentils. Drain the raisins of any excess liquid and stir them into the batter along with the dried apricots.

BAKE THE COOKIES: Scoop about 1 tablespoon of batter and roll it into a ball. Repeat, placing the balls on the prepared sheet pans and leaving at least 1 inch of space between them (you'll have to bake these cookies in batches). Place the sheet pans in the oven, one on each rack, and bake until the cookies are light brown, 12 to 15 minutes.

SERVE: Remove the pans from the oven and allow the cookies to cool on the pans for 2 to 3 minutes. Then use a metal spatula to transfer them to a wire rack. Let the cookies cool for at least 5 to 10 minutes more before dusting with confectioners' sugar and serving. Store the cookies in a plastic container with a fitted lid at room temperature for up to 2 days.

Cherry Almond Cookies

Cherry and almond is one of my favorite combinations. The aroma of almond extract also creates that certain Italian-bakery effect. In fact, whenever I'm baking and I pull a bottle of the extract out of the cabinet, one whiff takes me straight back to childhood. Almond extract in a bakery is like that first sniff of perfume in a department store that sets the tone and makes you want to start shopping. In this case, the extract makes you want to start baking. These cookies are flourless, so the batter can be a bit loose. The taste of them, once they are baked, is worth it.

MAKES ABOUT 20 COOKIES

- 1⅔ cups almond flour
- ½ cup plus 1½ tablespoons granulated sugar
- Grated zest of 1 large lemon
- 1 teaspoon ground ginger
- ¼ teaspoon almond extract
- 1 teaspoon kosher salt
- Scant ½ cup dried cherries, coarsely chopped
- 2 large egg whites
- 1 tablespoon honey
- ½ cup confectioners' sugar

Preheat the oven to 350°F. Set oven racks in the upper-middle and lower-middle positions. Line two sheet pans with parchment paper.

START THE BATTER: Put the almond flour, granulated sugar, lemon zest, ginger, almond extract, salt, and dried cherries in a large bowl and stir to combine.

ADD THE MERINGUE: In the bowl of a stand mixer fitted with the whisk attachment, beat the egg whites and honey on medium-high speed until they reach fairly stiff peaks, 5 to 8 minutes. Using a rubber spatula, gently fold the meringue into the almond flour mixture.

FORM THE COOKIES: Place the confectioners' sugar in a medium bowl. Wet your hands to keep the batter from sticking (and this batter is sticky!), then use your hands to form the batter into 1-tablespoon balls. Flatten the balls slightly into thick coins, roll them generously in the confectioners' sugar, and set them on the prepared sheet pans, leaving 1 inch of space between each cookie and wetting your hands as needed. You should end up with about 20 cookies.

BAKE THE COOKIES: Bake until the cookies are light brown on the top and edges, 10 to 12 minutes. Remove the pans from the oven and allow the cookies to cool on the pans for 2 to 3 minutes. Then use a metal spatula to transfer them to a wire rack. Let the cookies cool for another 5 to 10 minutes before serving. Store the cookies in a plastic container with a fitted lid at room temperature for up to 2 days.

Blondies

I think blondies are more layered, textured, and tasty than their far more famous cousin, brownies. With a blondie, there is room for flavor beyond the taste of chocolate—there is an exciting contrast between the toasted nuts, the salt, and the occasional chocolate chips. For extra-deep flavor, I brown the butter before adding it to the batter. You don't need to get out any fancy equipment to make these. You don't even need a stand mixer. All you need is a bowl, a saucepan, and a spoon.

MAKES 16 TO 24 SQUARES

- 8 tablespoons (1 stick) unsalted butter, plus extra at room temperature for greasing the pan
- 1 cup pecans
- 1 cup all-purpose flour
- ¼ teaspoon baking powder
- ¼ teaspoon baking soda
- 1 teaspoon kosher salt
- ⅔ cup packed dark brown sugar
- ¼ cup granulated sugar
- 1 large egg
- 1 large egg yolk
- 1 tablespoon light corn syrup
- 1 teaspoon vanilla extract
- 1 cup semisweet chocolate chips

Preheat the oven to 350°F. Position a rack in the center of the oven. Line the bottom of an 8-inch square baking dish with two long sheets of foil, allowing an inch or two of excess foil to hang over each edge. Grease the foil with butter.

TOAST THE PECANS: Place the pecans on a rimmed sheet pan and bake until they become toasty and golden brown, 5 to 8 minutes. Transfer the nuts to a plate to cool, then finely chop them.

BROWN THE BUTTER: In a large saucepan, melt the butter over medium heat, then cook, swirling the pan often, until the white bits at the bottom of the pan turn light brown and the butter smells nutty, 2 to 3 minutes. Immediately pour the brown butter into a medium bowl and let it cool for at least 10 minutes.

FINISH THE BATTER: In a large bowl, whisk together the flour, baking powder, baking soda, and salt. To the bowl with the brown butter, add both sugars, egg, egg yolk, corn syrup, and vanilla, and stir to combine. Pour the wet ingredients over the dry ingredients, add the chopped pecans and the chocolate chips, and stir only enough to combine. (The less the batter is mixed, the tenderer the blondie will be.)

BAKE: Pour the batter into the prepared baking dish, spreading it out evenly into the corners, and place the dish in the oven on the center rack. Bake until a small knife inserted into the center of the blondie emerges clean, 30 to 35 minutes. Remove the baking dish from the oven and set it aside to cool for at least 10 to 15 minutes.

SERVE: Grip the overhanging foil and use it to lift the entire blondie square out of the pan. Transfer the blondie to a cutting board and cut it into small squares. Then use a metal spatula to transfer the squares to a wire rack. Let the blondies cool for another 10 to 15 minutes before serving. Store the blondies in a plastic container with a fitted lid at room temperature for up to 2 days.

Pistachio Brittle

I honestly love taking a bite of this brittle, catching the chewy, roasted, salty notes from the pistachios . . . and the unavoidable consequence of them getting stuck in my teeth. It's the perfect reason to take a sip of hot coffee and re-experience all the flavors at once. Besides eating it as is, there is a lot you can do with this brittle. For a dipped effect, try dunking large shards in melted dark chocolate and cooling them, or pulse the brittle in a food processor to break it up into a coarse powder and sprinkle it over ice cream or use it to decorate a frosted cake or cupcakes. I even put wedges of it on a cheese platter next to some fresh fruit.

MAKES ABOUT 1 POUND BRITTLE

Nonstick cooking spray
1⅓ cups sugar
¼ cup light corn syrup
2½ tablespoons unsalted butter
¼ teaspoon almond extract
¼ teaspoon baking soda
2 teaspoons kosher salt
1½ cups roasted, salted, shelled pistachios

MAKE THE BRITTLE: Line a rimmed half sheet pan with parchment paper and spray a spatula (ideally a silicone one) with cooking spray.

In a large nonstick skillet, combine the sugar with ½ cup of water, the corn syrup, butter, and almond extract. Cook over low heat, stirring only occasionally with a wooden spoon, until the sugar melts and turns a light caramel color, 12 to 15 minutes. Remove the pan from the heat and stir in the baking soda, 1 teaspoon of the salt, and the pistachios. Immediately pour the mixture onto the parchment-lined sheet pan and use the greased spatula to spread it out as thin as possible. Sprinkle with the remaining 1 teaspoon salt and set aside for 5 to 10 minutes to cool and harden.

SERVE: Cover the brittle with a layer of plastic wrap or seal it in a large plastic bag, and break it into pieces by hitting it with a rolling pin. Store the brittle in a sealed container at room temperature for up to 3 days.

Coconut-Ginger Tuiles

What I love about thin, wafer-like tuiles is that they stay pliable while they are warm and can be molded into lots of shapes that end up being an edible component of a dessert. *Tuile* means "tile" in French, and this cookie sort of looks like a traditional clay roof tile. You can insert the just-baked tuiles into the cups of a muffin tin to shape them into casual (i.e., not perfect) tart shells that can be filled with pastry cream and fresh strawberries or with chocolate mousse. Or you can turn a tuile into a homemade ice cream cone by wrapping it, hot from the oven and while it is still pliable, around a conical mold or even a small glass. Coconut milk and butter create a rich but light batter, while ground ginger gives the cookie a slight tingle on the palate, one you can't quite place—and that keeps you coming back for more.

MAKES ABOUT 18 TUILES

- 1 cup all-purpose flour
- 1 cup packed dark brown sugar
- 1 teaspoon ground ginger
- 4 tablespoons (½ stick) unsalted butter, melted
- ⅔ cup unsweetened coconut milk
- Nonstick cooking spray

MAKE THE BATTER: In a medium bowl, whisk together the flour, brown sugar, and ginger. Stir in the melted butter and the coconut milk. Whisk the batter until it is smooth, and then set it aside to rest for 10 to 15 minutes.

GET READY: Preheat the oven to 375°F. Line two sheet pans with parchment paper and lightly spray each one with cooking spray.

BAKE: Place a tablespoon of the batter directly on one of the lined sheet pans, and use the back of a spoon to spread it out into an oval about 2 inches wide and 2 to 3 inches long. Spread a few more on the pan, leaving at least 1 inch of space between them. Repeat with the second sheet pan. Place the first pan in the oven and bake until the tuiles are golden brown, 5 to 7 minutes.

SERVE: Act quickly! Using a metal spatula, peel the tuiles off one by one and leave them flat or gently curl them into any shape. If the tuiles harden before you have a chance to shape them, return the sheet pan to the oven for a minute, until they soften again, then continue shaping. Cool the tuiles for a few minutes before serving. Repeat the process with the second pan. You can make the batter in advance and store it in the fridge for up to 2 days. It's best to bake the tuiles only as you need them. The tuiles can be stored in a sealed plastic container at room temperature overnight—that's all.

Raspberry Walnut Rugelach

Rugelach originated in Poland, and the word means "little twists" in Yiddish—I used to enjoy them at friends' houses over the holidays, and now I make them for Ava because they're just so good. The little flaky "twists" are filled with chewy raisins and crunchy walnuts, while the cinnamon-laced raspberry jam offers tang and makes the cookies addictive. You can bake all of the cookies at once, or freeze some of the dough and bake them as needed. I keep the dough in the refrigerator and work with just one portion at a time because when it gets warm, the dough can be difficult to handle. If this happens, rather than struggle, just pop it back in the fridge for a few minutes.

MAKES 2 DOZEN COOKIES

- 1 cup (2 sticks) unsalted butter, at room temperature
- 6 ounces cream cheese, at room temperature
- 2¼ cups all-purpose flour, plus extra for shaping
- ⅓ cup sugar
- 1½ teaspoons ground cinnamon
- ¾ cup seedless raspberry jam
- ¾ cup golden raisins, coarsely chopped
- ¾ cup walnuts, coarsely chopped

MAKE THE DOUGH: In the bowl of a stand mixer fitted with the paddle attachment, cream the butter and cream cheese on high speed until mixed and fluffy, about 2 minutes. Reduce the speed to medium and slowly add the flour, mixing just until it is incorporated. Turn the dough out onto a floured surface and divide it into thirds. Place each third on a piece of plastic wrap and press it to form a round. Enclose each round in the plastic wrap and refrigerate for at least 30 minutes.

MAKE THE CINNAMON SUGAR: In a small bowl, combine the sugar and cinnamon. Set aside.

ROLL THE DOUGH: Line three sheet pans with parchment paper. Lightly flour a rolling pin, the work surface, and the dough itself. Roll one portion of the dough into a 6-inch round that's about ½ inch thick. Use a brush to remove any extra flour from the surface of the dough.

ASSEMBLE: Spread ¼ cup of the jam over the dough, leaving a ½-inch border around the edge. Sprinkle one-third of the cinnamon sugar over the jam. Top it with about one-third of the raisins and one-third of the walnuts. Cut the round into 8 even triangles (like 8 slices of pizza), and roll each triangle from the wide end inward. Place the rugelach on one of the lined sheet pans, leaving 1 inch of space between them and making sure the tips of the triangles are on the bottom. Refrigerate the first pan and repeat with the remaining 2 dough rounds. Refrigerate the rugelach for at least 1 hour or up to 12 hours before baking (or freeze for up to 2 months).

GET READY: Preheat the oven to 350°F. Position a rack in the center of the oven.

BAKE THE COOKIES: Bake one pan of rugelach at a time. Place the pan in the oven on the center rack and bake until light brown, about 10 minutes. Rotate the pan and bake until the bottoms are golden brown, another 10 to 12 minutes. Remove the pan from the oven, set aside to cool slightly, and add another pan to the oven. Transfer the cookies to a wire rack to cool completely. The cookies can be stored in a sealed plastic container at room temperature for up to 3 days.

Jasmine Shortbread

Buttery shortbread comes to life with jasmine tea's floral notes and lemon zest. Don't be afraid to dig a little deep when you zest the lemon: grate the top layer of the skin and then some of the bitter white pith underneath as well. It's nice paired with the tannins from the tea. I keep a log of this dough in my freezer at all times for a slice-and-bake moment, such as when I need something sweet to serve on the fly or something fresh-baked and homey to bring to a friend's house.

MAKES 30 TO 36 COOKIES

- 2 cups all-purpose flour
- ½ teaspoon ground allspice
- 1 teaspoon kosher salt
- ½ cup plus 2 tablespoons confectioners' sugar
- 2 jasmine tea bags, cut open
- Grated zest and some bitter pith of 1 large lemon
- 2 teaspoons vanilla extract
- 1 cup (2 sticks) unsalted butter, cubed and chilled

MAKE THE DOUGH: In a food processor fitted with the metal blade, combine the flour, allspice, salt, confectioners' sugar, and the contents of the tea bags, and pulse to blend. Pulse in the lemon zest, vanilla, butter, and 1 tablespoon of water. Continue to pulse until the dough forms a loose ball. Do not overmix or the shortbread will be tough and chewy.

ROLL: Place a piece of plastic wrap on your work surface and place half of the dough on top. Mold and roll the dough into a 2-inch-thick log, and enclose it in the plastic wrap. Flatten the log against the counter on four sides to square it off. Repeat with the remaining dough. Refrigerate the dough logs for at least 30 minutes and up to 4 hours.

GET READY: Preheat the oven to 350°F. Set oven racks in the upper-middle and lower-middle positions. Line two sheet pans with parchment paper.

BAKE THE COOKIES: Slice the logs crosswise into ½-inch-thick slices and place the squares of dough on the prepared sheet pans, leaving at least 1 inch of space between them so they have room to spread. Place one sheet pan on the upper rack and the other on the lower rack and bake until the shortbread squares are light brown on the tops and edges, 8 to 10 minutes. Remove the pans from the oven and let the cookies cool on the pans for at least 5 to 10 minutes. Then use a metal spatula to transfer them to a wire rack. Let them cool for another 5 to 10 minutes before serving. Store the cookies in a plastic container with a fitted lid at room temperature for up to 2 days.

Dark Chocolate–Dipped "Pretzel" Butter Cookies

Making these pretzel-shaped butter cookies is a fun activity to do with kids. Ava and I have made them together, and to be honest, she shapes a far better pretzel than I do. A cookie plate needs variety, and this changes up the classic butter cookie with an unusual shape and some pleasant bitterness from that quick dunk in dark chocolate. It's also a fun cookie to eat, with its twists and curves and the crunch from the coarse sugar. You can also dunk the baked cookies in white chocolate for a richer version.

MAKES 30 TO 36 COOKIES

½ cup whole blanched almonds

1¾ cups all-purpose flour, plus 2 tablespoons for rolling

⅓ cup confectioners' sugar

1 teaspoon kosher salt

1 large egg, lightly beaten

¾ cup (1½ sticks) unsalted butter, chilled and cubed

Grated zest of 1 large lemon

¼ cup whole milk

8 ounces bittersweet chocolate (70% cacao), coarsely chopped

½ cup coarse sugar or pearl sugar

Preheat the oven to 350°F.

TOAST THE ALMONDS: Place the almonds on a rimmed sheet pan and bake until they become toasty and golden brown, 5 to 8 minutes. Transfer the almonds to a plate to cool.

MAKE THE DOUGH: In a medium bowl, mix together the flour, confectioners' sugar, and salt. In a food processor fitted with the metal blade, pulse the cooled almonds until they resemble coarse meal. Add the flour mixture and pulse to blend. Then pulse in the egg, butter, and lemon zest until combined. Place half of the dough on a piece of plastic wrap and enclose it in the wrap. Repeat with the other half. Refrigerate the dough for at least 1 hour and up to 4 hours.

GET READY: Preheat the oven to 350°F. Set oven racks in the upper-middle and lower-middle positions. Line two sheet pans with parchment paper.

FORM THE COOKIES: Remove one of the dough halves from the fridge. On a floured surface, roll the dough into a 1-inch-thick log, and then slice the log crosswise into 16 equal pieces. Roll each of those pieces into a log about 7 inches long. Press down on each end of one of the logs to flatten them. Now shape the log as if you were bringing the ends together into a circle, but cross each end up and over the other, forming a pretzel shape. Place the shaped cookie on one of the lined sheet pans, and repeat with the remaining dough logs, leaving at least 1 inch of space between them. Once the first sheet pan is full, place it in the refrigerator. Remove the second ball of dough from the fridge, and repeat the process, placing the second batch of "pretzels" on the second lined sheet pan.

BAKE: Set one sheet pan on the upper rack and the other on the lower rack, and bake the cookies for 6 minutes. Open the oven, rotate the pans, and bake until they are light brown, 6 to 8 additional minutes. Remove the pans from the oven and let the cookies cool for 5 minutes. Then use a metal spatula to transfer them to a wire rack. Cool the cookies for another 30 minutes before dipping them in the chocolate.

MELT THE CHOCOLATE AND DIP THE COOKIES: Line a sheet pan with parchment paper. In a medium saucepan, warm the milk over medium heat; then add the chocolate and stir until it melts. Transfer the chocolate to a small bowl and dunk the top of each cookie in the warm chocolate to coat. (Alternatively, dunk half of each cookie in the chocolate.) Arrange the cookies on the prepared sheet pan, sprinkle with the coarse sugar, and let stand at room temperature for at least 15 minutes for the chocolate to set. Store the cookies in a plastic container with a fitted lid at room temperature for up to 2 days.

FRUIT CRISPS, CRUMBLES & CUSTARDS

In this chapter you'll find a lot of fruit, sometimes mixed with herbs, tea, or even jam. These recipes are exciting because in addition to flavor, we're experiencing the wonderful textures that dessert can offer. Like a luxurious crème brûlée or flan, a Jell-O cake hearkens back to the 1970s, and the tender/crisp balance of a fruit crumble. There are some cool risks we take, like layering a chocolate custard on top of a layer of vanilla custard to make a silky dessert oddly reminiscent of the flavors of a Boston cream doughnut or a black-and-white cookie. This is about Americana and those classic, nostalgic feelings we turn to throughout our lives. These are desserts that you generally serve family-style. Put the dish in the center of the table, let people ooh and ahh, and don't forget to take a little bow.

Blueberry Crumble

My mother made blueberry crumble throughout my childhood, mostly in the summer when blueberries were in season. My mom's a New England gal and she grew up eating bowls of summer blueberries in a pool of heavy cream; in fact, she would often eat a small bowlful while she was baking this dessert. Lighter and crunchier than a cobbler, a crumble is topped with buttery spiced bread crumbs rather than biscuits. Mom made her own bread crumbs, but I happen to love the texture of panko and it saves me a step, too. I also veer from her recipe by adding red wine vinegar and blueberry jam to the filling, and by cooking the blueberries to intensify their flavor *before* assembling and baking the crumble. I like baking this in a 4-quart rectangular baking dish that offers ample surface area for more crunchy topping.

SERVES 10 TO 12

- 10 tablespoons (1¼ sticks) unsalted butter, chilled, plus 1 tablespoon at room temperature for greasing the baking dish
- 2 pounds (about 7 cups) fresh blueberries
- 1 tablespoon red wine vinegar
- 1 cup blueberry jam
- 3 cups packed dark brown sugar
- 1 teaspoon kosher salt
- Grated zest and juice of 1 large lemon
- 1½ cups panko bread crumbs
- 1 teaspoon ground cinnamon
- ⅛ teaspoon ground nutmeg (preferably freshly grated)
- ⅛ teaspoon ground allspice
- ¼ teaspoon ground cloves

Preheat the oven to 350°F. Position a rack in the center of the oven. Grease a 10 by 15-inch baking dish with the room-temperature butter.

SAUTÉ THE BLUEBERRIES: Heat a large sauté pan over medium heat and add 1 tablespoon of the chilled butter. Sauté half of the blueberries over medium heat until they start to release their liquid, 2 to 3 minutes. Transfer the berries to a large bowl. Repeat with another 1 tablespoon of the chilled butter and the remaining blueberries. Set the cooked berries aside.

MAKE THE FILLING: In a large bowl, gently stir together the red wine vinegar, jam, ½ cup of the brown sugar, ½ teaspoon of the salt, the lemon zest and juice, and the cooked blueberries. Set the filling aside.

MAKE THE TOPPING: Cut 8 tablespoons (1 stick) of the butter into cubes and place them in a large bowl. Add the bread crumbs and use your hands to work them together until the mixture resembles coarse crumbs. Add the remaining ½ teaspoon salt and 2½ cups brown sugar and the cinnamon, nutmeg, allspice, and cloves. Continue to work the ingredients in with your hands until the mixture looks like wet, buttery sand.

ASSEMBLE: Spread the filling in the dish and top it with the spiced bread crumbs.

BAKE: Cover the dish tightly with foil and place it in the oven on the center rack. Bake until the topping is cooked and tender, 12 to 15 minutes. Remove the foil and raise the oven temperature to 425°F. Bake until the top browns, 8 to 10 minutes. Let the crumble cool in the baking dish and serve it warm or at room temperature.

Peach Crisp

WITH CHAMOMILE

The undertone of apricot jam in this peach crisp adds a flavor that reminds me of the intensity of eating a peach as a child, the kind of peach where you bite into it and the juice drips down to your elbow. I prefer yellow peaches; I think they have more natural peach flavor than white peaches. All the same, buy what looks best. The cinnamon and the chamomile are such great flavors to pair with this fruit, giving both acidity and warmth. Serve the crisp with vanilla, salted caramel, or pistachio ice cream or even lemon sorbet. Note: My mother has made this with half fresh peaches and half canned (drained) peaches, too.

SERVES 8 TO 10

8 yellow peaches (about 3 pounds), halved, pitted, and each half cut into 8 equal wedges

1 cup apricot jam

2½ cups packed dark brown sugar

1 tablespoon blackstrap molasses

Grated zest and juice of 1 large lemon (you'll need 2 tablespoons grated zest)

Grated zest and juice of 1 large orange

2 teaspoons kosher salt

1 teaspoon ground cinnamon

⅛ teaspoon ground nutmeg (preferably freshly grated)

2 chamomile tea bags

1½ cups all-purpose flour

¾ cup (1½ sticks) unsalted butter, chilled and cubed, plus 1 tablespoon at room temperature for greasing the baking dish

Preheat the oven to 375°F. Position a rack in the center of the oven.

MAKE THE FILLING: Put the peach slices in a bowl and toss them with the apricot jam, ½ cup of the brown sugar, the molasses, lemon juice, 1 tablespoon of the lemon zest, the orange zest and juice, 1 teaspoon of the salt, the cinnamon, and the nutmeg. Cut the tea bags open and sprinkle the tea over the mixture. Toss to combine.

MAKE THE TOPPING: In another bowl, combine the flour and the remaining 2 cups brown sugar and 1 teaspoon salt. Add the cubed butter to the bowl and break it up with your fingers, integrating the flour with the butter until it forms crumbs the size of small peas. Refrigerate.

ASSEMBLE: Grease the bottom and sides of a 9 by 11-inch baking dish with the room-temperature butter. Add the peach filling and any juices from the bowl to the baking dish and sprinkle the topping over it evenly.

BAKE: Place the baking dish in the oven on the center rack and bake until the fruit is tender when pierced with the tip of a knife and the topping is golden brown, 40 to 45 minutes. Set the dish aside to cool for a few minutes before serving. Top the crisp with the remaining tablespoon of lemon zest.

Seventies Raspberry Jell-O "Cake"

This is a classic Jell-O mold from the seventies, which has a special place in my heart because it hearkens back to a time of bell-bottomed jeans, sandy beach picnics, and no cell phones. My mom made this only once or twice when I was a kid—and when she did it looked like she had achieved the impossible. You have to start by admitting to yourself that you love the way tangy Jell-O mixes with fresh fruit and whipped cream. Here, I elevate this childhood throwback by adding red wine for a tart note and cranberry sauce for bitterness, plus mint for freshness. Lining the Bundt pan with plastic wrap creates a barrier between the pan and the fruit, making the "cake" far easier to unmold. Slice this into thick pieces and serve them with the unsweetened whipped cream. The cream will counter the sweetness of the Jell-O. It's also oddly delicious with a scoop of vanilla ice cream or lemon sorbet.

SERVES 8 TO 10

- 1 (750mL) bottle fruity red wine, such as Merlot or Cabernet Sauvignon
- 1 cup sugar
- 3 (3½-ounce) boxes raspberry Jell-O
- 2¼ cups boiling water
- 1 (14-ounce) can jellied cranberry sauce, chopped into small pieces
- 2 pints fresh raspberries
- ½ cup medium-size fresh mint leaves, plus extra for serving
- 1½ cups unsweetened whipped cream (recipe follows)

REDUCE THE RED WINE: In a medium saucepan, combine the red wine and the sugar, and simmer over medium heat until it has reduced to ¾ cup, 18 to 20 minutes. Turn off the heat and cover the pot to keep the reduction warm.

MAKE THE JELL-O: In a large bowl, combine the Jell-O with the boiling water and the still-warm reduced red wine. Stir until the Jell-O granules have dissolved. Add the cranberry sauce to the hot mixture and stir until it has melted.

MOLD THE DESSERT, PART 1: Place a 6-cup Bundt mold on a sheet pan and line it with a layer of plastic wrap that overhangs the edges of the mold. Scatter 1 cup of the raspberries over the bottom of the mold. Gently pour half of the Jell-O mixture over the fruit, taking care not to disturb its placement (you can pour the mixture into a liquid measuring cup if that helps you retain control), adding just enough to cover the layer of fruit. Place the Bundt mold, on the sheet pan, on a shelf in the center of the refrigerator. Chill for 1 hour.

MOLD THE DESSERT, PART 2: Remove the Bundt mold from the fridge. Gently arrange another cup of the raspberries on top of the set Jell-O layer. Add mint leaves wherever there are gaps between the berries. Pour the remaining Jell-O mixture carefully over the fruit. Gently reposition any fruit or mint leaves that moved when you poured it in. Return the mold to the sheet pan in the refrigerator and chill it for another hour.

SERVE: Invert the Bundt mold onto a serving platter and remove the mold from the "cake." Top the "cake" with more mint leaves and arrange the remaining raspberries in the center. Serve it in slices, topped with whipped cream. The "cake" will keep, covered, in the refrigerator for up to 3 days.

recipe continues

WHIPPED CREAM

This is such a simple recipe: Whip the cream with sugar (or without) and you're done. You can vary the amount of sugar you put in the cream according to how sweet a dessert you pair it with. Sometimes I call for unsweetened whipped cream because the dessert is already very sweet. For example, I like unsweetened cream with the Key Lime Pie on page 309. For best results, chill the metal mixer bowl and the whisk in the freezer so that you begin with ice-cold cream, which will whip up more quickly. You can double or halve the recipe as needed.

MAKES 1½ TO 2 CUPS

1 cup heavy cream, chilled

2 tablespoons sugar (optional)

In the bowl of a stand mixer fitted with the whisk attachment (or in a large metal bowl using a whisk or a handheld mixer), beat the cream and sugar (if using) until the cream reaches stiff peaks.

Use right away or store in an airtight container in the refrigerator for up to 12 hours. When you are ready to serve it, simply whisk the cream a few times to fluff up the texture.

Crème Caramel

WITH APRICOT JAM

This is a classic from my childhood. My mother would somehow pull off a dessert like this on a weeknight! The hardest part for me was waiting for the custard to cool and set up enough to eat. The moment when you lift off the ramekin and the custard slips out, with the caramel pooling almost poetically around it, is so dramatic. It's also great with fresh strawberries in place of the apricot jam.

SERVES 8

1¾ cups sugar
5 large eggs
1 teaspoon kosher salt, plus extra for serving
3 cups whole milk
2 teaspoons vanilla extract
3 to 4 tablespoons apricot jam

MAKE THE CARAMEL: Add 1 cup of the sugar and ⅓ cup of water to a medium stainless-steel saucepan, swirling the pan to blend them together. Cook over medium heat, without stirring, until the liquid forms a clear syrup, 3 to 5 minutes. Continue cooking, watching it constantly and swirling the pan occasionally, until the caramel turns an amber to golden-brown color, 3 to 5 minutes. Carefully remove the pan from the heat and pour a little of the caramel over the bottom of eight 6-ounce ramekins. You want to pour the caramel on the bottom and not so much on the sides. (If the caramel hardens slightly and is hard to pour, simply warm it up again to loosen it.) Set the ramekins aside long enough for the caramel to harden and cool, about 20 minutes.

Preheat the oven to 325°F.

MAKE THE CUSTARD: In a medium bowl, whisk the eggs with the remaining ¾ cup sugar and the salt. In a medium saucepan, bring the milk to a gentle simmer over medium heat. Add the vanilla, and then pour the hot milk over the egg mixture, whisking to blend and ensuring that the sugar completely dissolves. Pour the custard into a large liquid measuring cup and evenly distribute it over the caramel in the ramekins.

BAKE THE CUSTARDS: Set the ramekins in a baking dish or roasting pan and carefully fill the baking dish about one-third full with warm water. Cover the baking dish with foil, crimping it tightly around the sides. Poke a few holes in the foil to allow steam to escape as the custards bake. Place the baking dish in the oven and bake until the custards are firm in the center, 40 to 45 minutes (shake a ramekin to make sure the custard isn't liquidy). Remove the baking dish from the oven, set it on a flat surface, and use tongs to carefully lift the ramekins from the water bath. Set them aside to cool for 15 minutes at room temperature, and then refrigerate until fully chilled, 3 to 4 hours or up to 12 hours (if refrigerating for more than a few hours, cover each ramekin with plastic wrap).

SERVE: Carefully run a small knife around the edge of each ramekin. Turn each ramekin upside down onto a small plate and shake it a little to unmold the custard. The caramel should ooze out over the custard. Top with a spoonful of apricot jam and the tiniest pinch of salt before serving.

Chocolate and Honey-Vanilla Crème Brûlée

Crème brûlée, French for "burned cream," is a classic that never goes out of style. One of the very first desserts I made in a professional kitchen was a raspberry crème brûlée. The fruit was hidden beneath the custard like a treasure—I loved the way the raspberry seeds created such a subtle and wonderful texture. Here, instead of raspberries, I bury chocolate beneath the vanilla cream, like a rich, dark secret. The honey almost acts like a translator, enabling the vanilla and chocolate to talk to each other. The only way for the honey-vanilla custard not to sink and combine with the chocolate custard is to pour it on top while the custard is frozen! Have patience with this one . . . you'll be rewarded.

SERVES 6

CHOCOLATE CUSTARD

3 large egg yolks

4 tablespoons sugar

½ teaspoon kosher salt

2 tablespoons unsweetened Dutch-process cocoa powder

1 cup heavy cream

2 teaspoons vanilla extract

HONEY-VANILLA CUSTARD

1 cup heavy cream

¼ cup honey

1 teaspoon vanilla extract

3 large egg yolks

2 tablespoons sugar

BRÛLÉE TOPPING

¾ to 1 cup sugar

MAKE THE CHOCOLATE CUSTARD: In a heatproof medium bowl, whisk the egg yolks with 2 tablespoons of the sugar and the salt; set aside. In a small bowl, whisk the remaining 2 tablespoons sugar with the cocoa powder; set aside.

In a medium saucepan set over medium heat, bring the cream and vanilla to a simmer. Turn off the heat and whisk in the cocoa-sugar mixture until it has dissolved, then slowly whisk half of this hot chocolate-cream mixture into the egg mixture to temper the eggs. Then whisk in the rest of the chocolate-cream mixture. Pour the custard into six 6-ounce ramekins. Cover the tops with plastic wrap and freeze the custards for *at least* 8 hours or up to 12 hours.

MAKE THE HONEY-VANILLA CUSTARD: In a medium saucepan, combine the cream, honey, and vanilla and bring the mixture to a simmer over medium heat. In a medium bowl, whisk the egg yolks and sugar together until smooth. Slowly whisk half of the hot cream mixture into the yolks to temper the eggs, and then whisk in the remaining cream. Set the custard aside to cool for 15 minutes.

Preheat the oven to 325°F.

COMBINE THE CUSTARDS: Remove the ramekins from the freezer and slowly pour the honey-vanilla custard over the chocolate custard, filling the ramekins almost to the top.

BAKE THE CUSTARDS: Place the ramekins in a baking dish, leaving some space between them, then fill the baking dish about one-third full with warm water. Cover the baking dish with foil, crimping it around the sides. Poke a few holes in the foil to allow steam to escape as the custards bake. Place the baking dish in the oven and bake for 20 minutes. Then

recipe continues

carefully lift the foil to release any steam, replace the foil, and bake until the custards are firm but still slightly jiggly in the center, 10 to 15 minutes. Remove the baking dish from the oven and use a pair of tongs to carefully lift the ramekins from the water bath. Set them aside to cool at room temperature for 15 minutes, and then refrigerate them for at least 1 hour or up to 12 hours (if refrigerating for more than a few hours, cover each ramekin tightly with plastic wrap).

BRÛLÉE AND SERVE: Sprinkle each custard with an even layer of sugar (about 2 tablespoons per ramekin), and use a kitchen torch to burn the sugar to somewhere between amber and dark brown.

Alternatively, if you don't have a torch, place an oven rack 2 inches from the broiler element and preheat the broiler. Place the ramekins on a sheet pan and set them under the broiler to caramelize the sugar. This will take 2 to 3 minutes, but watch the custards closely since broiler intensities vary. Remove the sheet pan from the broiler and set it aside for a few minutes to allow the hot sugar top to cool and harden. (You always have the option to serve this crème brûlée without the burnt sugar topping on it. In that case, it's a delicious two-layer custard.)

Serve the crème brûlée with small spoons to crack the burnt sugar topping.

TARTS, PIES & DESSERTS À LA MODE”

Pies and tarts never go out of style. I consider tarts to be more of a French bistro dessert, while pies seem so American to me. I first fell in love with tarts as a teenager. I went to France with my parents and marveled at how restaurants often put out a spread of fruit tarts on the table near the entrance. You are thinking about dessert before the meal has begun! My dad would always walk in, pull the waiter aside, and “reserve” his preferred slice of tart. I don’t think he would have been able to relax otherwise. He did this at diners, too, with large slabs of pie. I think of pie seasonally. The pumpkin pie means fall and Thanksgiving are in full swing. A blueberry or cherry pie means I have likely just finished the last bites of a sandy PB&J sandwich at the beach. Of course, nothing tops off a pie (or tart) better than ice cream or sorbet, so naturally I include some fun options here (as well as stand-alone ice cream desserts). These are all the types of dessert that you make in advance—or at least have all of the elements at the ready—so you can imagine eating it before you have even begun to cook the main meal! There are also parts of recipes that you can use for a larger dessert, for example, a caramel that can go on ice cream.

Pink Grapefruit Sorbet

WITH EARL GREY CARAMEL

This was inspired by a dish that I'd watch Guy Savoy eat every night before service at his restaurant in Paris: a scoop of Earl Grey tea sorbet on top of a spoonful of vanilla custard sauce. It was so interesting to me, like a variation on a cup of sweet tea with cream! This pink grapefruit sorbet is really tasty and light, and the caramel is so unique tinged with the tea. I like to use the caramel in other places, too, like drizzled on ice cream or cookies.

MAKES ABOUT 1 QUART SORBET AND ½ CUP CARAMEL

SORBET

- 1 quart (4 cups) freshly squeezed pink grapefruit juice, at room temperature
- ¼ cup sugar
- ¼ cup light corn syrup
- 6 grates of lemon zest
- 1 tablespoon fresh lemon juice

CARAMEL

- 3 Earl Grey tea bags
- ¾ cup sugar
- 2 teaspoons light corn syrup

MAKE THE SORBET: In a medium saucepan, combine 1 cup of the pink grapefruit juice with the sugar and corn syrup. Bring to a simmer over medium heat, whisking until all of the ingredients are combined, 2 to 3 minutes. Remove the pan from the heat and transfer the mixture to a medium bowl. Whisk in the remaining 3 cups grapefruit juice and the lemon zest and juice. Refrigerate for 30 minutes.

Churn the grapefruit sorbet in an ice cream machine according to the manufacturer's instructions. Transfer the sorbet to the freezer and let it harden for at least 1 hour or up to 8 hours.

STEEP THE TEA: In a small saucepan, bring ¾ cup of water to a boil. Turn off the heat and add the tea bags. Allow them to steep for 10 minutes to create a strong tea flavor. Discard the tea bags and pour the brewed tea into a medium saucepan.

FINISH THE CARAMEL: Add the sugar and corn syrup to the pan with the tea and bring to a simmer over medium heat (don't stir it). Simmer, stirring with a clean wooden spoon, until the mixture forms a fairly thick, light-amber caramel, 5 to 8 minutes. Remove the pan from the heat.

SERVE: Scoop the sorbet into individual serving bowls and drizzle with the caramel.

Chocolate, Caramel, and Praline Sundae

While I am providing a recipe here for the way I like to build a sundae, there really aren't any rules to follow other than making it the way you love to eat it—and for me that means homemade sauces. I am all for homemade sauces because you can better control and develop the sweetness and richness and vary the textures. I think this is especially true for chocolate sauce, which has to have the right balance of bitter and sweet, and when made right, can be as satisfying as a fantastic cup of morning coffee. I like to keep a small batch of the hot fudge sauce and the caramel sauce in the door of the fridge (it keeps for a good month, though it doesn't usually last that long) so I'm always prepared to whip up a dessert when friends come over—or even when I am home alone and want to treat myself! You can also make this into a giant sundae and serve it family-style in the center of the table with lots of spoons for sharing.

MAKES 4 TO 6 SUNDAES OR 1 GIANT ONE (1 CUP CHOCOLATE SAUCE; ¾ CUP CARAMEL SAUCE; ¾ CUP CRUSHED PRALINE)

CHOCOLATE SAUCE

½ cup heavy cream

1 tablespoon unsalted butter

½ cup (4 to 5 ounces) chopped semisweet chocolate

1 tablespoon dark rum

CARAMEL SAUCE

½ cup sugar

4 tablespoons (½ stick) unsalted butter

¼ cup heavy cream

2 teaspoons vanilla extract

⅛ teaspoon kosher salt

MAKE THE CHOCOLATE SAUCE: In a medium saucepan set over medium heat, bring the heavy cream to a gentle simmer. Remove the pan from the heat and whisk in the butter, chocolate, and rum. Stir until smooth and set aside.

MAKE THE CARAMEL SAUCE: Spread the sugar in a thin, even layer over the bottom of a small heavy-bottomed saucepan. Slowly pour in ¼ cup of water. Bring the mixture to a simmer over low heat and cook until it is light golden brown, 15 to 20 minutes. Remove the pan from the heat and add the butter, cream, vanilla, and salt. Then return the pan to low heat and simmer, stirring often, until the ingredients come together, 2 to 3 minutes. Remove from the heat and set aside.

MAKE THE PRALINE: Coat a rimmed sheet pan generously with cooking spray. In a medium heavy-bottomed saucepan, combine ½ cup of water with the sugar and cream of tartar. Bring the mixture to a gentle simmer over medium heat. Using a candy thermometer or instant-read thermometer, bring the mixture to 236°F and then stir in the walnuts, coating the nuts with the caramel. Immediately turn the praline out onto the prepared sheet pan, tilting the pan to encourage it to spread out. Set the praline aside to cool completely, about 30 minutes. Then turn the praline out onto a cutting board and crush it into bits by chopping it with a knife. Alternatively, transfer the praline to a food processor and pulse to break it up. Transfer the crushed praline to a medium bowl.

PRALINE

- Nonstick cooking spray
- ¼ cup sugar
- ⅛ teaspoon cream of tartar
- ½ cup walnut halves

FOR THE SUNDAE

- 1 pint vanilla ice cream
- ¾ cup fresh strawberries, hulled and sliced
- Whipped cream (page 294)
- 12 marshmallows (or more mini marshmallows)

ASSEMBLE INDIVIDUAL SUNDAES: Using an ice cream scoop or a large spoon, form 3 generous scoops of vanilla ice cream, roll them through the chopped praline, and then arrange them together in a sundae dish. Serve the caramel sauce, strawberries, whipped cream, marshmallows, and chocolate sauce in bowls on the side so people can assemble their sundaes as they like. Store the praline in a plastic container with a fitted lid at room temperature. The caramel sauce and chocolate sauce should be stored separately in covered containers in the refrigerator.

Pear, Banana, and Dark Rum Tart

My dad worked as a waiter for two years when he was just out of school. He was, as he proudly described it, "the main flambé captain in the dining room of the Garden City Hotel." That meant he was in charge of cooking all of the classic desserts tableside: cherries jubilee, crêpes suzette, and, his favorite, bananas Foster. Considering this was the only time either of my parents ever touched the restaurant industry, I thought I would make a tart celebrating some of those flavors in his honor. Because Dad loved pears so much, I wanted to include them, imagining that the meaty, sweet fruit would be wonderful with the flavors of banana and rum. I like Bosc or Anjou pears for this because they are tasty and stay firm when baked. If you're feeling ambitious, use twice the number of smaller Forelle pears instead: the presentation, with lots of the smaller pear halves, is dramatic.

The banana-rum filling replaces a more traditional cream filling with a fruity and slightly boozy center. This makes the ice cream or whipped cream you serve alongside even tastier.

SERVES 10 TO 12

CRUST

- 6 tablespoons (¾ stick) unsalted butter, melted, plus 1 tablespoon at room temperature for greasing the pan
- 1½ cups (12 to 14 ounces) slivered almonds, finely ground in a food processor
- ¾ cup granulated sugar

FILLING

- Scant ½ cup dark rum
- 1 cup packed dark brown sugar
- 1 tablespoon vanilla extract
- 8 tablespoons (1 stick) unsalted butter
- 4 medium-size ripe bananas, peeled
- Kosher salt

Preheat the oven to 375°F. Position a rack in the center of the oven. Grease the sides and bottom of a 9-inch tart pan with a removable bottom with the room-temperature butter.

MAKE THE CRUST: In a medium bowl, mix together the melted butter, ground almonds, and granulated sugar until the mixture resembles coarse crumbs. Add the crumbs to the buttered tart pan and spread them out evenly, using the bottom of a drinking glass or measuring cup to press the crumbs into a solid, even layer over the bottom of the pan and up the sides. (The sides are not high on this tart; the crumbs should rise just high enough to hold the fruit—they may not reach the top of the pan.) Place the tart pan on a sheet pan, put it in the oven on the center rack, and bake until the crust is firm and golden brown, 15 to 18 minutes. Remove the tart pan from the oven and set it aside; keep the oven on.

MAKE THE RUM MIXTURE: In a small saucepan, combine the rum, brown sugar, and vanilla. Bring the mixture to a simmer over medium heat and stir to dissolve the brown sugar. Shut off the heat and cover the pan to keep the mixture warm.

FINISH THE FILLING: In a medium skillet, melt the butter over medium heat, then cook, swirling the pan often, until the white bits on the bottom of the pan turn light brown and the butter smells nutty, 2 to 3 minutes. Add the whole bananas, arranging them in a single layer. Sprinkle the bananas with a tiny pinch of salt and cook on one side until they have softened, 3 to 5 minutes. Turn them over and cook for an additional minute. Remove the skillet from the heat and pour the rum mixture over

recipe and ingredients continue

PEARS

1 cup granulated sugar

2 tablespoons blackstrap molasses

1 teaspoon ground cinnamon

1 teaspoon ground ginger

6 medium-size ripe Bosc or Anjou pears (about 2½ pounds), unpeeled, halved and cored

1 tablespoon red wine vinegar

Whipped cream (page 294) or ice cream, for serving

the bananas. Add 2 tablespoons of water, return the skillet to the heat, and cook until the bananas become tender, 3 to 5 minutes. Mash the bananas into the rum mixture with the tines of a fork, and set it aside to cool.

COOK THE PEARS: In a large ovenproof skillet, heat the granulated sugar over low heat until it melts and turns a very light brown, 10 to 12 minutes. Carefully remove the skillet from the heat and add the molasses, cinnamon, and ginger. Arrange the pear halves, flesh-side down, in a single layer on top. Return the skillet to medium heat and cook, moving the pears around from time to time with a wooden spoon, until they brown and start to soften, 10 to 12 minutes. Add the vinegar and carefully transfer the skillet to the oven. Bake until the pears are tender when pierced with the tip of a knife, 8 to 10 minutes. (Pears vary in cooking time according to ripeness and variety; when they are cooked, the knife will slip in and out of the pears with little effort.) Remove the skillet from the oven and set it aside to cool.

ASSEMBLE THE TART: Remove the ring from the edge of the tart pan. Place the tart crust (still attached to the pan bottom) on a serving platter. Spoon the banana-rum filling into the crust, leaving a 1-inch border. Top with the pears in a single layer, flesh-side up, and pour the cooking liquid from the pears over them. Let the tart set for about 1 hour at room temperature before serving.

SERVE: Serve the tart at room temperature, topping each slice with whipped cream or ice cream. Serve at room temperature. Leftover tart will keep in the refrigerator for a day or two.

Lemon Cream Tart

Though I will always consider myself a lifelong native New Yorker, I was born in St. Louis and we moved to NYC when I was ten days old. My mother told me one of the things she missed most about my true hometown was its signature gooey butter cake. I kept that cake in mind while working on this tart, which reminds me of a butter cake because it has a sturdy crust and a gooey, sugary center. My family *loves* lemon and tartness, so this mash-up makes perfect sense to me: the flavors of a butter cake and the tart and creamy notes of a lemon tart. This can be served with dollops of lightly whipped cream or with fresh berries on top. The tart is also a good foil for a puckery sorbet like pineapple or lime or even Pink Grapefruit Sorbet (page 300).

SERVES 8 TO 10

- ¾ cup (1½ sticks) unsalted butter, at room temperature, plus 1 tablespoon for greasing the pan
- ½ cup confectioners' sugar
- 5 large egg yolks
- 1½ cups all-purpose flour, plus more for rolling
- ½ cup plus 3 tablespoons heavy cream
- 3 large lemons
- ¾ cup plus 1½ tablespoons granulated sugar
- Whipped cream (page 294), for serving

MAKE THE DOUGH: In the bowl of a stand mixer fitted with the paddle attachment, mix the ¾ cup (1½ sticks) butter and confectioners' sugar on low speed just until blended. Mix in 2 of the egg yolks, one by one, blending after each addition. Add the flour and 2 tablespoons of the cream and blend until the flour is barely incorporated—it should look like a batter in which the ingredients are not fully mixed together. The goal is not to overmix, so it will yield a tender crust. Place the dough on a piece of plastic wrap, place another piece of plastic wrap on top, and flatten the dough into a ½-inch-thick disk. Enclose the dough in the plastic wrap and refrigerate it.

MAKE THE FILLING: Grate the zest of one of the lemons, and then juice all of the lemons, straining the juice through a fine-mesh sieve into a medium bowl to remove any pulp or seeds. In another medium bowl, whisk together the remaining 3 yolks and the granulated sugar. Whisk in the lemon zest and juice and the remaining ½ cup plus 1 tablespoon cream. Cover with plastic wrap and refrigerate.

Preheat the oven to 350°F. Grease the sides and bottom of a 9-inch tart pan with the 1 tablespoon room-temperature butter.

ROLL AND BAKE THE TART SHELL: Set the dough on a flat, lightly floured surface and, using a rolling pin, roll the dough into a 9- to 10-inch round that is about ⅛ inch thick. Fit the dough into the prepared tart pan, pressing it into the corners and sides, and pinch off the excess at the rim. Place a sheet of parchment over the dough and fill it with pie weights or dried beans; bake until the edges of the crust are somewhat firm, 10 to 12 minutes. Remove the parchment and weights, return the tart pan to the oven, and bake until the crust is golden, 15 to 18 minutes more.

recipe continues

BAKE THE TART: Remove the pan from the oven and place it on a rimmed sheet pan. Reduce the oven temperature to 250°F. Remove the filling from the refrigerator and whisk it just to blend. Pour the filling into the hot tart shell and bake the tart until the filling puffs and jiggles only slightly when you shake the sheet pan, 50 to 55 minutes. Let the tart cool completely at room temperature.

SERVE: Cut the tart into wedges (like a pie) and serve at room temperature with whipped cream on the side. The tart will keep, wrapped in plastic wrap, in the fridge for up to 3 days.

Key Lime Pie

I made many key lime pies before I found *the one*. It had to have the proper "tang" factor and a silky-smooth, rich texture. And here it is! I serve slices of this pie dolloped with an excessive amount of unsweetened whipped cream to offset the sweetness. Because the recipe requires 2 cups of condensed milk, you may have some extra. Pour that excess into a small pot and simmer until it caramelizes and turns golden brown—it takes only about three minutes. Serve the rich, sweet caramel with the whipped cream or simply drizzle it over the pie before serving.

SERVES 8 TO 10

CRUST

4 tablespoons (½ stick) unsalted butter, melted, plus 1 tablespoon at room temperature for greasing the pie plate

1½ cups finely ground graham cracker crumbs (from about 10 graham crackers)

¼ cup sugar

6 light grates of lemon zest

FILLING

2 cups sweetened condensed milk (use any left over to make caramel; see headnote)

½ cup sour cream

2 tablespoons grated lime zest (from about 2 limes)

¾ cup fresh lime juice (from 8 to 10 limes)

Unsweetened whipped cream (page 294), for serving

Preheat the oven to 350°F. Position a rack in the center of the oven. Grease the bottom and sides of a 9-inch pie plate with the room-temperature butter.

MAKE THE CRUST: In a medium bowl, mix together the graham cracker crumbs, sugar, melted butter, and lemon zest. The texture should resemble wet sand. Use the bottom of a glass or measuring cup to press the crust into an even layer over the bottom and up the sides of the pie plate. Place the pie plate in the oven and bake until the crust firms up and browns lightly, 10 to 12 minutes. Remove it from the oven and set it aside to cool; keep the oven on.

MAKE THE FILLING: In a medium bowl, whisk together the condensed milk, sour cream, lime zest, and lime juice until smooth. Pour the filling into the cooled pie crust.

BAKE: Place the pie plate in the oven on the center rack and bake until the filling is somewhat firm in the center, 20 to 22 minutes. Let the pie cool completely at room temperature, then refrigerate it for at least 1 hour (or cover the cooled pie with plastic wrap and refrigerate it for up to 12 hours).

SERVE: Cut the pie into wedges and serve them with unsweetened whipped cream on the side. You can also serve dollops of the whipped cream right on top of the wedges to accentuate the contrast between the rich cream and the sweet-tart filling. The pie can be refrigerated, covered, for up to 3 days.

COCKTAILS & MOCKTAILS

These are cocktails that I make at home when I'm cooking with friends. That's why I start with a list of what's in my own liquor cabinet. My daughter, Ava, likes to get in on the fun of mixing and shaking drinks, so some of these are specifically mocktails that she can help prepare (and almost all of the cocktails have alcohol-free variations for anyone who isn't partaking). I also include some drinks that work as fun brunch ideas—like lattes, ice cream lattes, and iced tea with matcha ice cubes!

CHERRY VODKA SODA

MAKES 4 DRINKS (WITH EXTRA CHERRY SYRUP)

This is great as a tart (but also sweet) vodka cocktail. Eliminate the vodka and you have a fun nonalcoholic drink with an amazing real cherry taste and stunning color. Yuzu is a Japanese citrus fruit, and the juice is very special. It tastes like a lemonade crashed into a cherry soda. If unavailable, substitute lemon juice.

2 cups cherry juice

2 cups sugar

½ cup bottled yuzu juice or fresh lemon juice (from 3 lemons)

Ice cubes

16 ounces (2 cups) soda water

8 ounces (1 cup) vodka

MAKE THE CHERRY SYRUP: In a medium saucepan, combine 1 cup of the cherry juice, 1 cup of water, and the sugar, and bring to a boil over medium heat. Stir to dissolve the sugar. Strain the mixture through a fine-mesh sieve into a medium bowl and chill completely in the refrigerator. Then add the remaining 1 cup cherry juice and the yuzu juice, and mix to blend.

MIX: Fill four rocks glasses with ice. Put a long-handled spoon in each glass and fill with 4 ounces (½ cup) of soda water and 2 ounces (¼ cup) of vodka. Pour about 2 ounces (¼ cup) of the cherry syrup into the glasses and stir vigorously with the spoon to combine. Taste, and adjust as needed. Serve immediately.

The remaining cherry syrup can be refrigerated in a sealed plastic or glass container for up to 2 weeks.

MELON TEQUILA COOLER

MAKES 4 TO 6 DRINKS (OR 1 PITCHER)

This is such a good blender drink. It works with any fleshy melon: cantaloupe, Galia, honeydew, Canary. The most important thing is that the melon is sweet and ripe. When it links up with the tequila, it makes for a powerful cocktail that is also very refreshing. Omit the tequila and add 1 to 2 cups more cider for a no-alcohol version.

1 large cantaloupe

½ cup lemon juice (from 3 lemons)

1 cup sparkling cider (nonalcoholic), chilled

1 tablespoon honey

8 to 16 ounces (1 to 2 cups) blanco tequila, chilled

MAKE THE MELON PUREE: Cut the melon in half and scoop out and discard the seeds. Use a spoon to scoop out the flesh in small balls and tightly pack a 4-cup liquid measuring cup with the melon balls. Transfer the melon to a blender, add the lemon juice, cider, and honey, and puree until smooth. Refrigerate until chilled.

MIX: For each drink, pour about ⅓ cup (about 5 ounces) of the melon puree into a highball glass and stir in 2 to 3 ounces (about ¼ cup) of the tequila.

SETTING UP YOUR BAR

There are so many choices when it comes to booze, so first things first: What kind of cocktails do you like to order most? That should direct you in choosing which kinds of alcohol to stock in your bar. This is what my liquor cabinet looks like:

Aperol and Campari

Carpano Antica Formula sweet and dry vermouths

Pimm's Cup No. 1

Ketel One and Hangar 1 vodka

Casamigos and Casa Dragones tequila

Hendrick's gin (all flavors); I also like Bombay Sapphire for neutral gin notes

Bulleit bourbon

WhistlePig rye

White rum

Angostura bitters

Luxardo Maraschino cherries

STRAWBERRY JAM DAIQUIRI
(PAGE 320)

SPICY SPIKED LEMONADE
(PAGE 315)

CHERRY VODKA SODA
(PAGE 311)

MELON TEQUILA COOLER
(PAGE 311)

MINT JULEP
(PAGE 314)

MINT JULEP

MAKES 4 DRINKS

One of my favorite cocktails is the mint julep. I love chewing on the crushed ice to offset the punch of alcohol from the bourbon and the tingle from the mint leaves as they mix with the ice. It reminds me of an adult snow cone, like the fruity, icy ones I used to get from the ice cream truck as a kid. Substitute lemon soda for the bourbon and you have a nice mocktail that both grown-ups and kids can get behind.

1 cup granulated sugar

3 cups loosely packed fresh mint leaves

Grated zest and juice of 3 large lemons

12 to 16 ice cubes

10 to 12 ounces (1¼ to 1½ cups) bourbon (or lemon soda for a no-alcohol version)

Maple syrup

1 to 2 tablespoons raw sugar, such as Demerara

MAKE THE MINT SYRUP: In a small saucepan, heat 2 cups of water and the granulated sugar over medium heat, stirring, until the sugar dissolves completely, 2 to 3 minutes. Remove from the heat and pour the sugar syrup into a bowl. Add 2 cups of the mint leaves and let steep while the sugar syrup cools for about 15 minutes, then strain out the mint leaves (or use a slotted spoon to remove them). Stir in the lemon zest and juice, and refrigerate until completely chilled.

CRUSH THE ICE: The ice for this drink is very important. I like to wrap regular ice cubes in a kitchen towel and crush them with a rolling pin until fairly fine. I fill a bowl with this ice and keep it in the freezer until I'm ready to serve the drinks.

SERVE: Juleps are traditionally served in silver cups, but any fun cup will do. Mix the remaining 1 cup mint leaves into the crushed ice, and fill each julep cup amply with the mint ice, mounding the ice above the rim of the cup. Pour about ½ cup of the chilled mint syrup over the ice in each cup, add 2 to 2½ ounces (4 to 5 tablespoons) of the bourbon, and top with a splash of maple syrup and a sprinkle of the raw sugar for texture.

SPICED NEGRONI

MAKES 2 DRINKS

A traditional Negroni is famous for being magically sweet and pleasantly bitter at the same time. It's honestly as refreshing as lemonade was to me as a kid. I like to spice mine to match an amazing version that I once tasted in Rome: it was spiced with cinnamon, anise, and ginger and had a warmth from those flavors that made me drink one after another. I really like this flavor combination—it rides the perfect line between bitter and sweet. For me, this means it goes well with salty snacks as well as a full meal. Make sure everything, including the glasses, is as cold as possible.

8 ounces (1 cup) Campari

2 cinnamon sticks, about 3 inches long

2 whole star anise pods

1 teaspoon ground ginger

4 (½-inch-thick) slices of tangerine (skin and all), seeds removed

8 to 12 ice cubes

3 ounces (¼ cup plus 2 tablespoons) dry gin

2 ounces (¼ cup) sweet vermouth

SPICE THE CAMPARI: In a small saucepan, bring the Campari, cinnamon sticks, star anise, and ginger to a simmer over medium heat. Stir, remove from the heat, and let the spices steep for 10 minutes. Then strain out the spices (or use a slotted spoon to remove them) and refrigerate the spiced Campari until it is completely chilled.

GET READY: Choose two smallish rocks glasses and rub a tangerine slice around the rim of each one. Add 2 pieces of tangerine and 2 or 3 ice cubes to each glass.

SHAKE: In a cocktail shaker (or any container with a fitted lid), combine 2 or 3 ice cubes, the gin, 4 ounces (½ cup) of the spiced Campari, and the vermouth and shake vigorously for about 15 seconds. Divide the drink between the two glasses. Reserve the remaining spiced Campari for more drinks.

FROZEN MOJITO

MAKES 4 DRINKS

I think college spring break has given the mojito an unwarranted bad rap. This cocktail is one of my go-tos for its refreshing, clean taste of rum that's brought to life by fresh mint leaves. While alcohol can never fully freeze, I love mojitos somewhat frozen and slushy, like a Moscow Mule.

"Muddle" means to crush the mint leaves to bring out their flavor. If you get serious about mixology, invest in a muddler or use a mortar and pestle to crush your mint leaves. The taste of the mint is so much more vibrant and pronounced as a result.

2 cups sugar

1½ cups fresh mint leaves, stemmed

14 ounces (1¾ cups) white rum

1 cup fresh lime juice (from 8 to 10 limes)

MAKE THE MINT SYRUP: In a medium saucepan, combine 2 cups of water with the sugar and simmer over medium heat, stirring, until the sugar dissolves, 1 to 2 minutes. Add ½ cup of the mint leaves and remove from the heat. Let the syrup cool to room temperature. Strain the syrup (or use a slotted spoon to remove the mint leaves) into a bowl and refrigerate until well chilled.

MIX: Place about half of the remaining mint leaves in a bowl, add 1½ cups of the chilled mint syrup, and use a wooden spoon to muddle the leaves. In a baking dish, combine the muddled mint syrup, the rum, and the lime juice. Taste, and adjust if needed. Freeze until firm-ish, 2 to 3 hours.

SERVE: Scrape and flake the ice with a fork. Fill four rocks glasses with some of the slush, add the remaining mint leaves, and spoon more slush on top.

SPICY SPIKED LEMONADE

MAKES 4 DRINKS

The kick from black pepper in this lemonade stimulates the appetite, while the lemon and lime juice give it a wonderfully refreshing quality. I mix a pitcher at a time (usually in the morning so it has ample time to chill) rather than making individual drinks, because it goes *that* quickly. If you are making a large batch, it's best to pour the lemonade over ice just before serving rather than filling the pitcher with ice ahead of time; if it sits too long on the ice, the flavor gets diluted. You can make this into a zippy nonalcoholic soda by cutting out the vodka and Pimm's. Simply replace them with lemonade.

12 ounces (1½ cups) vodka, plus extra if needed

4 ounces (½ cup) Pimm's No. 1

1 cup fresh lemon juice (from 5 to 6 lemons)

½ cup fresh lime juice (from 4 to 6 limes)

½ cup honey

2 teaspoons coarsely ground black pepper

1 lemon, sliced into ½-inch-thick rounds

1 cup lemon-lime soda, chilled

MIX: In a large container with a fitted lid, combine the vodka, Pimm's, lemon juice, lime juice, honey, and black pepper. Cover and shake to blend. Refrigerate for at least 1 hour or up to 12 hours.

SERVE: Fill a pitcher with ice cubes and the lemon slices. Shake the chilled vodka mixture and pour it into the pitcher. Using a long wooden spoon, stir while pouring in the lemon-lime soda, reaching down to the bottom of the pitcher with the spoon to make sure everything is well blended. Taste: you may find you want to add another splash of vodka. Serve immediately.

A CHILLED BOULEVARDIER

MAKES 2 DRINKS

This innocent-looking drink was said to have been invented by Erskine Gwynne, the founder of a Parisian magazine called *The Boulevardier,* in the 1920s. The drink outlasted the magazine by decades, and I don't wonder why. It's a strong drink that sneaks up on you (which I love). Fortified with bourbon, this is a really refreshing terrace drink that looks, from a distance, like an innocent Negroni but is much stronger. I like it ice-cold and served up.

1½ ounces (3 tablespoons) Campari, chilled
4 ounces (½ cup) bourbon, chilled
1½ ounces (3 tablespoons) sweet vermouth, chilled
2 lemon twists

In a cocktail shaker filled with ice, combine the Campari, bourbon, and vermouth. Shake, then divide the drink between two coupe or rocks glasses. Garnish each glass with a lemon twist.

TASTY MANHATTAN

MAKES 4 DRINKS

This is such a strong drink—I can only have one (or even just half)! That said, it's one of my all-time favorites. Rye gives the cocktail more layers of flavor than bourbon, and it has to be served at an "ice cream headache" level of coldness. I always have to have crunchy snacks on the side, like some super-salty peanuts or pretzels.

6 ounces (¾ cup) rye whiskey
2½ ounces (⅓ cup) sweet vermouth
3 or 4 dashes Angostura bitters
Ice cubes
4 orange twists
Maraschino cherries, for garnish
Salted peanuts or pretzels, for serving

In a 2-cup liquid measuring cup, combine the rye, vermouth, and bitters. Taste, and adjust the mix if needed. In a cocktail shaker filled with ice, shake half of the drink mixture. Divide the mixture between two rocks glasses and garnish each one with an orange twist and a few cherries. Repeat with the remaining drink mixture. Serve with salty snacks.

MULLED WHITE WINE

MULLED WHITE WINE

MAKES 4 DRINKS

This recipe came about when I realized how much I appreciate the lightness of white wine, even in the winter months. Here I infuse it with spices and serve it warm, perfect for holidays and parties. There is something about the lightness of the color that conveys the idea that the drink is both refreshing and belly warming. I don't use expensive wine here because its nuance will get lost among all the other flavors.

4 cinnamon sticks, about 3 inches long

3 whole star anise pods

¼ cup honey, plus extra if needed

1 (750mL) bottle dry Chardonnay

1 large lemon, zested, then cut into rounds (seeds removed)

1 tablespoon dark brown sugar

INFUSE THE WINE: In a medium pot, combine the cinnamon sticks, star anise, and honey. Bring the mixture to a simmer over medium heat and let it froth and turn light brown, 3 to 5 minutes. Remove the pot from the heat and slowly add the wine. Return the pot to the burner, add the lemon slices, and bring to a simmer over medium heat. Remove it from the heat and let the spices steep, like tea, for 15 to 20 minutes. Strain the spiced wine through a fine-mesh sieve into a large bowl (discard the spices and lemon slices). Taste and stir in more honey, if needed.

SERVE: In a small shallow bowl, use your fingers to rub the lemon zest into the brown sugar. Dip the rims of four heatproof glasses or mugs in the lemon sugar. Ladle the wine into the glasses and serve it steaming warm.

MULLED CIDER

SERVES 4 TO 6

A "straight" apple cider (an alcohol-free cider, not a hard cider) is often made from mixed varieties of apples and is sometimes enriched with crabapples for a little pucker. For this recipe, I like a cloudy and murky sweet cider.

1 quart (4 cups) apple cider

5 whole cloves

5 large cinnamon sticks

½ teaspoon ground nutmeg (preferably freshly grated)

¼ cup packed dark brown sugar

1 knob fresh ginger, cut into 1-inch-thick slices

Grated zest and juice of 1 large lemon

1 medium applesauce-type apple, such as a McIntosh or Macoun, cored and diced

In a medium saucepan, heat the cider until it is hot but not boiling. Add the cloves, cinnamon sticks, nutmeg, brown sugar, ginger, and lemon juice, and stir to combine and dissolve the sugar. Bring to a gentle simmer over low heat and cook for about 10 minutes. Shut off the heat and let it steep for 10 to 15 minutes. I leave the whole spices in there because they are rustic. If you prefer the cider without, simply strain them out. Divide the lemon zest and diced apple among four to six mugs, ladle the spiced cider into the mugs, and serve.

STRAWBERRY JAM DAIQUIRI

MAKES 5 COCKTAILS (OR 1 PITCHER)

Daiquiris are sweet, and as a result, they don't get taken seriously in the cocktail world. I find that if you add the floater of dark rum on top of each glass, it heightens the alcohol note, allowing the fruit and sweetness to take a back seat. Strawberry jam, an untraditional addition, brings a deep cooked-fruit note that heightens the taste of both the strawberries and the rum. I think if we served drinks in metal cups at the restaurant so no one could see what anyone else was drinking, many more of these would be consumed. Make them when strawberries are sweet and in season, which is late June into August in New York (though frozen berries are fine, too).

12 ounces frozen strawberries

7 ounces (¾ cup plus 2 tablespoons) light rum, plus extra if needed

2 tablespoons strawberry jam

1 cup sugar

½ cup fresh lime juice (from 4 to 5 limes), plus extra if needed

Ice cubes

Fresh strawberries, for garnish

Dark rum (optional)

In a blender, combine the frozen strawberries, light rum, jam, sugar, lime juice, and a few ice cubes and blend until smooth. Taste, and adjust with more lime juice or more light rum if necessary. Put a few ice cubes into five highball glasses and fill the glasses with the mixture. Garnish the drinks with fresh strawberries and top with a floater of dark rum, if desired.

CONCORD GRAPE SODA

MAKES ABOUT 6 SODAS

You can use Concord or white grape juice for this soda. The novelty (and great taste) of using frozen grapes as ice cubes is really fun for kids and grown-ups alike. Use all kinds of grapes—anything seedless is best. Note: If the honey won't mix with the grape juice, warm the honey with a little grape juice to dissolve it and then stir it into the remaining grape juice.

1 quart (4 cups) grape juice, chilled

1 tablespoon honey

2 cups seltzer or naturally sparkling water, chilled

24 to 30 grapes, stemmed, washed, and frozen

Mix the grape juice and honey together in a pitcher. Fill six highball or rocks glasses three-fourths full with the grape juice and top with the sparkling water. Stir a few frozen grapes into each glass. Note: Grapes can be a choking hazard for younger children, so leave them for the older kids.

COCONUT SODA

MAKES 3 OR 4 DRINKS

This is such a tasty soda because it's light and bubbly yet has a rich flavor. It's satisfying and addictive once you start drinking it. Ava and I make this on many afternoons when we're hanging out together after school.

1 (15.5-ounce) can unsweetened coconut milk

¼ cup honey

1 tablespoon sugar

Juice of ½ large lemon

Ice cubes

6 to 8 ounces sparkling water

In a blender, blend the coconut milk, honey, sugar, and lemon juice on low speed until combined. Fill each rocks glass with ice, pour the mixture over the ice, and stir about 2 ounces (¼ cup) of the sparkling water into each glass.

COCONUT SODA
CONCORD GRAPE SODA

MELTED COFFEE ICE CREAM LATTE

MAKES 4 LATTES

This is kind of like an Italian *affogato,* a dessert treat where espresso gets poured over vanilla ice cream—except here, the ice cream is melted and becomes part of the drink. *Affogato* means "drowned," referring to the ice cream drowning in the hot coffee; here I like to think it's more like the ice cream and coffee meet in a kiddie pool and agree to be friends. It's this ideal combination of a great coffee drink made even better by a scoop of great coffee ice cream. Skim milk makes better froth when you already have all the cream from the melted ice cream.

1 cup skim milk

1 pint coffee ice cream

1 cup brewed espresso, hot

In a small saucepan, heat the milk with the ice cream over medium heat, whisking as it heats, until the mixture simmers and becomes foamy. (Alternatively, microwave the milk mixture until it is hot and then whisk until it is foamy; or if you have an espresso maker that froths milk, you can use it to simultaneously froth the milk and melt the ice cream in a medium pitcher.) Divide the hot espresso among four cups and pour some of the frothed milk mixture over each one. Serve immediately.

ICED GREEN TEA WITH MATCHA ICE CUBES

MAKES 4 ICED TEAS

This is a fun drink because the subtle sweetness from the honeydew melon in the ice cubes is great with the tartness of the tea—and it also turns the cubes a beautiful grassy green. This is a strong iced tea, meaning it has a lot of flavor. It stands up to anything, from grilled fish to fruity desserts. It's also very beautiful to look at!

MATCHA ICE CUBES

2 cups 2-inch chunks honeydew melon

2 tablespoons matcha powder

1 cup boiling water

ICED TEA

6 green tea bags

MAKE THE ICE CUBES: Puree the honeydew in a blender until smooth; keep the melon in the blender. Put the matcha powder in a medium heatproof bowl, pour the boiling water over it, and whisk until it is very well blended and there aren't any lumps. Pour the liquid over the melon in the blender, and puree until combined. Pour the mixture into the cups of a 14-cube ice cube tray, filling them to the brim. Freeze until solid.

MAKE THE ICED TEA: In a medium pot, bring 1 quart (4 cups) of water to a simmer over medium heat. Add the tea bags, remove from the heat, and steep for 6 to 8 minutes (we are steeping the tea for an extra-long time because it will be diluted and combined with other ingredients). Remove and discard the tea bags. Refrigerate the tea until it is well chilled.

SERVE: Put 3 matcha ice cubes in each glass and fill the glasses with the tea. Serve immediately.

ICED GREEN TEA WITH MATCHA ICE CUBES

DAIRY-FREE MATCHA LATTE (page 324)

HORCHATA ICED COFFEE (page 325)

CLASSIC LATTE

MAKES 2 LATTES

Latte is a fancy-pants term for an espresso mixed with frothed milk. You can also make it with regular brewed coffee, which is technically a *café au lait*. Experiment with different espresso flavors and blends until you find the one you like. Personally, I love a nutty coffee bean with some cocoa-y notes.

2 cups whole milk

⅔ cup brewed espresso, hot

In a small saucepan, heat the milk, whisking as it heats, until it comes to a simmer and becomes foamy. (Alternatively, microwave the milk until hot and then whisk until foamy; or if you have an espresso maker that froths milk, you can use it to froth the milk.)

Divide the hot espresso between two cups and pour half of the frothed milk over each. Serve immediately.

DAIRY-FREE MATCHA LATTE

MAKES 2 LATTES

Matcha tea tastes like a cup of great green tea crashed into a fresh lime. I love the tang of the matcha combined with the almond and coconut notes from the two milks in this recipe. I make this latte unsweetened and then add honey to it before drinking. I also sometimes like to sweeten it with dark brown sugar.

1 cup unsweetened almond milk

1 cup unsweetened coconut milk

2 tablespoons matcha powder

MAKE THE LATTE: In a small saucepan, heat the almond and coconut milks, whisking as they come to a simmer and become foamy. (Alternatively, microwave the milks until hot and then whisk until foamy; or if you have an espresso maker that froths milk, you can use it to froth the milks.)

MAKE THE TEA: Heat ½ cup of water to a simmer in a small saucepan. Remove the pan from the heat and whisk in the matcha powder until smooth. Divide the hot matcha between two cups and pour half of the frothed milk over each. Serve immediately.

ROSE WATER LATTE

MAKES 2 LATTES

There are a lot of recipes that call for steeping dried (or even fresh) rose petals in water for a latte. But food-grade, unsprayed rose petals can be hard to find and vary dramatically in taste (and unpleasant bitterness), so I use rose water instead. I find the color of the latte is as important as the flavor of the rose, which is why I add raspberry sorbet. The sorbet enhances the color *and* adds great tang to the floral rose water (which is available in any Middle Eastern or Indian market, and in most health food stores, too).

1 cup unsweetened coconut milk
1 cup skim milk
2 raspberry tea bags
½ cup raspberry sorbet, melted
1 teaspoon rose water

MAKE THE LATTE: In a small saucepan, heat the milks together, whisking constantly and vigorously as they heat, until the mixture simmers and becomes foamy. (Alternatively, microwave the milks together until they are hot and then whisk until foamy; or if you have an espresso maker that froths milk, you can use it to froth the milks.)

MAKE THE TEA: In a small saucepan, heat ½ cup of water to boiling and add the tea bags. Remove the pan from the heat and steep the tea for 3 minutes; then discard the tea bags. Whisk in the raspberry sorbet and the rose water until smooth. Divide the rose mixture between two cups and pour half of the frothed milk over each.

HORCHATA ICED COFFEE

MAKES 4 COFFEES

Horchata is a tasty rice-based drink you can find in most Mexican dining establishments in the United States. It reminds me of light rice pudding with almost roasted nutty notes. There are powdered forms of horchata, but making it the "real" way yields super tasty results. The drink has a cooling effect when paired with spicy foods; I love serving it with al pastor tacos or spicy corn nuts! The combination of the rice, honey, and coffee is a hit. No one will guess how you made this!

½ cup long-grain white rice, rinsed and drained
1 teaspoon ground cinnamon
¼ cup honey
2½ cups strong brewed coffee, at room temperature

MAKE THE HORCHATA: In a blender, combine the rice and cinnamon with 4 cups of water. Pulse to coarsely blend the rice and water. Then set the mixture aside, still in the blender, to soak for 3 hours at room temperature.

COOK THE HONEY: In a small skillet, bring the honey to a simmer over medium-low heat. Let it bubble and froth, and cook until it turns light amber, 2 to 3 minutes. Remove the pan from the heat and set it aside to cool slightly.

SERVE: Add the cooked honey and the coffee to the rice mixture in the blender, and puree until smooth. Strain the liquid through a fine-mesh sieve into a pitcher, and refrigerate until chilled. Serve the drink over ice in tall glasses. The horchata can be refrigerated for up to 5 days.

MANGO AND GREEN BUBBLE TEA

MAKES 2 OR 3 BUBBLE TEAS

I love the chewy texture of tapioca, so of course I am into bubble tea (also known as boba). I always find comfort in the almost gluey sweetness of the tapioca balls, and I love them even more when they are part of a drink that is so thick you can eat it with a spoon, almost like an ice cream sundae. If you like, you can puree other fruits to make the base of this drink—strawberries and raspberries are both great. Mango will always be my favorite, however, because it reminds me of the wonderful sweet Indian yogurt drink called *lassi*.

Fresh and frozen mango both work here. This recipe makes about 1½ quarts of the tea base. You can cut the ingredient amounts in half if you want to make a smaller batch.

2 green tea bags

½ cup large tapioca pearls, rinsed

2 cups chopped fresh very ripe mango

Juice of 1 medium lemon

1 cup whole milk

1 tablespoon honey

MAKE THE TEA: In a small saucepan, bring 1 cup of water to a boil and add the tea bags. Remove the pan from the heat and let the tea steep for 2 minutes. Then discard the tea bags and set the tea aside to cool completely.

COOK THE TAPIOCA: In a large sauté pan, cover the tapioca pearls with cool water and stir until they float to the surface. Bring to a simmer over low heat and cook, stirring from time to time to make sure they don't stick to the pan, until they are gluey-looking, 5 to 8 minutes. Remove the pan from the heat, cover the pan, and let the tapioca sit for 15 minutes. Then remove the cover, drain the tapioca in a colander, and rinse it under cool water. Transfer the drained tapioca to a medium bowl and set it aside.

MAKE THE DRINK: In a blender, combine the mango, lemon juice, milk, and honey, and puree until completely smooth. Blend in the cooled tea and refrigerate for at least 30 minutes to chill or for up to 4 hours.

SERVE: Spoon the tapioca into tall glasses and then fill the glasses with the mango mixture. Serve the bubble tea with large straws and long-handled spoons for scooping up the tapioca.

JJT-6469

ACKNOWLEDGMENTS

The most important person in my life is my daughter, Ava. That said, this book is also a lot about two people I no longer have anymore: my dad and my aunt Aggie. I had little family growing up, and they were two of the most important people to me. The other is my mother. She is, thank God, still around and took a dark red pencil to every word of this book. She is the Quincy Jones of editors, and this is her opus.

Another important person in my life is Michael Castellon. You cut my father's hair and gently shaved his face when he was really sick. That bought a lifetime of love and loyalty from me. You also make a great cauliflower lasagna.

My most important mentor (and friend) is Bobby Flay, who is truly like a mob boss with a heart of gold. I can't put a value on how many times he has saved me from my own choices and cooked me some incredible food, too. He brought me into Food Network, showed me the ropes, and fed me scallops on crispy tortillas with corn and avocado along the way. He also reminds me of the essentials (in no particular order):

1. *Remember every time you're on TV, your daughter is watching you.*

2. *Believe in yourself and do the work.*

3. *Don't be a knucklehead.*

4. *Taste your food.*

Thanks also to Giada De Laurentiis for being a great friend. So supportive. Such a great lover of chocolate cake and frank conversation. Great mom. Amazing restaurateur. Great TV personality and entrepreneur. You honestly inspire me.

Special thanks to Guy Fieri, who has invited me to be a part of countless shows on Food Network: from *Grocery Games* to *Guy's Ranch Kitchen* to *Guy's Big Project,* he always makes me feel like an important part of his great work. Thanks to Brian Lando. He is the reason I am on a couple of shows called *Chopped* and *Iron Chef America*. A special thanks to Steve Kroopnik and John Bravakis from Triage and to Vivian Sorensen, the Queen of *Chopped*, too.

The most important chef I worked for is Guy Savoy. He told this scrappy American girl it was okay to cook in his three-Michelin-star joint in Paris in 1992, and I watched six years go by in a blink. He truly taught me what flavor is—how to find it, harness it, and not throw it away. He taught me what a great ingredient is and why I should care. Okay, so he might have broken a few plates and yelled a bit along the way. The most rewarding moments were when he would make a beeline for the "American girl's" station and take a huge ladle of whatever soup I was making. I came to expect it. I loved watching the color return to his face. Watching him dunk bread in the soup. I think it fed me more than it actually fed him.

Other than my daughter, my other great life achievement is Butter. A force of nature. Somehow a team has formed and we won't let it be broken by anything. It's mostly because we all want to be Alvaro Buchelly when we grow up. He's our Crown Prince of Butter. Thanks go to these hooligans, too: the extraordinary chef Michael "Butter is an Italian restaurant" Jenkins and the incredible Jamaal "Edward 40hands" Dunlap. They are two incredible men whom I have watched grow, mature (somewhat), and run this great restaurant. It honestly brings tears to my eyes. Without Michael there would simply be no soul, and without Jamaal there would be no heart or food. The very special bunny Antonio "à la Morales" Morales, pastry chef extraordinaire Kevin O'Brien, Miguel "Mango" Angel Cruz, Flaviano "Muscle Milk" Sosa, Michael "Inspired Vision chef" Chatman, Steak Master David Rim, Jon "I have Nothing!" Boros, Max Castro, DJSerge1 "You're really probably fired this time" Ramirez, Stephanie "Cinnamon Rolls" Galan, Wirt "I need to take a gin break and run a juice bar because I now have ten children" Cook, Diane "Can I just give you a light punch on the arm, Michael?" Vista-Wayne, Lucas "Sniffles" Marino, Alexandria "Is Kevin coming in tonight?" Ventrella, and Manuel "Grumpypants" Duarte. While general manager Lauren Basco is technically "front of house," she may as well be a kitchen staff member. Lauren seamlessly rose from Dancing Queen hostess to literally running the joint. I'm so proud to know you and call you a friend. I'll drive you through an artichoke field anytime. To amazing purveyors and friends: Louis Rozzo, Pat LaFrieda, Mark Pastore, and Lou Di Palo.

Thanks to my editor, Raquel Pelzel, and her staff at Clarkson Potter for painstakingly editing this book. Raquel managed to clarify my language and thoughts into recipes that make sense to people other than just me. A critical thing and the work of a great editor.

Shout-out to the copy editors, too. They never get the thanks they deserve!

Thanks to Marysarah Quinn and Ian Dingman for the stunning and unique design of the book. Thanks to Irika Slavin and Lauren Mueller at Food Network for their amazing support and patience. Special thanks to Courtney White, Kathleen Finch, Mark Levine, and Allison Page for taking a chance on me more than once!

Special thanks to Jon Steinlauf, Karen Grinthal, and Jon Sichel for their great friendship.

Thanks to Josh Bider, Jeff Googel, Strand Conover, Jon Rosen, and Andy McNichol at William Morris Endeavor.

Thanks to the farmers at the Union Square Greenmarket: Alex Paffenroth, Northshire Farms, Windfall Farms, Stokes Farms, Cherry Lane Farm, Eckerton Farms, and Keith's Farm.

Thanks to great Hamptons farmers Marilee Foster, Pike Farms, Green Thumb Organic, Balsam Farms, Amber Waves, and Mecox Bay Dairy. Thanks to Carissa's Breads for inspiring me, too.

The main recipe tester is none other than the great Ashley Archer, with whom I have worked for years. She is a force of nature and brilliant. Thank you.

A special thanks to my assistant, Christina Caruana, and pastry chef, Kevin O'Brien, for also testing so many of these recipes again and again. Christina: you are becoming a great cook! Thanks to Michael Castellon for his smart suggestions, skilled cooking, and patient discussion about so much of this book.

Johnny Miller is a uniquely great photographer. He mixed his own view with mine in the most brilliant and generous way. He came to my house and I didn't want him to leave. What an artist! Thanks to Luc Decker for the critically important

digital piece of the images. Thanks to Rebecca Jurkevich for the transcendent cooking, gifted hands, and otherworldly food styling. Thanks to Cybelle Tondu for her amazing cooking and assistance with the food. Thanks to Sarah Smart for prop styling.

Thanks to Colleen Grapes for really being the greatest friend I have.

Thanks to Gretta Monahan, Ricky Goldin, Randy Kolhoff, Peter Cook, Karen "Kiki" Mullane, MP Styles, Bruce Bronster, Bruce Seidel, Annie Washburn, Emily Giske, Patti Jackson, Missy Robbins, Michael Symon, Lee Schrager, Geoffrey Zakarian, Scott Conant, Alton Brown, Mikey "Bagels," Vivian Sorenson, Dave Mechlowicz, Madi Clark, and fellow chefs everywhere.

Thanks to Cobi Levy, Tony Ramirez, Tim Gunyon, and Ashley Marshal for doing nothing short of amazing work at Butter.

Lastly, a shout-out to dishwashers and short-order diner cooks. The Great American Diner is a dying art in this country. Breakfast shifts and washing dishes are the hardest stations to work in any restaurant setting. Next time you eat a perfectly poached egg on a warm, clean plate, think about it. Respect.

INDEX

Note: Page references in italics indicate photographs.